In the Name of Democracy

In the Name
of Democracy

AMERICAN WAR CRIMES IN IRAQ AND BEYOND

EDITED BY

Jeremy Brecher, Jill Cutler,
AND Brendan Smith

Metropolitan Books
HENRY HOLT AND COMPANY
NEW YORK

Metropolitan Books
Henry Holt and Company, LLC
Publishers since 1866
175 Fifth Avenue
New York, New York 10010
www.henryholt.com

Metropolitan Books® and ® are registered trademarks of
Henry Holt and Company, LLC.

Distributed in Canada by H. B. Fenn and Company Ltd.

Library of Congress Cataloging-in-Publication Data

In the name of democracy: American war crimes in Iraq and beyond / edited by
Jeremy Brecher, Jill Cutler, and Brendan Smith.—1st ed.
    p. cm.
Includes bibliographical references.
ISBN-13: 978-0-8050-7969-2
ISBN-10: 0-8050-7969-6
    1. Iraq War, 2003—Atrocities.   2. United States—Armed forces—Iraq.
3. War crimes.   I. Brecher, Jeremy.   II. Cutler, Jill.   III. Smith, Brendan.

KZ6795.173.15 2005
956.7044'38—dc22   2005046528

Henry Holt books are available for special promotions and premiums.
For details contact: Director, Special Markets.

First Edition 2005

Designed by Meryl Sussman Levavi

Printed in the United States of America

1 3 5 7 9 10 8 6 4 2

To those everywhere who resist
the crimes of their governments

CONTENTS

Part III ■ Beyond Iraq:
The Future of U.S. War Crimes

Part IV ■ Perspectives on American War Crimes

Part V ▪ The Resisters: "Conscience, Not Cowardice"

Part VI ▪ Halting War Crimes: A Shared Responsibility

In the Name of Democracy

INTRODUCTION

The ultimate step in avoiding periodic wars, which are inevitable in a system of international lawlessness, is to make statesmen responsible to law.

> —Opening statement of Justice Robert Jackson, chief American prosecutor at the Nuremberg Tribunal, 1945

It is a big mistake for us to grant any validity to international law even when it may seem in our short-term interest to do so—because, over the long term, the goal of those who think that international law really means anything are those who want to constrict the United States.

> —John Bolton, Under Secretary of State, nominated 2005 for American ambassador to the United Nations

Brandon Hughey was a private at Fort Hood when he discovered that his army unit was about to be sent to Iraq. The eighteen-year-old from San Angelo, Texas, was desperate—not because he was afraid to go to war but because he was convinced that the Iraq war was immoral. He considered solving the problem by taking his own life. Instead, he got in a car and drove to Canada. He explained, "I would fight in an act of defense, if my home and family were in danger. But Iraq had no weapons of mass destruction. They barely had an army left, and [UN Secretary-General] Kofi Annan actually said [attacking Iraq was] a violation of the UN charter. It's nothing more than an act of aggression. You can't go along with a criminal activity just because others are doing it."

If, as the Bush administration has maintained, the United States is fighting in Iraq to protect itself from terrorism, free the people of Iraq from tyranny, enforce international law, and bring peace and democracy to the Middle East, then war resisters like Brandon Hughey appear deluded if not cowardly and criminal.

But what if Private Hughey is right? What if the U.S. operation in Iraq is "nothing more than an act of aggression"? What if it indeed constitutes "criminal activity"? What, then, is the culpability of President George W. Bush, Defense Secretary Donald Rumsfeld, and other top U.S. officials? And what is the responsibility of ordinary Americans?

Until recently, the possibility that top U.S. officials were responsible for war crimes seemed to many Americans nothing but the invidious allegations of a few knee-jerk anti-Americans. But as more and more suppressed photos and documents have been disclosed, and as more and more eyewitness accounts from prisons and battlefields have appeared in the media, Americans are undergoing an agonizing reappraisal of the Iraq war and the broader *war on terror* of which it is allegedly a part.

The *Washington Post*, once an avid supporter of the U.S. attack on Iraq, headlined an end-of-2004 editorial "War Crimes." It addressed the actions not of Saddam Hussein or Slobodan Milošević, but rather of U.S. defense secretary Donald Rumsfeld: "Since the publication of photographs of abuse at Iraq's Abu Ghraib prison in the spring the administration's whitewashers—led by Defense Secretary Donald H. Rumsfeld—have contended that the crimes were carried out by a few low-ranking reservists." These whitewashers have similarly contended that "no torture occurred at the Guantánamo Bay prison." But "New documents establish beyond any doubt that every part of this cover story is false." The documents "confirm that interrogators at Guantánamo believed they were following orders from Mr. Rumsfeld." The *Post* charges that violations of human rights "appear to be ongoing in Guantánamo, Iraq and Afghanistan." And "the appalling truth is that there has been no remedy for the documented torture and killing of foreign prisoners by this American government."

The purpose of this book is to help Americans face up to what our country has been doing in Iraq and more broadly in the *war on terror*—and to face up to the responsibilities those realities entail for us. It explores the evidence for U.S. war crimes. It addresses the question of who is responsible for them. It examines the plans to continue them. It opens up the historical, legal, and moral questions

they pose. It presents the story of those who have refused to participate in them. Finally, it looks at the responsibility of ordinary citizens
to halt war crimes and how that responsibility might be met.

WHAT ARE WAR CRIMES?

There are many bad things in the world, but nearly all countries in
the world have joined to single out certain acts as *war crimes*—
crimes so heinous that they are offenses not just against their immediate victims but against all of humanity. As a U.S. federal judge said
of one type of war criminal, "The torturer, like the pirate of old, has
become *hostis humanis generis*, the enemy of mankind."

Several overlapping strands have come together in the contemporary popular concept of war crimes. One, with roots in many cultures around the world, including the "just war" doctrines of medieval
Europe, is that armed attack on another country is a crime. As the
Nuremberg Tribunal put it, "To initiate a war of aggression" is "*the
supreme international crime* differing only from other war crimes in
that it contains within itself the accumulated evil of the whole." The
UN Charter provided that "all members shall refrain in their international relations from the threat or use of force against the territorial integrity or political independence of any state." Violations of this
principle are crimes against peace.

A second strand is *humanitarian law*, which protects combatants and civilians from unnecessary harm during war. In 1863, U.S.
president Abraham Lincoln promulgated the Lieber Code defining
protections for civilians and prisoners of war. The next year a number of countries agreed to the Geneva Convention for the Amelio-
ration of the Condition of the Wounded and Sick in Armies in the
Field.[1] Diplomatic conferences in 1899 and 1907 produced the "Law
of the Hague," which prohibited attacks on undefended towns, use
of arms designed to cause unnecessary suffering, poison weapons,
collective penalties, and pillage.[2]

[1] Frank Newman and David Weissbrodt, *International Human Rights*, 2nd ed. (Cincin-
nati: Anderson, 1969), p. 3.
[2] Steven R. Ratner and Jason S. Abrams, *Accountability for Human Rights Atrocities in
International Law*, 2nd ed. (Oxford: Oxford University Press, 2001), p. 81.

The devastation associated with World War II led to the recognition of a new category of international crimes, *crimes against humanity*, which involved acts of violence against a persecuted group in either war or peacetime. The Nuremberg Charter defined these acts as "murder, extermination, enslavement, deportation, and other inhumane acts committed against civilian populations, before or during the war; or persecutions on political, racial or religious grounds in execution of or in connection with any crime within the jurisdiction of the Tribunal, whether or not in violation of the domestic law of the country where perpetrated." The definition of crimes against humanity has since been expanded to include rape and torture.

These three strands came together after World War II in the Nuremberg and Tokyo war crimes trials. *Crimes against peace*, *war crimes*, and *crimes against humanity* have come to be summed up as *war crimes*.[3] War crimes were codified in the four Geneva Conventions of 1949 and have been further developed in subsequent protocols and agreements.

By agreeing to the UN Charter, the Geneva Conventions, and other such treaties, nations agreed to bind themselves to limitations on their sovereign prerogatives. But as Lisa Hajjar explains in her contribution to the present volume: "Enforcement depended on the willingness of individual states to conform to the laws they signed, and on the system of states to act against those that did not. While some states instituted domestic reforms and pursued foreign policies in keeping with their international obligations, most refused to regard human rights and humanitarian laws as binding." Despite Nuremberg, ours has been "an age of impunity."

But as Richard Falk writes in this book, the 1990s saw "a dramatic revival of the idea that neither states nor their leaders were above the law with respect to war making and crimes against humanity." International tribunals tried war crimes in the former Yugoslavia, Rwanda, and Sierra Leone. The International Criminal Court was

[3] The law of war crimes has continued to evolve. The Geneva Conventions of 1949 built on the early conventions but provided far greater protections to civilians in armed conflicts. Two protocols in 1977 defined *war crimes* as "grave breaches" of the Geneva agreements.

created—despite massive opposition from the Bush administration.[4] Henry Kissinger—himself a target of that revival—wrote in alarm in 2001 that "in less than a decade an unprecedented movement has emerged to submit international politics to judicial procedures" and has "spread with extraordinary speed."[5] War crimes prosecution, once a dimming historical memory, became a living contemporary presence.

War crimes have several characteristics that make them different from other crimes. War criminals are subject to *universal jurisdiction*, meaning that they can be tried not just in their own country but anywhere in the world. War crimes are likely to be the acts of high government officials, and such officials are likely to be in a position to prevent the courts of their own country from bringing them to justice. While international law prefers that each country deal with its own war criminals, international tribunals and the courts of other nations have been given authority to try war crimes cases where national courts fail to act.

Many laws, such as the laws against killing people, are suspended in times of war. But the law of war crimes applies even under conditions of emergency.[6] It is designed for conditions of war; absence of normal legality is no defense for war crimes. The Convention Against Torture, for example, provides that "no exceptional circumstances whatsoever, whether a state of war of a threat of war, internal political instability or any other public emergency, may be invoked as a justification of torture."[7]

The prohibition on war crimes is absolute, not relative. U.S. Justice Robert Jackson proclaimed at Nuremberg, "No grievances

---

4. For an account of this "dramatic revival," see Geoffrey Robertson, *Crimes Against Humanity: The Struggle for Global Justice* (New York: New Press, 2002).

5. Henry Kissinger, "The Pitfalls of Universal Jurisdiction: Risking Judicial Tyranny," *Foreign Affairs*, July–August 2001.

6. "Humanitarian law applies specifically to emergency situations." Newman and Weissbrodt, *International Human Rights*, p. 17. For a discussion of the Bush administration's claims that law does not apply in an emergency, see Sanford Levinson's contribution to the present volume.

7. Convention Against Torture and Other Cruel, Inhuman or Degrading Treatment or Punishment, adopted and open for signature, ratification, and accession by General Assembly resolution 39/46 of December 10, 1984, article 16. Quoted in Human Rights Watch, *The Road to Abu Ghraib*, reprinted in this volume.

or policies will justify resort to aggressive war. It is utterly renounced and condemned as an instrument of policy."[8] The same applies to other war crimes as well. The war crimes of one's opponents are no justification for one's own.

Charges that opponents have committed war crimes have become common currency of international conflict. But *war criminal* is more than an epithet. Today there is a body of law that is clearly enough formulated and widely enough accepted to be interpreted by courts based on procedures similar to those used for judging other crimes. Those are the standards by which allegations of American war crimes must be judged.

THE EVIDENCE

Part I summarizes the rapidly accumulating evidence of U.S. war crimes. This evidence comes from official government investigations; official documents released under court order; information leaked by participants and whistle-blowers; eyewitness accounts; and victims' experiences.

There are three sets of questions regarding possible U.S. war crimes in Iraq. The first set of questions concerns the legality of the U.S. attack on Iraq under international law. Secretary-General Kofi Annan of the United Nations stated shortly before the attack that the UN Charter is "very clear on the circumstances under which force can be used. If the U.S. and others were to go outside the Council and take military action, it would not be in conformity with the charter."[9] He subsequently stated that the invasion of Iraq was "not in conformity with the UN Charter, from our point of view, and from the Charter point of view, it was illegal." The U.S. admission that Iraq had no weapons of mass destruction, and the growing evidence that the United States fabricated the evidence on which that charge was based, has provided added weight to Annan's view.

The second set of questions involves the possible illegality of

[8.] Statement by Justice Jackson on War Trials Agreement, August 12, 1945.
[9.] This is an excerpt taken from a BBC interview with Kofi Annan on September 16, 2004.

the U.S. occupation of Iraq and its conduct. The seriousness of such questions was recently underlined by the warning of Louise Arbour, the UN High Commissioner for Human Rights, that those guilty of violations of international humanitarian and human-rights laws—including deliberate targeting of civilians, indiscriminate and disproportionate attacks, killing of injured persons, and the use of human shields—must be brought to justice, "be they members of the Multinational Force or insurgents."

The military technology the United States is using in Iraq, such as cluster bombs and depleted uranium, may be illegal in itself. Under Article 85 of the Geneva Conventions it is a war crime to launch "an indiscriminate attack affecting the civilian population in the knowledge that such an attack will cause an excessive loss of life or injury to civilians." A UN weapons commission described cluster bombs as "weapons of indiscriminate effects." A reporter for the *Mirror* (United Kingdom)[10] wrote from a hospital in Hillah, "Among the 168 patients I counted, not one was being treated for bullet wounds. All of them, men, women, children, bore the wounds of bomb shrapnel. It peppered their bodies. Blackened their skin. Smashed heads. Tore limbs. A doctor reported that 'All the injuries you see were caused by cluster bombs' . . . The majority of the victims were children who died because they were outside."

The third set of questions has to do with the torture and abuse of prisoners in U.S. custody. This has been a huge but unresolved issue since it was first indelibly engraved in the public mind by the photos from Abu Ghraib prison. Cascading disclosures have revealed that torture and other forms of prisoner abuse have been endemic not only in Iraq but in Afghanistan, Guantánamo, and many other U.S. operations around the world.

CULPABILITY

One of the most important principles established at Nuremberg is that individuals are responsible for their own actions, even if they were obeying orders, and that those in a position to give orders

[10.] As reported in the April 3, 2003, issue.

are responsible for the actions of those under them. "Complicity in the commission of a crime against peace, a war crime, or a crime against humanity" is "a crime under international law." Furthermore, "the fact that a person who committed an act which constitutes a crime under international law acted as Head of State or responsible Government official does not relieve him of responsibility under international law."

In those few instances where the Bush administration has admitted that wrongdoing may have occurred in connection with Iraq and the war on terror, it has consistently blamed low-level personnel and denied its own responsibility. But there are growing indications that, from the initial manipulation of evidence to justify the attack on Iraq to the latest cover-up of memos justifying torture, the highest levels of the Bush administration have been involved. Part II presents evidence that the trail of responsibility for the policies that led to such actions runs to the highest levels of the Pentagon and the door of the Oval Office.

As *International Herald Tribune* columnist William Pfaff wrote, "Proposals to authorize torture were circulating even before there was anyone to torture. Days after the Sept. 11 attacks, the administration made it known that the United States was no longer bound by international treaties, or by American law and established U.S. military standards concerning torture and the treatment of prisoners."[11] In January 2002, White House counsel Alberto Gonzales advised the president that if he "simply declared 'detainees' in Afghanistan outside the protection of the Geneva conventions, the 1996 U.S. War Crimes Act—which carries a possible death penalty for Geneva violations—would not apply." Later a legal task force from the Department of Defense concluded that the president, as commander in chief, had the authority "to approve any technique needed to protect the nation's security." As Pfaff observed, "Subsequent legal memos to civilian officials in the White House and Pentagon dwelt in morbid detail on permitted torture techniques, for

[11.] William Pfaff, "Torture: Shock, Awe, and the Human Body," *International Herald Tribune*, December 21, 2004.

practical purposes concluding that anything was permitted that did not (deliberately) kill the victim."

The Bush administration has systematically tried to block accountability for war crimes. It has refused to join the International Criminal Court and has pressured countries around the world to exempt Americans from prosecution. It pressured Belgium to repeal the law granting Belgian courts universal jurisdiction to try international law cases. As the *New York Times* put it, the Bush administration "drags its feet on public disclosure, stonewalls Congressional requests for documents and suppressed the results of internal investigations."[12]

The United States has promoted war crimes prosecutions starting with the Nuremberg trials after World War II and continuing to the recent trials in Rwanda, the current trials of Slobodan Milošević, and the impending trial of Saddam Hussein. These trials have all emphasized the accountability of top officials for acts committed under their authority. Is there any reason the same standard should not be applied to the top officials in the Bush administration?

FUTURE WAR CRIMES

Part III indicates that the problem of U.S. war crimes is not simply one of correcting misdeeds of the past. The Bush administration's actions in Iraq are part of a broader set of policies it refers to as the *war on terror*. These policies lay the groundwork and provide the justification for U.S. war crimes to continue in the future.

The Bush administration's security doctrine, as articulated in the 2002 *National Security Strategy*, declared a war on terror "of uncertain duration." It enunciated a doctrine of preventive war in which "the United States will act against such emerging threats before they are fully formed." It "will not hesitate to act alone, if necessary, to exercise our right of self defense by acting preemptively." As Senator Robert Byrd commented, "Under this strategy, the President lays claim to an expansive power to use our military to strike other nations first, even if we have not been threatened or provoked."

12. "Time for Accounting," editorial, *New York Times*, February 19, 2005.

The investigative journalist Seymour Hersh recently discovered that President Bush had signed "a series of findings and executive orders authorizing secret commando groups and other Special Forces units to conduct covert operations against suspected terrorist targets in as many as ten nations." Threats against Iran, Syria, North Korea, and other countries are repeatedly uttered by the Bush administration. Officials in the Department of Defense told the *New York Times* they are making plans for "fighting for intelligence," that is, commencing combat operations chiefly to obtain intelligence. U.S. officials are making plans to hold captives for their lifetimes without trial in countries around the world. And they are planning to create assassination teams—modeled on the "death squads" of El Salvador—to eliminate their opponents in Iraq.

FACING THE IMPLICATIONS

The possibility that high U.S. officials may be guilty of war crimes and may be preparing to commit more raises questions that few Americans have yet faced. These questions go far beyond technical legal matters to the broadest concerns of international security, democratic government, morality, and personal responsibility. Part IV presents perspectives from a variety of disciplines and political viewpoints designed to help us address those questions.

The UN Charter, the Geneva Conventions, and the principles of international law, while all too often violated, have provided some basis for international peace and security. What is the likely result of following the advice of the Bush administration's John Bolton that it is "a big mistake for us to grant any validity to international law"? Is it likely to be greater freedom and security, or an unending war of all against all? Are the American people—not to mention the people of the world—ready to abandon the international rule of law and return to what Justice Jackson called "a system of international lawlessness"?

The Bush administration has made extraordinary claims regarding the authority of the president to act without legal restraint. This questions the very idea of the United States as a democracy governed by a constitution. As Sanford Levinson writes in this volume: "The debate about torture is only one relatively small part of a far more profound debate that we should be having. Do 'We the People,' the ostensible sovereigns within the American system of government, accept the vision of the American president articulated by the Bush administration? And if we do, what, then, is left of the vaunted vision of the rule of law that the United States ostensibly exemplifies?"

The United States has vast power, but it includes only 5 percent of the world's people. If its leaders engage in war crimes with impunity, what is apt to happen to its relations with the rest of the world's peoples and governments? Can it gain cooperation to meet its national objectives and the needs of its people? Or will it face growing scorn and isolation?

And what about the moral questions raised by war crimes? Is there a limit to the behavior we are prepared to accept? As Bob Herbert asks in a recent article, "As a nation, does the United States have a conscience? Or is anything and everything O.K. in post-9/11 America? If torture and denial of due process are O.K., why not murder? . . . Where is the line that we, as a nation, dare not cross?"[13]

RESISTERS

Some of the most difficult issues are faced by those in the military and the government who may be directly complicit in war crimes. Some have said no to participation in the war in Iraq and the cover-up of related criminal activity. Part V presents statements by, interviews with, and articles about military and civilian resisters.

Specialist Jeremy Hinzman of Rapid City, South Dakota, joined the Eighty-second Airborne as a paratrooper in 2001. He wanted a career in the military and did a stint in Afghanistan. Then he was ordered to Iraq. "I was told in basic training that, if I'm given an illegal or immoral order, it is my duty to disobey it. And I feel that invading and occupying Iraq is an illegal and immoral thing to do."

In September 2004, Stephen Funk, a marine reservist of Filipino and Native American origin, was tried for refusing to fight in Iraq. "In the face of this unjust war based on deception by our leaders, I could not remain silent. In my mind that would have been true cow-

[13] Bob Herbert, "It's Called Torture," New York Times, February 28, 2005.

ardice . . . I spoke out so that others in the military would realize that they also have a choice and a duty to resist immoral and illegitimate orders."

In December 2004, the Hispanic sailor Pablo Paredes, wearing a T-shirt reading "Like a cabinet member, I resign," refused to board his Iraq-bound ship in San Diego Harbor. At his court-martial, Paredes said, "I am convinced that the current War on Iraq is illegal." As a member of the armed forces, "beyond having a duty to my chain of command and my President, I have a higher duty to my conscience and to the supreme Law of the land. Both of these higher duties dictate that I must not participate in any way, hands on or indirect, in the current Aggression that has been unleashed on Iraq. . . . I am guilty of believing that as a service member I have a duty to refuse to participate in this War because it is illegal." Astonishingly, the military judge, Lt. Cmdr. Robert Klant, accepted Paredes' war crimes defense and refused to send him to jail. The government prosecutor's case was so weak that Klant declared ironically, "I believe the government has just successfully proved that any seaman recruit has reasonable cause to believe that the wars in Yugoslavia, Afghanistan and Iraq were illegal."[14]

Resistance has also taken the form of unauthorized leaking of secret information about U.S. war crimes by military and government whistle-blowers. For example, in May 2003 a group of military lawyers went to visit a leader of the Association of the Bar of New York. They told him of the justifications for torture and other violations of the Geneva Conventions being propounded at high levels of government. The resulting report was one of the first public disclosures of the role of high government policy makers in torture and prisoner abuse.

These various kinds of resisters have taken a risk and often paid a price for their actions. Those actions may contribute to a greater or lesser degree to bringing war crimes to a halt. Beyond that, they pose to all Americans the question of what their own responsibility to halt war crimes may be.

[14] Lynn Gonzalez, "The Case of Pablo Paredes," ZNet, http://www.zmag.org/content/print_article.cfm?itemID=7973&sectionID=51.

HALTING WAR CRIMES

Under the principles established by the Nuremberg and Tokyo war crimes tribunals, those in a position to give orders are responsible for war crimes and crimes against humanity conducted under their authority. But responsibility does not end there. Anyone with knowledge of illegal activity and an opportunity to do something about it is a potential criminal under international law unless the person takes affirmative measures to prevent the commission of the crimes.[15] Part VI explores the responsibility of ordinary citizens and what "affirmative measures" they might take to bring war crimes to a halt.

Crimes are ordinarily dealt with by the institutions of law enforcement. But those institutions are largely in the hands of people who may be complicit in the very crimes that need to be investigated. Can they be held accountable? Or can war criminals forever act with impunity?

The problem of a government that is ostensibly democratically elected but that defies actual accountability is one that citizens in many countries have faced at one time or another. We can take inspiration from the way citizens from Serbia to the Philippines and from Chile to Ukraine have utilized "people power" to block illegal action and force accountability on their leaders. We can similarly take inspiration from resistance to illegitimate authority in our own country from the American Revolution to the Watergate investigations that ultimately brought the Nixon administration to account for its criminal abuse of power.

Part VI examines the failure of established institutional structures to restrain criminality on the part of the Bush administration. It considers how the processes of law enforcement could be revitalized to address war crimes. It also examines institutional forms that could be invoked, such as the U.S. War Crimes Act of 1996, congressional investigatory powers, a 9/11-style independent commission, and a special prosecutor, to establish accountability for these crimes. It de-

[15.] Francis Boyle, *Defending Civil Resistance Under International Law* (Dobbs Ferry, N.Y.: Transnational, 1987), p. 237.

scribes the role that military and governmental personnel and ordinary citizens can play in catalyzing change by refusing to obey illegal "law." It examines efforts to encourage and support such resistance. And it emphasizes the role of civil society and ordinary citizens in bringing American war crimes to a halt.

WAR CRIMES AND DEMOCRACY

If war crimes are being committed, they are being committed in the name of democracy. Their ostensible purpose is to extend democracy throughout the world. They are committed by a country that proudly proclaims itself the world's greatest democracy.

Such acts in Iraq and elsewhere represent, on the contrary, the subversion of democracy. They reflect the imposition by violence and brutality of a rule that is not freely chosen.

Such acts also represent a subversion of democracy at home. They represent a presidency that has denied all accountability to Congress, courts, or international institutions. As Elizabeth Holtzman puts it in her contribution to this volume: "The claim that the President . . . is above the law strikes at the very heart of our democracy. It was the centerpiece of President Richard Nixon's defense in Watergate—a defense that was rejected by the courts and lay at the foundation of the articles of impeachment voted against him by the House Judiciary Committee." It denies the constitutional constraints that have made the United States a government under law. It subverts democracy in the name of democracy.

War crimes represent the defiance not only of international but also of U.S. law. The effort to halt them is at once a movement for peace and a struggle for democracy.

Note: Wherever possible we have indicated both text and Internet sources for the full original documents we have excerpted.

The Evidence

INTRODUCTION

For the last sixty years, the U.S. Supreme Court, military judges, international lawyers, and American-sanctioned war crimes tribunals have engaged in investigation and prosecution of war crimes activity. As early as 1946, the U.S. Supreme Court affirmed the criminal liability of a Japanese commander who failed to prevent atrocities by his troops.[1] U.S. military operations manuals regularly incorporate Geneva Conventions provisions, with, for example, clauses for mandatory POW tribunals set up in the battlefield.[2] And in the last decade alone, U.S. administrations have supported war crimes tribunals in the former Yugoslavia, Rwanda, Sierra Leone, and East Timor. As U.S. troops readied their attack on Baghdad, President Bush proclaimed that if Iraqis "take innocent life, if they destroy infrastructure, they will be held accountable as war criminals . . . War crimes will be prosecuted. War criminals will be punished."[3]

What happens when the same standards are applied to U.S. activities in Iraq and other aspects of the war on terror? The answer is obscured by the fact that reliable, independent information is difficult to acquire. In Iraq, American journalists are restricted to the fortified "Green Zone," free to attend Pentagon press briefings but often too threatened to independently investigate or talk to average Iraqis. It is further obscured by an Administration that, according to the *New York Times*, "drags its feet on public disclosure, stonewalls Congressional requests for documents and suppresses the results of internal investigations."[4]

Indeed, the Bush administration is engaged in a large-scale

---

[1] "The law of war imposes on any . . . commander a duty to take such appropriate measures as are within his power to control the troops under his command for the prevention of acts which are violations of the law of war . . . he may be charged with personal responsibility for his failure to take such measures when violations result." *In re Yamashita*, 327 U.S. 1 (1946) at 14. See also W. Hays Parks, "Command Responsibility for War Crimes," 62 *Military Law Review* 1 (1973).

[2] See *United States Army Operations Law Handbook*, JA 422 at 272 (1997).

[3] Barry Schweid, "War Planning Includes Targeting Saddam Hussein; Top Prospects Uncertain," Associated Press, February 26, 2003; Vivienne Walt, "U.S. Officials Expect to Find Evidence of War Crimes," *USA Today*, March 18, 2003.

[4] "Time for Accounting," editorial, *New York Times*, February 19, 2005.

cover-up of war crimes. Its suppression of information ranges from denying the use of illegal napalm on the battlefield and refusing to track the Iraqi civilian death toll to hiding "ghost detainees" from the International Committee of the Red Cross and withholding executive orders relating to the prisoner abuse at Abu Ghraib. These activities culminate in the systematic refusal of the Administration to open full and proper investigations into allegations of war crimes. In the words of John Dean, the former whistle-blowing Nixon counsel, this is a cover-up "worse than Watergate."[5]

Despite the obstacles, intrepid journalists, lawyers, and investigators—aided by courageous whistle-blowers inside the government—have revealed evidence of terrible crimes, including civilian killings, use of illegal, indiscriminate weapons, and deliberate attacks on ambulances and residential areas. They show the now notorious prisoner abuse scandal to be the mere tip of the iceberg, indicating an administration engaged in large-scale and systematic criminal activity.

A court of law is the appropriate place to determine legal culpability. But the evidence presented in part I makes an overwhelming case that serious war crimes have been committed, and that those responsible for them should be removed from all positions of honor and authority and charged with criminal offenses.

"An Illegal War" tracks the Administration's launching of an illegal, aggressive war, deemed the ultimate crime by the Nuremberg Tribunal and the UN Charter. Drawing on the expertise of renowned international lawyers and scholars, it examines in detail U.S. arguments for invading Iraq, including claims of self-defense, humanitarianism, and implied authorization by the UN Security Council.

"Crimes of War and Occupation" illustrates that the Bush administration's crimes are not confined to aggression and torture, but rather extend to its conduct of the war and subsequent occupation of Iraq. For example, the Administration's bombing of residential neighborhoods, use of banned napalm, and denial of water to civilians violate the Geneva Conventions' primary requirement

5. John W. Dean, *Worse than Watergate* (New York: Little, Brown, 2004).

that occupying forces protect civilian populations from the brutalities of war.

Finally, "Tantamount to Torture" tracks the Administration's systematic use of torture to fight the war on terror. This emerging scandal is woven together with victims' statements, news articles, classified FBI memos, and investigative reports by the Department of Defense.

Part I does not seek to evoke a "shock effect" by presenting the most gruesome examples available. Rather, its goal is to provide the information needed to evaluate the legality of U.S. policies and practices. Later parts of this book will explore the social, political, and moral implications of these realities. This part presents the law and the facts.

AN ILLEGAL WAR

Following the attacks on the World Trade Center in 2001, key members of the Bush administration began pushing for the invasion of Iraq. Richard Clarke, the former counterterrorism chief for President Bush, recalls Secretary of Defense Donald Rumsfeld saying in the days after September 11, "We needed to bomb Iraq . . . There aren't any good targets in Afghanistan."[1] This was despite clear evidence provided by the CIA and the U.S. State Department that Iraq played no role in the Trade Center bombings. But the war plans of the Pentagon faced a serious hurdle: it is illegal to invade another country.

Principle VI of the Nuremberg Charter states that it is a crime to engage in the "planning, preparation, initiation or waging of a war of aggression or a war in violation of international treaties, agreements or assurances."[2] Of course nations still resort to war. But in the face of a general rule against the use of force, such violence must fall within one of two narrowly defined exceptions: either the attack has been authorized by the UN Security Council, or it is justified under the doctrine of self-defense.

Well aware of this prohibition, the Bush administration argued both exceptions simultaneously. First, asserting self-defense, it claimed Iraq to be a threat to the United States based on "evidence" of Iraq's stockpiling of weapons of mass destruction (WMD)—despite UN weapons inspectors' inability to find such evidence.[3] Second, unable to garner support at the UN Security Council, the Adminis-

---

[1] Leslie Stahl, "Interview with Richard Clarke," *Sixty Minutes*, March 21, 2004.

[2] Charter of the Nuremberg Tribunals, principle VI. Full text published in *Report of the International Law Commission Covering Its Second Session, 5 June–29 July 1950*, document A/1316, pp. 11–14.

[3] The strict limitations on self-defense as a justification for war were well established in international law long before the UN Charter. As Michael Byers, Associate Professor at Duke University Law School, explained, "customary law traditionally recognized a limited right of pre-emptive self-defense according to what are known as the '*Caroline criteria*.'" These date back to an incident in 1837, during a rebellion against British

tration argued an "implied" right to invade Iraq drawn from former UN Security Council resolutions.

The response by the national and international legal communities to these arguments was clear and resounding. A letter sent to the White House on behalf of more than one thousand law professors and U.S. legal organizations stated, "We consider that any future use of force without a new U.N. Security Council Resolution would constitute a crime against peace or aggressive war in violation of the U.N. Charter."

The selections in this section examine in detail U.S. arguments for going to war. "Tearing Up the Rules: The Illegality of Invading Iraq," a report prepared by the Center for Economic and Social Rights, addresses the Bush administration's self-defense claims, as well as subsequent humanitarian justifications. Also included is a short excerpt of a BBC interview with UN Secretary-General Kofi Annan, in which he unequivocally states, more than a year after the invasion, that the U.S. war "was illegal." Finally, in *Some Legal Aspects of the Military Operation in Iraq,* Christian Dominice, the Secretary-General of the Institute of International Law, examines and rejects U.S. arguments for implied authorization for the war by the UN Security Council.

If the Administration's legal case for war rested on stronger footing, this section might have required documents uncovered after the invasion that reveal the United States' misrepresentation of Iraq's WMD. These post-invasion documents include the secret "Downing Street Memo," which disclosed the minutes of a July 23, 2002, meeting of Tony Blair and his top military and intelligence of-

---

rule in Canada, when British troops attacked a ship (the *Caroline*) that was being used by private citizens in the United States to ferry supplies to the rebels. After a long diplomatic correspondence between the U.S. Secretary of State, Daniel Webster, and the British Foreign Office minister, Lord Ashburton, a form of words was agreed upon to govern acts of anticipatory self-defense: there must be "a necessity of self-defense, instant, overwhelming, leaving no choice of means, and no moment for deliberation" and the action taken must not be "unreasonable or excessive." "Iraq and the Bush Doctrine of Pre-emptive Self-Defense," Crimes of War Project, http://www.crimesofwar.org/ experts/bush-intro.html.

ficials. The head of the British intelligence service, MI6 (identified in the memo as "C"), reported on his recent trip to Washington: "Military action was now seen as inevitable. Bush wanted to remove Saddam, through military action, justified by the conjunction of terrorism and WMD. But the intelligence and facts were being fixed around the policy." Such documents revealing the Bush administration's intention to attack Iraq, and the failure to find WMD, merely heap excess evidence onto an already open-and-shut case.

Most of the following excerpts were written in 2003 during the lead-up to war and operate on the assumption that the Administration's factual claims were true. They clearly establish that the United States planned, prepared, and initiated a war of aggression.[4]

The invasion of Iraq is illegal for good reason. International law forbids aggressive war in any form, whether under the cloak of "military security," "democracy," or "fighting terrorism." It forces nations to present their claims and build consensus; and with a few but firm binding laws it works to contain raw, self-interested aggression.

---

[4] This section does not address the illegality of the U.S. invasion of Afghanistan. As Richard Falk states in part VI, footnote 36, of this book: "The Afghanistan war was undertaken without Security Council authorization, but at least there was a plausible case for American claims of self-defense, provided by the 9/11 attacks . . . [However,] even though the [Afghan war] had a legal basis, it was undertaken in a manner that makes it legally questionable."

Selected Principles of International Law

CHARTER OF THE UNITED NATIONS

Article 2(3): All Members shall settle their international disputes by peaceful means in such a manner that international peace and security, and justice, are not endangered.

Article 2(4): All Members shall refrain in their international relations from the threat or use of force against the territorial integrity or political independence of any state, or in any other manner inconsistent with the Purposes of the United Nations.

CHARTER OF THE NUREMBERG TRIBUNALS

PRINCIPLE VI: (a) Crimes against peace:

(i) Planning, preparation, initiation or waging of a war of aggression or a war in violation of international treaties, agreements or assurances;

(ii) Participation in a common plan or conspiracy for the accomplishment of any of the acts mentioned in (i).

PRINCIPLE VII: Complicity in the commission of a crime against peace, a war crime, or a crime against humanity as set forth in Principle VI is a crime under international law.

SOURCE: UN Charter, chapter 1, article 2. Available at http://www.un.org/aboutun/ charter. English text of the charter of the Nuremberg Tribunal published in *Report of the International Law Commission Covering Its Second Session, 5 June–29 July 1950,* document A/1316, pp. 11–14.

Tearing Up the Rules:
The Illegality of Invading Iraq

CENTER FOR ECONOMIC AND SOCIAL RIGHTS

As the United States and the United Kingdom prepared to invade Iraq, their officials made statements at the UN and elsewhere justifying their attack. Many international law scholars condemned their arguments and maintained that such an attack would be aggression and a crime against peace. The following excerpt is from a report that summarizes their main arguments. The report was prepared in March 2003 by the Center for Economic and Social Rights, an international human rights organization supported by the Ford and MacArthur foundations. Based in New York, the center holds consultative status with the United Nations.

PROHIBITION AGAINST FORCE IN INTERNATIONAL LAW

The United Nations was created in a mood of popular outrage after the horrors of World War II. Its central purpose was to serve as an instrument for maintaining peace in order "to save succeeding generations from the scourge of war, which twice in our lifetime has brought untold sorrow to mankind."[1] Leading jurists consider the U.N. Charter as the highest embodiment of international law — codifying and superseding existing laws and customs.[2]

Under Article 1(1) of the Charter, the world organization's central purpose is "to bring about by peaceful means and in conformity with the principles of justice and international law, adjustment or settlement of international disputes or situations which might lead to a breach of the peace." Similarly, Article 2(3) obligates member

SOURCE: Available at http://www.cesr.org/filestore2/download/523. Copyright © 2005 by Roger Normand and Center for Economic and Social Rights.

[1.] Preamble, Charter of the United Nations, June 26, 1945, entered into force October 24, 1945.

[2.] After the establishment of the United Nations, a number of influential international jurists argued that its charter superseded all previous customary international law. See, e.g., Hans Kelsen, *The Law of the United Nations* (London: Institute of World Affairs, 1950), p. 914; Ian Brownlie, *International Law and the Use of Force by States* (Oxford: Oxford University Press, 1948), p. 264; Philip Caryl Jessup, *A Modern Law of Nations—An Introduction* (New York: Macmillan, 1948), p. 165.

states to "settle their international disputes by peaceful means," while Article 2(4) provides that:

> All members shall refrain in their international relations from the threat or use of force against the territorial integrity or political independence of any state, or in any other manner inconsistent with the Purposes of the United Nations.

Only *two exceptions*, specified in the Charter and supplemented by customary international law, permit the lawful use of force. First is the right of individual or collective self-defense in response to an armed attack, under Article 51. Second is the specific authorization of force by the Security Council as a last resort to maintain international peace and security, under Chapter VII. If the planned attack by the U.S. and U.K. against Iraq fails to meet the specific criteria set forth in these exceptions, or under principles of customary international law, then it will be an unlawful act of aggression—defined and condemned by the Nuremberg Military Tribunal as "the supreme international crime."[3]

RIGHT OF SELF-DEFENSE IN INTERNATIONAL LAW

Limits of Self-Defense in the UN Charter

Article 51 of the UN Charter recognizes that member states have the "inherent right of individual or collective self-defense *if an armed attack occurs*" (emphasis added). The urgency of responding to such attack entitles a state to defend its sovereignty through the unilateral use of retaliatory force—but only "until the Security Council has taken measures necessary to maintain peace and security."[4] As discussed in Section IV below, once the Security Council formally determines the existence of a threat to international peace and security, individual states may no longer exercise the right of self-defense without the Council's express prior approval (as happened in the 1991 Gulf War).

[3] 6 Federal Rules Decisions (FRD) 69, 109.
[4] UN Charter, article 51.

Article 51 applies only in the event of an actual armed attack. As Iraq has not attacked the U.S. or U.K., and there is no credible, substantiated evidence connecting Iraq to the September 11th attacks, the U.S. and U.K. may not invoke self-defense under the U.N. Charter to justify attacking Iraq. They must therefore rely on the disputed doctrine of preemptive self-defense under customary law.

Preemptive Self-Defense in Customary International Law

Although the Charter itself does not provide legal authority to use force against a perceived threat of imminent attack,[5] there does exist a disputed customary international law right of preemptive self-defense. According to the famous formulation of U.S. Secretary of State Daniel Webster, adopted by the seminal *Caroline* case, the legitimate exercise of this right requires "a necessity of self-defense, instant, overwhelming, leaving no choice of means, and no moment for deliberation."[6]

This has been interpreted to establish a red line between "anticipatory" self-defense in response to an attack that *might* occur at an unknown point in the future, and "interceptive" self-defense in response to an *imminent and unavoidable* attack. It is generally accepted that "in the case of anticipatory self-defense, it is more judicious to consider such action as *legally prohibited*."[7] Only in the rare case where interceptive self-defense can be shown, through clear and convincing evidence, as necessary to avoid a greater harm might it arguably be lawful to use force outside the limits of the Charter.[8]

The U.S. and U.K. seek to justify war on the grounds that Iraq intended to acquire and use weapons of mass destruction against

---

[5] R. Singh, A. Macdonald, and Matrix Chambers (public interest lawyers on behalf of Peacerights), *Opinion on the Legality of the Use of Force Against Iraq*, para. 17, p. 8 (September 10, 2002).

[6] Letter from U.S. Secretary of State Daniel Webster to Lord Ashburton, August 6, 1842, quoted in John Bassett Moore, *A Digest of International Law*, vol. 2 (1906), p. 412.

[7] A. Cassese, *International Law* (Oxford: Oxford University Press, 2001), p. 311.

[8] See, e.g., Yoram Dinstein, *War, Aggression and Self-Defence*, 2nd ed. (Cambridge: Cambridge University Press, 1994), p. 188.

them at an unspecified point in the future. Yet despite advanced intelligence-gathering capabilities, neither country has presented any credible evidence that Iraq possessed any proscribed weapons, let alone the intent and capacity to use them in an imminent attack. After conducting more than 550 inspections in almost four months, UNMOVIC teams failed to uncover evidence that Iraq maintained either stocks of such weapons or the operational capacity to deploy and deliver them against the U.S. or U.K.[9] Even Iraq's neighbors rejected the argument that military intervention from outside powers was necessary under the right of collective self-defense to protect them from an imminent Iraqi threat.

Under these circumstances, war against Iraq violated any reasonable interpretation of either the Charter's limited provision for self-defense exception or the customary law principle of preemptive self-defense. The potential threat Iraq posed to the U.S. and U.K. was not imminent, unavoidable, or even particularly credible. Launching a massive invasion to overthrow its government and occupy its territory in response to a dubious hypothetical future threat was neither a necessary nor proportionate response. In essence, the U.S. and U.K. argument for preemptive strike closely resembles the long-discredited doctrine of preventive war, definitively abolished after World War II.

Nuremberg Ban on Preventive War

Preventive war is unequivocally illegal. In 1946, the International Military Tribunal at Nuremberg rejected Germany's argument that it had been compelled to attack Norway and Denmark in self-defense to prevent a future Allied invasion.[10] The Tribunal concluded that these attacks violated customary law limits on self-defense and instead constituted wars of aggression whose prohibition was demanded by the conscience of the world.[11] As the Tribunal stated:

---

9. *Twelfth Quarterly Report of the Executive Chairman of UNMOVIC*, S/2003/232 (February 28, 2003).
10. 6 FRD 69, 83.
11. Ibid., 88, 117–18.

To initiate a war of aggression, therefore, is not only an international crime; it is *the supreme international crime* differing only from other war crimes in that it contains within itself the accumulated evil of the whole.[12]

Nuremberg's condemnation of preventive war was incorporated into the U.N. Charter, affirmed by the General Assembly,[13] and accepted by the Security Council. In 1978, the U.S. mobilized the Security Council to condemn Vietnam's invasion of Cambodia and overthrow of the violently repressive Khmer Rouge regime, terming it a breach of the Charter and an act of aggression in violation of international law. Similarly, in 1981, the Council unanimously condemned Israel's "preventive" attack against an Iraqi nuclear plant as a "clear violation of the Charter of the UN and the norms of international conduct."[14] A Council member explained the consensus:

The concept of preventive war, which for many years served as a justification for the abuses of powerful States, since it left to their discretion to define what constituted a threat to them, was definitively abolished by the Charter of the U.N.[15]

The German argument in favor of preventive war was judged and condemned by the Nuremberg Tribunal, and German leaders held individually accountable as war criminals. Any return to this doctrine by powerful states such as the U.S. and U.K. would undermine world public order, and in the process encourage states and non-state actors alike to launch unilateral acts of aggression unconstrained by longstanding principles of international law.

Humanitarian Intervention

The U.S. and U.K. have also sought to justify war under the legally dubious doctrine of humanitarian intervention, a new concept that

---

[12.] Ibid., 109 (emphasis added).
[13.] General Assembly resolution 95(I) (December 11, 1946).
[14.] Security Council resolution 487 (1981), operative paragraph 1; International Legal Materials (ILM) 965 (1981).
[15.] ILM (1981), Mexico, 991–92.

has not gained the support of the international law community. This doctrine—recently advocated by several Western countries and human rights organizations—proposes that the international community has the right and duty to use military force for humanitarian purposes such as stopping egregious violations of human rights.[16] This concept has aroused considerable skepticism from most international lawyers, in part because it circumvents well-established procedures and principles of the U.N. Charter and international law.[17] Even supporters concede that humanitarian intervention is a moral argument rather than a legal right.

The attraction of humanitarian intervention lies in its capacity to redress gross human rights abuses that otherwise might fall outside the scope of Security Council action—the genocide in Rwanda, for example. However, this is a misreading of the Council's authority. Major crises like the Rwandan genocide have regional and international repercussions. The Council is therefore already empowered, under Chapter VII, to respond with force if necessary as a final resort to maintain peace and security and uphold the U.N.'s fundamental purposes, which include "encouraging respect for human rights and fundamental freedoms."[18] As a matter of historical record, the Security Council did consider military intervention in Rwanda but was blocked repeatedly by its permanent members, including the U.S., the U.K, and France.[19]

The obvious danger of humanitarian intervention is that it enables individual states to intervene wherever and whenever they perceive a compelling humanitarian necessity, unaccountable to established legal limits on the use of force. There is no safeguard to

[16.] Human Rights Watch, Report on Kosovo Bombing, *Civilian Deaths in the NATO Air Campaign* (2000).

[17.] B. Simma, "NATO, the UN and the Use of Force: Legal Aspects" (1999) 10 *European Journal of International Law* 1 at 22; A. Cassese, *"Ex iniuria ius oritur:* Are We Moving towards International Legitimation of Forcible Humanitarian Countermeasures in the World Community?" (1999) 10 *European Journal of International Law* 23 at 25; M. Koskenniemi, "'The Lady Doth Protest Too Much': Kosovo, and the Turn to Ethics in International Law" (2002) 65 *Modern Law Review* 159 at 162.

[18.] UN Charter, article 1.

[19.] Samantha Power, *A Problem from Hell: America and the Age of Genocide* (New York: Basic Books, 2002).

prevent states from manipulating this concept to serve narrow political interests rather than universal humanitarian concerns. From the standpoint of preventing human rights abuses, it would seem more effective, morally and legally, to promote principled and consistent enforcement of the existing legal framework of the U.N. Charter, the Universal Declaration of Human Rights, the Geneva Conventions, and international law in general.

In the case of Iraq, this controversial new doctrine is being interpreted by the U.S. and U.K. to circumvent the Charter altogether and justify war against Iraq without Security Council approval. The U.S. has openly called for "regime change" in Iraq—ostensibly in response to the government's well-documented record of political repression, human rights abuses, and chemical weapons use—despite having systematically ignored these abuses during the 1980s when President Saddam Hussein was actively serving U.S. interests in the region.[20]

> The human rights situation in Iraq is being invoked with unusual frequency by some Western political leaders to justify military action. This selective attention to human rights is nothing but a cold and calculated manipulation of the work of human rights activists.[21]
>
> —Irene Khan, Secretary-General of Amnesty International, September 25, 2002

By invoking the concept of humanitarian intervention to justify an otherwise unlawful use of force, the U.S. and U.K. would effectively overturn the established hierarchy of international law. The practical outcome would be to shift decision-making on basic issues of peace and security from multilateral U.N. mechanisms to individual states, empowering them to use force without accountability to general principles of law.

[20] Patrick E. Tyler, "Officers Say U.S. Aided Iraq in War Despite Use of Gas," *New York Times,* August 17, 2002.
[21] Irene Khan, "Iraq II: Who Cares About the People?" *International Herald Tribune,* September 25, 2002.

U.S. policy towards Iraq poses a direct challenge to the central purpose of the United Nations, in particular the Charter's prohibition on the use of preventive force. While Prime Minister Blair has hesitated to pursue open defiance of the U.N. and sought legal justification for war, the Bush administration has publicly insisted that the U.S. will invade Iraq and pursue "regime change" under any and all circumstances, including opposition in the Council. As President Bush recently declared, "we really don't need anybody's permission."[22]

Alarmed by the imminent threat to global security and the U.N. system as a whole, international lawyers have rapidly developed a consensus that war against Iraq violates the outer limits of laws regulating the use of force.[23] Legal associations and human rights groups around the world have condemned the threatened used of force by the U.S., U.K., and states acting in concert with them, and initiated actions to hold such governments accountable for war crimes and crimes against the peace.

> The Administration has made clear that such an attack is based on long-term foreign policy, if not moral reasons, and not on any concept of defending the United States from [an] imminent military threat . . . The Committee concludes, therefore, that Resolution 678 does not provide authorization for the invasion contemplated by the Bush Administration.[24]
>
> —The New York City Bar Committee on
> International Security Affairs, Fall 2002

---

[22] "U.S. Says U.N. Could Repeat Errors of 90's," *New York Times*, March 11, 2003.

[23] World Editorial and International Law, "International Law Scholars Appeal to U.N. Secretary-General," press release, March 11, 2003; International Association of Lawyers Against Nuclear Arms, "International Appeal by Lawyers and Jurists Against the 'Preventive' Use of Force," February 14, 2003; letter of European law professors, "War Would Be Illegal," *Guardian*, March 7, 2003.

[24] The Committee on International Security Affairs of the Association of the Bar of the City of New York, *The Legality and Constitutionality of the President's Authority to Initiate an Invasion of Iraq*, vol. 57, no. 4, at 382, 390 (Fall 2002).

We consider that any future use of force without a new U.N. Security Council Resolution would constitute a crime against
peace or aggressive war in violation of the U.N. Charter.[25]

> —Center for Constitutional Rights, on behalf of
> over one thousand law professors and U.S.
> legal organizations, January 24, 2002

The U.S. Administration has offered several different justifications for a war against Iraq. Yet, in essence, the planned military
action comes down to an act of aggression against Iraq, the
characterization of which as a "preventive" war does nothing to
alter its illegality under international law.[26]

> —Freiburg Lawyers Declaration, on behalf of
> over one hundred German jurists, February
> 10, 2003

As this report demonstrates, war against Iraq cannot be justified
under any reasonable interpretation of international law. U.S. and
U.K. arguments in support of attacking Iraq are based, in essence,
on the unilateral right of powerful states to preempt even the possibility of future threats from other states, no matter how speculative
or remote. This position is manifestly illegal, and constitutes an act
of aggression within the legal definition of a crime against peace.

[25] Center for Constitutional Rights, "Letter to President George W. Bush on Consequences of Future Use of Force Against Iraq," January 24, 2002.
[26] Kai Ambos, "Freiburg Lawyers Declaration of 10 February 2003—On German Participation in a War Against Iraq," 4 *German Law Journal* 3 (2003).

An Illegal War

BBC Interview with Kofi Annan

The BBC interviewed United Nations Secretary-General Kofi Annan on September 16, 2004, more than a year after the United States invaded Iraq. In his remarks, excerpted below, the normally cautious and diplomatic Annan stunned the world by declaring the U.S. invasion illegal under the UN Charter and international law.

Q: Are you bothered that the U.S. is becoming an unrestrainable, unilateral power?

A: Well, I think over the last year, we've all gone through lots of painful lessons. I'm talking about since the war in Iraq. I think there [have] been lessons for the U.S. and there [have] been lessons for the UN and other member states and I think in the end everybody is concluding that it is best to work together with our allies and through the UN to deal with some of these issues. And I hope we do not see another Iraq-type operation for a long time . . .

Q: . . . Do you think that the resolution that was passed on Iraq before the war did actually give legal authority to do what was done?

A: Well, I'm one of those who believe that there should have been a second resolution because the Security Council indicated that if Iraq did not comply there will be consequences. But then it was up to the Security Council to approve or determine what those consequences should be.

Q: So you don't think there was legal authority for the war?

A: I have stated clearly that it was not in conformity with the Security Council—with the UN Charter.

Q: It was illegal?

A: Yes, if you wish.

Q: It was illegal?

A: Yes, I have indicated it is not in conformity with the UN Charter, from our point of view, and from the Charter point of view it was illegal.

SOURCE: Interview originally appeared on the BBC, September 16, 2004. Available at http://news.bbc.co.uk/2/hi/middle_east/ 3661640.stm.

Some Legal Aspects of the Military Operation in Iraq

CHRISTIAN DOMINICE

As national and international opposition to the attack on Iraq grew, the Bush administration dispatched Secretary of State Colin Powell to the UN to argue that Iraq was in "material breach" of existing UN Security Council resolutions, thereby granting an implied U.S. right to attack. In the following article, Christian Dominice considers and refutes this claim. Dominice is an emeritus professor at the University of Geneva and the Secretary-General of the Institute of International Law, an organization that plays a key advisory role to the United Nations.

The United States attempted, particularly during the first months of 2003, to convince the Members of the Security Council to adopt a Resolution authorizing the use of force against Iraq, but without success. The main opponents, France, Germany, and Russia, argued that the disarmament of Iraq was to be achieved through the work of UN inspectors, as stipulated by CS Resolution 1441 (2001). Without an expressed authorization by the Security Council, the invasion of Iraq was manifestly contrary to the Charter, hence illegal. However, it has been argued that an implied authorization could be deduced from previous CS Resolutions.

For example Resolution 1441, which has been so much discussed, was invoked. It is a text which, *inter alia*, decides that Iraq "has been and remains in material breach of its obligations under relevant resolutions, including resolution 687 (1991), in particular through Iraq's failure to cooperate with United Nations inspectors and the IAEA [International Atomic Energy Agency] . . ." It imposes on Iraq various obligations concerning inspections and cooperation with UN inspectors. It then concludes with the paragraph: "Recalls, in that context, that the Council has repeatedly warned

SOURCE: Article originally written in July 2003 and published in Irwin Abrams and Wang Gungwu, eds., *The Iraq War and Its Consequences* (London, Singapore: World Scientific Publishing Co., 2003). Available at http://www.worldscibooks.com/general/ 5381.html. Copyright © 2005 by World Scientific Publishing Co. This article expresses the personal opinion of the author and not that of the institute.

that it will face serious consequences as a result of its continued violations of its obligations."

Neither the decision that Iraq is in material breach of its obligation, nor the warning at the end of the Resolution, can really be considered as constituting an authorization given by any Member State to go to war against Iraq. Resolution 1441 is no argument. The "serious consequences" are measures to be decided by the Security Council.

It has also been attempted, but with no convincing force, to argue that Resolution 678 (1990), which authorized the use of force to restore Kuwait's Sovereignty, or Resolution 687 (1991), which imposed a set of obligations on Iraq—with its agreement—afforded a legal basis for the war against Iraq. The purpose for which the use of force had been authorized by the first one had been achieved in 1991, and the second one did not authorize the use of force against Iraq.

Our conclusion is that the invasion of Iraq was not justified by either of the two exceptions to the prohibition of the use of force. It was illegal.

CRIMES OF WAR AND OCCUPATION

On March 20, 2003, the United States began bombing Iraq. The strategy was to "shock and awe" the enemy, dropping nearly three thousand bombs in the first few days of the war.[1] As one Pentagon strategist boasted to CBS News, "There will not be a safe place in Baghdad." Immediately, reports of civilian casualties began to pour in. The *Los Angeles Times* surveyed Baghdad hospitals and found records of 1,700 civilians killed and 8,000 injured in the battle for Baghdad alone.[2] The Associated Press deemed its hospital footage of babies cut in half and children with their limbs blown off too upsetting to air on television.[3]

The laws of war—as codified in the Geneva Conventions—prescribe rules for conducting battle as humanely as possible. They are guided by the principle that persons who do not take part in armed hostilities are entitled to special protection and humane treatment. In practice this means shielding civilians from battle, protecting the civilian infrastructure, and assuming responsibility for essential services as an occupying power. Both in conducting the war and as an occupying power, the United States has failed to comply with these laws of war, and as a result, unknown numbers of Iraqi civilians have been killed or maimed.

The reports and articles in this section present evidence of these crimes. The United States has used cluster bombs in residential neighborhoods, where injured survivors watched as the bombs "fell like grapes from the sky . . . bounc[ing] through the windows and doors of their homes."[4] Two British journalists report the U.S. use of napalm, infamous from the Vietnam War, as well as depleted uranium-tipped weapons, which cause high

---

[1.] "Baghdad Wakes Up to Explosions," Fox News, March 22, 2003. Available at http://www.foxnews.com/story/0,2933,81791,00.html.

[2.] Laura King, "Baghdad's Death Toll Assessed," *Los Angeles Times*, May 18, 2003.

[3.] Amnesty International, *Iraq: Civilians Under Fire* (April 2002), p. 2. Available at http://www.web.amnesty.org/library/index/engmde140712003.

[4.] Ibid., p. 1.

rates of birth deformities, blood infections, and cancer. According to a study by Johns Hopkins University researchers, an estimated 100,000 Iraqi civilians have died as a result of the U.S. bombing and invasion.

Alarmed by the rising civilian death toll and the U.S. use of illegal weaponry, the preeminent human rights group Amnesty International issued an urgent report titled *Iraq: Civilians Under Fire*, calling for "an immediate moratorium on the use of cluster bombs by the U.S./U.K. forces . . . that are inherently indiscriminate."[5] Such weapons are illegal under the Geneva Conventions, which expressly forbid "arms, projectiles or materials calculated to cause unnecessary suffering" to civilians.[6]

The United States has also deliberately targeted medical facilities. In Fallujah, U.S. troops began their attack on "insurgent strongholds" by storming the local hospital to assuage the U.S. Department of Defense's concerns about "inflated civilian casualty figures" coming from the medical facilities.[7] In response, Congressman Jim McDermott and Dr. Richard Rapport wrote an op-ed, reprinted here, that calls for an investigation of this serious violation of the Geneva Conventions.

The law of war also mandates that all military action must be necessary and proportionate to the threat being faced.[8] Nevertheless, Amnesty International and other human rights organizations document routine use of disproportional force at checkpoints and during house searches. In the words of one senior British officer in Iraq: "The view of the British chain of command is that the Americans' use of violence is not proportionate and is over-responsive to the threat they are facing. They are not concerned about the Iraqi

---

5. Ibid.
6. Hague Convention IV, Respecting the Laws and Customs of War on Land, article 23. Available at http://www.yale.edu/lawweb/avalon/lawofwar/hague04.htm.
7. See the petition submitted to the Inter-American Commission on Human Rights at the Organization of American States by the Association of Humanitarian Lawyers, November 24, 2004. Available at http://www.brusselstribunal.org/Lawsuit_OAS.htm.
8. See the "Protocol Additional to the Geneva Conventions of 12 August 1949, and Relating to the Protection of Victims of International Armed Conflicts (Protocol I), 8 June 1977." Available at http://www.icrc.org/ihl.nsf/7c4d08d9b287a421412567390003e 636b/f6c8b9fee14a77fdc125641e0052b079.

loss of life . . . It is trite, but American troops do shoot first and ask questions later."[9]

But it is not only bombs and bullets that kill or maim civilians in war zones. According to the Columbia University professor Jeffrey Sachs, Iraqi "children in urban war zones die in vast numbers from diarrhea, respiratory infections and other causes, owing to unsafe drinking water, lack of refrigerated foods, and acute shortages of blood and basic medicines in clinics and hospitals." The Geneva Conventions require that when one nation invades another, the invading nation assumes responsibility for caring for the civilian population. As a result, under occupation law, the United States is legally bound to provide services such as electricity, medical care, food, and education. *U.S. Violations of Occupation Law in Iraq*, prepared by the Center for Economic and Social Rights, carefully documents the persistent failure of American forces to secure these fundamental rights for Iraqis; and in *Denial of Water in Iraqi Cities*, Daniel O'Huiginn and Alison Klevnas present evidence of a "deliberate U.S. policy of denying water to the residents of cities under attack."

Although much attention has been paid to the buildup to war and the prisoner abuse scandal, the crimes associated with the conduct of the war and occupation have gone largely unreported. The articles and reports in this section begin to correct this imbalance, presenting some of the clearest war crimes committed by the Bush administration. For these various crimes of occupation—whether targeting residential neighborhoods with cluster bombs or deliberately attacking hospitals—are not mere technical or minor breaches of international law. Rather, they violate the core principle of the Geneva Conventions—protection of civilians regardless of emergency.

[9.] Sean Rayment, "U.S. Tactics Condemned by British Officers," *Telegraph*, April 11, 2004. Available at http://www.telegraph.co.uk/news/main.jhtml?xml=/news/2004/04/11/wtact11.xml.

Iraq: Civilians Under Fire

Amnesty International

In April 2003, one month into the "Shock and Awe" campaign in Iraq, Amnesty International issued the report *Iraq: Civilians Under Fire*. It documents the brutal effect of American use of illegal cluster bombs on residential areas and presents examples of Iraqi civilian deaths at the hands of U.S. troops. Amnesty International is a human rights organization with more than 1.8 million members located in 150 countries around the world.

Amnesty International (AI) is deeply concerned about the mounting toll of civilian casualties in Iraq and the reported use of cluster bombs by U.S. forces in heavily populated areas. Despite repeated assurances from U.S. and U.K. authorities that they would do everything possible to protect the Iraqi people, since 20 March hundreds of civilians have reportedly been killed. Some have been victims of cluster bombs; some have died in attacks in disputed circumstances. AI urges all the warring parties to make the safety of Iraqi civilians a top priority.

CLUSTER BOMBS AND OTHER INDISCRIMINATE WEAPONS

The scenes at al-Hilla's hospital on 1 April showed that something terrible had happened. The bodies of the men, women and children—both dead and alive—brought to the hospital were punctured with shards of shrapnel from cluster bombs. Videotape of the victims was judged by *Reuters* and *Associated Press* editors as being too awful to show on television. *Independent* newspaper journalists reported that the pictures showed babies cut in half and children with their limbs blown off. Two lorry-loads of bodies, including women in flowered dresses, were seen outside the hospital.

Injured survivors told reporters how the explosives fell "like grapes" from the sky, and how bomblets bounced through the

SOURCE: Available at http://www.amnestyusa.org/countries/iraq/document.do? id= 66FAC9972223B83180256D03003C478D. Copyright © 2005 by Amnesty International.

windows and doors of their homes before exploding. A doctor at al-Hilla's hospital said that almost all the patients were victims of cluster bombs.

Many of the cluster bombs reportedly dropped from the air by U.S. forces on a civilian area of al-Hilla were of the type BLU97 A. Each canister contains 202 small bomblets the size of a soft drink can. These cluster bombs scatter and spray over a large area about the size of two football fields. At least 5 per cent of the bomblets do not explode on impact, turning them into *de facto* anti-personnel mines as they continue to pose a threat to people, including civilians, who come into contact with them.

The devastating consequences of using cluster bombs in civilian areas are utterly predictable. If, as accounts suggest, U.S. forces dropped cluster bombs in residential areas of al-Hilla, even if they were directed at military targets, such an action could constitute a disproportionate attack. This would be a grave breach of international humanitarian law. An independent and thorough investigation must be held and those found responsible for any violations of the laws of war should be brought to justice. The U.S. and U.K. authorities should order the immediate halt to further use of cluster bombs.

The rules of war prohibit the use of inherently indiscriminate weapons. These are weapons which are incapable of being used in a manner that complies with the obligation to distinguish between civilians and combatants.

CIVILIAN KILLINGS

The U.S. and U.K. governments have repeatedly stated that they have "no quarrel with the Iraqi people." However, the reality is that prolonged and intense bombardment in or near residential areas has destroyed homes and livelihoods, and has maimed and killed civilians, including children. "Fatal errors" have cost lives. Hospitals around the country say they are overwhelmed by the number of injured people arriving at their doors, and can no longer cope. The International Committee of the Red Cross said on 7 April that several hundred wounded Iraqis had been admitted to Baghdad hospitals after U.S. troops reached the city and fighting erupted.

Detailed information about the killing and wounding of Iraqi civilians is hard to verify. However, there have been a number of incidents in which U.S. and U.K. forces may have breached international humanitarian law.

The following incidents demand investigation. They are by no means a comprehensive list of all the civilian casualties reported, but serve to highlight the extent of the suffering and the urgent need to establish the truth and ensure that such tragedies are not repeated.

6 April: Ali Ismaeel Abbas, 12, was asleep when a missile obliterated his home and most of his family, leaving him orphaned, badly burned and without arms, according to a *Reuters* report. The boy's father, pregnant mother, brother, aunt, three cousins and three other relatives were killed in night-time missile strikes on their house in Diala Bridge district east of Baghdad.

31 March: A U.S. Apache helicopter reportedly fired on and destroyed a pickup truck in the region of al-Haidariya near al-Hilla. The sole survivor, Razeq al-Kadhem al-Khafaji, told an *AFP* journalist how 15 members of his family were killed in the attack. He said the family was fleeing fierce fighting in al-Nasiriya, further south, when their truck was blown up. Sitting among the 15 coffins at the local hospital, he said he had lost his wife, six children, his father, his mother, his three brothers and their wives. The circumstances of the attack have not been clarified to AI's knowledge.

31 March: Soldiers with the U.S. Army's 3rd Infantry Division killed seven women and children when they opened fire on an unidentified four-wheel-drive vehicle as it approached a U.S. checkpoint near al-Najaf. According to a Pentagon spokesman, initial reports indicated that "the soldiers responded in accordance with the rules of engagement to protect themselves." However, this does not appear to be consistent with the version reported in the *Washington*

Post, which indicated that the officer in command at the scene believed at the time that no warning shots were fired. It asserts that the officer roared at the platoon leader, "You just [expletive] killed a family because you didn't fire a warning shot soon enough!"

28 March: A shattering explosion reportedly killed at least 62 people in a market in Baghdad's poor al-Shu'la neighbourhood. A distraught mother, Sumaya' Abed, said that three of her sons had been killed by pieces of shrapnel that cut through their chests and heads. The youngest was just 11 years old. Both the U.S. and U.K. governments publicly suggested that the explosion was "probably" caused by an ageing Iraqi anti-aircraft missile. However, according to the *Independent* newspaper, the remains of a serial number of a missile were found at the scene, identifying it as one manufactured in Texas, the U.S.A., by Raytheon, the world's biggest producer of "smart armaments," and sold to the U.S. Navy. AI believes that in such disputed circumstances independent investigation is vital.

RECOMMENDATIONS

Throughout the crisis AI has sought to focus attention on the rights of the Iraqi people. AI has sought assurances from all parties to the conflict that they will do their utmost to comply with their obligations under international human rights and humanitarian law. AI reiterates its appeal to the parties, in particular for: an immediate moratorium on the use of cluster bombs by U.S./U.K. forces and on other weapons that are inherently indiscriminate or otherwise prohibited under international humanitarian law; all parties involved to declare their readiness to avail themselves of the services of the International Humanitarian Fact-Finding Commission[1] regarding incidents of alleged serious violations of international humanitarian law.

[1.] In order to secure the guarantees afforded to the victims of armed conflicts, article 90 of the First Additional Protocol to the Geneva Conventions of 1949 provides for the establishment of an international fact-finding commission. This commission was officially constituted in 1991 and is a permanent international body whose main purpose is to investigate allegations of grave breaches and serious violations of international humanitarian law.

Use of Illegal Weapons by the U. S. Military

The following two excerpted articles by British journalists reveal the U.S. use of depleted uranium shells and napalm firebombs against Iraqi troops, insurgents, and civilians. Both of these weapons have been deemed illegal weapons of mass destruction under international treaties. Neil Mackay is a reporter for the *Sunday Herald,* and Andrew Buncombe works for the *Independent.*

U.S. Forces' Use of Depleted Uranium Weapons Is "Illegal"

NEIL MACKAY

American forces are using depleted uranium (DU) shells in the war against Iraq and flouting a United Nations resolution which classifies the munitions as illegal weapons of mass destruction.

DU contaminates land, causes ill-health and cancers among the soldiers using the weapons, the armies they target and civilians, leading to birth defects.

Professor Doug Rokke, ex-director of the Pentagon's depleted uranium project and onetime U.S. army colonel who was tasked by the U.S. department of defense with the post–first Gulf war depleted uranium desert clean-up, said use of DU was a "war crime."

Rokke said: "There is a moral point to be made here. This war was about Iraq possessing illegal weapons of mass destruction—yet we are using weapons of mass destruction ourselves." He added: "Such double-standards are repellent."

According to a August 2002 report by the UN [Subcommission on the Promotion and Protection of Human Rights], laws which are breached by the use of DU shells include: the Universal Declaration of Human Rights; the Charter of the United Nations; the Genocide Convention; the Convention Against Torture; [and] the four Geneva Conventions of 1949, which expressly forbid employing "poison or

SOURCE: Originally appeared in the *Sunday Herald,* March 30, 2003. Available at http://www.sundayherald/print32522.

poisoned weapons" and "arms, projectiles or materials calculated to cause unnecessary suffering." All of these laws are designed to spare civilians from unwarranted suffering in armed conflicts.

Rokke told the *Sunday Herald*: "A nation's military personnel cannot wilfully contaminate any other nation, cause harm to persons and the environment and then ignore the consequences of their actions . . . To do so is a crime against humanity."

U.S. Admits It Used Napalm Bombs in Iraq

ANDREW BUNCOMBE

American pilots dropped the controversial incendiary agent napalm on Iraqi troops during the advance on Baghdad. The attacks caused massive fireballs that obliterated several Iraqi positions.

The Pentagon denied using napalm at the time, but Marine pilots and their commanders have confirmed that they used an upgraded version of the weapon against dug-in positions.

The upgraded weapon, which uses kerosene rather than petrol, was used in March and April, when dozens of napalm bombs were dropped near bridges over the Saddam Canal and the Tigris River, south of Baghdad.

"We napalmed both those [bridge] approaches," said Colonel James Alles, commander. "Unfortunately there were people there . . . you could see them in the [cockpit] video. They were Iraqi soldiers. It's no great way to die. The generals love napalm."

At the time, the Pentagon insisted the report was untrue. "We completed destruction of our last batch of napalm on 4 April, 2001," it said.

The Pentagon said it had not tried to deceive. It drew a distinction between traditional napalm, first invented in 1942, and the weapons dropped in Iraq, which it calls Mark 77 firebombs.

Officials said that if journalists had asked about the firebombs their use would have been confirmed. A spokesman admitted they were "remarkably similar" to napalm.

John Pike, director of the military studies group GlobalSecurity.Org, said: "The U.S. is the only country that has used napalm for a long time."

SOURCE: Originally appeared in the *Independent*, August 10, 2003. Available at http://www.globalsecurity.org/org/news/2003/030810-napalm-iraq01.htm.

Investigate Alleged Violations of Law in Fallujah Attack

Congressman Jim McDermott and
Dr. Richard Rapport

In April and again in November 2004, the U.S. military launched full-scale attacks on the city of Fallujah, Iraq. The apparent goal was collective punishment against an entire city. According to one military analyst, "Even if Fallujah has to go the way of Carthage, reduced to shards, the price will be worth it," in order to break the back of the insurgency.[1] The following op-ed calls for an investigation of resulting war crimes in Fallujah, based on evidence of U.S. attacks on medical facilities, denial of vital water and electrical services to civilian populations, and deliberate bombing of religious buildings and residential neighborhoods.

Jim McDermott, M.D., represents Washington State's Seventh District in Congress. Richard Rapport, M.D., is in the neurological surgery department at Group Health.

At the beginning of their recent attack on Fallujah, U.S. Marines and Iraqi National Guard troops stormed Fallujah General Hospital, closing it to the city's wounded and confiscating cell phones from the doctors. A senior officer told the *New York Times* the hospital was "a center of propaganda."

Interviews with hospital personnel (which had revealed the extent of civilian casualties in an aborted April invasion) would not be a problem this time.

As the invasion proceeded, air strikes reduced a smaller hospital to rubble and smashed a clinic, trapping patients and staff under the collapsed structure. With the main hospital empty and other facilities destroyed, only one small Iraqi military clinic remained to serve the city.

U.S. forces cut off Fallujah's water and electricity. About 200,000 residents were forced to flee, creating a refugee population

SOURCE: Originally appeared in the *Seattle Post-Intelligencer*, January 11, 2005. Available at http://www.seattlepi.nwsource.com/opinion/207300_fallujahospital11.html. Copyright © 2005 by Jim McDermott and Richard Rapport.

[1] Ralph Peters, "And Now, Fallujah," *New York Post*, November 4, 2004.

the size of Tacoma. Those who remained faced a grim existence; they were afraid to leave their homes for fear of snipers and they had little to eat and only contaminated water to drink.

Public buildings, mosques and residences were subjected to assault by air and ground forces. The city now lies in ruins, largely depopulated, but still occupied by U.S. forces. Convoys sent by the Iraqi Red Crescent to aid the remaining population have been turned back. Diseases brought on by bad water are spreading in Fallujah and the surrounding refugee camps.

The means of attack employed against Fallujah are illegal and cannot be justified by any conceivable ends. In particular, the targeting of medical facilities and denial of clean water are serious breaches of the Geneva Conventions. Continuation of these practices will soon confirm what many already suspect: that the United States of America believes it is above the law.

Imagine a world where such ferocious attacks become common. Imagine the Puget Sound region's hospitals and clinics as targets, our water supply fouled. Imagine our outrage. Let's not walk any farther down that path.

Instead, we can reaffirm our commitment to a community of nations and to the laws that govern their relations. We can demonstrate respect for the diverse peoples of the world, while holding no life of lesser value than our own. Unfortunately, as a result of illegal U.S. actions, the former residents of Fallujah have lost respect for us. Without that respect, there is little our military can contribute.

To prevent more harm, we should support: 1) a withdrawal of U.S. troops from Fallujah, allowing unrestricted access for independent relief agencies such as the Red Crescent; 2) an independent investigation into violations of international law in Fallujah, as called for by Louise Arbour, the United Nations High Commissioner for Human Rights on Nov. 16; and 3) a campaign to deny any further supplemental budget requests that may, in fact, fund war crimes.

Join us in working to make respect for individual and collective rights, as expressed in international law and the U.S. Constitution, a central theme of our community's relations with the rest of the world.

Situation of Civilians in Fallujah, Iraq

Louise Arbour

As U.S. troops attacked Fallujah, the United Nations High Commissioner for Human Rights, Louise Arbour, came forward to express "deep concern" over the situation of Iraqi civilians and called for an investigation into possible war crimes violations. Arbour previously worked as chief prosecutor and investigator of the UN war crimes tribunal for the former Yugoslavia.

There have been a number of reports during the current confrontation alleging violations of the rules of war designed to protect civilians and combatants. [I am] particularly worried over poor access by civilians still in the city to the delivery of humanitarian aid and about the lack of information regarding the number of civilian casualties.

All violations of international humanitarian law and human rights law must be investigated and those responsible for breaches—including deliberate targeting of civilians, indiscriminate and disproportionate attacks, the killing of injured persons and the use of human shields—must be brought to justice, be they members of the Multinational Force or insurgents.

SOURCE: Statement read by José Luis Díaz, spokesperson, Office of the High Commissioner for Human Rights, at the regular press briefing held at the United Nations Office at Geneva, November 16, 2004. Available at http://www.unhchr.ch/huricane/huricane.nsf/view01/7472316E3570A216C1256F4E0046 EDC6?opendocument.

Mortality Before and After the 2003 Invasion of Iraq: Cluster Sample Survey

DRS. LES ROBERTS, RIYADH LAFTA, RICHARD GARFIELD, JAMAL KHUDHAIRI, AND GILBERT BURNHAM

The following article, published in October 2004 in the *Lancet,* the most highly respected medical journal in England, presents the findings of a Johns Hopkins University research team that compared Iraqi deaths before and after the U.S. invasion. Using advanced epidemiological sampling techniques, they estimated that at least 100,000 Iraqi civilians have died as a result of the invasion. Most were women and children who died from aerial bombing. The authors' affiliations are as follows: Drs. Les Roberts and Gilbert Burnham, Johns Hopkins Bloomberg School of Public Health; Drs. Riyadh Lafta and Jamal Khudhairi, College of Medicine, Al-Mustansiriya University, Iraq; Dr. Richard Garfield, Columbia University.

BACKGROUND

In March, 2003, military forces, mainly from the U.S.A. and the U.K., invaded Iraq. We did a survey to compare mortality during the period of 14.6 months before the invasion with the 17.8 months after it.

METHODS

A cluster sample survey was undertaken throughout Iraq during September, 2004. 33 clusters of 30 households each were interviewed about household composition, births, and deaths since January, 2002. In those households reporting deaths, the date, cause, and circumstances of violent deaths were recorded. We assessed the relative risk of death associated with the 2003 invasion and occupation by comparing mortality in the 17.8 months after the invasion with the 14.6-month period preceding it.

SOURCE: Available at http://www.thelancet.com/search/search.isa#summary. Reprinted with permission from Elsevier (*The Lancet,* vol. 364 [2004], pp. 1857–64).

FINDINGS

The risk of death was estimated to be 2.5-fold (95% CI 1.6–4.2) higher after the invasion when compared with the preinvasion period. Two-thirds of all violent deaths were reported in one cluster in the city of Fallujah. If we exclude the Fallujah data, the risk of death is 1.5-fold (1.1–2.3) higher after the invasion. We estimate that 98000 more deaths than expected (8000–194000) happened after the invasion outside of Fallujah and far more if the outlier Fallujah cluster is included. The major causes of death before the invasion were myocardial infarction, cerebrovascular accidents, and other chronic disorders whereas after the invasion violence was the primary cause of death. Violent deaths were widespread, reported in 15 of 33 clusters, and were mainly attributed to coalition forces. Most individuals reportedly killed by coalition forces were women and children. The risk of death from violence in the period after the invasion was 58 times higher (95% CI 8.1–419) than in the period before the war.

INTERPRETATION

Making conservative assumptions, we think that about 100000 excess deaths, or more have happened since the 2003 invasion of Iraq. Violence accounted for most of the excess deaths and air strikes from coalition forces accounted for most violent deaths. We have shown that collection of public-health information is possible even during periods of extreme violence. Our results need further verification and should lead to changes to reduce non-combatant deaths from air strikes.

DISCUSSION

U.S. General Tommy Franks is widely quoted as saying "we don't do body counts." The Geneva Conventions have clear guidance about the responsibilities of occupying armies to the civilian population they control. The fact that more than half the deaths reportedly caused by the occupying forces were women and children is cause for concern. In particular, Convention IV, Article 27 states that protected persons ". . . shall be at all times humanely treated, and shall be protected especially against acts of violence . . ." It seems difficult to understand how a military force could monitor the extent to which civilians are protected against violence without systematically doing body counts or at least looking at the kinds of casualties they induce. This survey shows that with modest funds, 4 weeks, and seven Iraqi team members willing to risk their lives, a useful measure of civilian deaths could be obtained. There seems to be little excuse for occupying forces to not be able to provide more precise tallies.

Iraq's Civilian Dead Get No Hearing in the United States

JEFFREY SACHS

The Pentagon has consistently refused to tally civilian casualties. In the words of U.S. General Tommy Franks, "We don't do body counts." The following op-ed by the U.S. economist Jeffrey Sachs examines the systematic refusal of American officials, with full complicity of the American media, to report high rates of civilian casualties in Iraq. Sachs is a Special Adviser to UN Secretary-General Kofi Annan and was voted by *Time* magazine as one of the one hundred most influential world leaders. Having advised dramatic reforms in Bolivia, Poland, and Russia, Sachs now serves as director of the Columbia University Earth Institute.

Evidence is mounting that America's war in Iraq has killed tens of thousands of Iraqi civilians, and perhaps well over 100,000. Yet this carnage is systematically ignored in the United States, where the media and government portray a war in which there are no civilian deaths, because there are no Iraqi civilians, only insurgents.

American behavior and self-perceptions reveal the ease with which a civilized country can engage in large-scale killing of civilians without public discussion. In late October [2004], the British medical journal *Lancet* published a study of civilian deaths in Iraq since the U.S.-led invasion began. The sample survey documented an extra 100,000 Iraqi civilian deaths compared to the death rate in the preceding year, when Saddam Hussein was still in power—and this estimate did not even count excess deaths in Fallujah, which was deemed too dangerous to include.

The study also noted that the majority of deaths resulted from violence, and that a high proportion of the violent deaths were due to U.S. aerial bombing. The epidemiologists acknowledged the uncertainties of these estimates, but presented enough data to warrant an urgent follow-up investigation and reconsideration by the Bush

SOURCE: Originally appeared in the *Daily Star*, December 2, 2004. Available at http://www.project.syndicate.org/commentaries/commentary_text.php4?id=1765+m= series. Copyright © 2004 by Project Syndicate.

administration and the U.S. military of aerial bombing of Iraq's urban areas.

America's public reaction has been as remarkable as the *Lancet* study, for the reaction has been no reaction. On Oct. 29 the vaunted *New York Times* ran a single story of 770 words on page 8 of the paper. The *Times* reporter apparently did not interview a single Bush administration or U.S. military official. No follow-up stories or editorials appeared, and no *Times* reporters assessed the story on the ground. Coverage in other U.S. papers was similarly meager. The *Washington Post*, also on Oct. 29, carried a single 758-word story on page 16.

Recent reporting on the bombing of Fallujah has also been an exercise in self-denial. On Nov. 6, the *New York Times* wrote that "warplanes pounded rebel positions" in Fallujah, without noting that "rebel positions" were actually in civilian neighborhoods. Another story in the *Times* on Nov. 12, citing "military officials," dutifully reported: "Since the assault began on Monday, about 600 rebels have been killed, along with 18 American and 5 Iraqi soldiers." The issue of civilian deaths was not even raised.

Violence is only one reason for the increase in civilian deaths in Iraq. Children in urban war zones die in vast numbers from diarrhea, respiratory infections and other causes, owing to unsafe drinking water, lack of refrigerated foods, and acute shortages of blood and basic medicines in clinics and hospitals (that is, if civilians even dare to leave their houses for medical care). The Red Crescent and other relief agencies were unable to relieve Fallujah's civilian population.

On Nov. 14, the front page of the *New York Times* led with the following description: "Army tanks and fighting vehicles blasted their way into the last main rebel stronghold in Fallujah at sundown on Saturday after American warplanes and artillery prepared the way with a savage barrage on the district. Earlier in the afternoon, 10 separate plumes of smoke rose from Southern Fallujah, as if etched against the desert sky, and probably exclaiming catastrophe for the insurgents."

There is, once again, virtually no mention of the catastrophe for civilians etched against that desert sky. There is a hint, though, in a brief mention in the middle of the story of a father looking over his wounded sons in a hospital and declaring: "Now Americans are shooting randomly at anything that moves."

A few days later, a U.S. television film crew was in a bombed-out mosque with American marines. While the cameras were rolling, a marine turned to an unarmed and wounded Iraqi lying on the ground and shot the man in the head. (Reportedly, there were a few other such cases of outright murder.) But the American media more or less brushed aside this shocking incident, too. The *Wall Street Journal* actually wrote an editorial on Nov. 18 that criticized the critics, noting that whatever the U.S. did, its enemies in Iraq did worse, as if this excused American abuses.

It does not. The U.S. is killing massive numbers of Iraqi civilians, embittering the population and many in the Islamic world, and laying the ground for escalating violence and death. No number of slaughtered Iraqis will bring peace. The American fantasy of a final battle, in Fallujah or elsewhere, or the capture of some terrorist mastermind, perpetuates a cycle of bloodletting that puts the world in peril.

Worse still, American public opinion, media, and the recent election victory of the Bush administration have left the world's most powerful military without practical restraint.

Denial of Water to Iraqi Cities

DANIEL O'HUIGINN AND ALISON KLEVNAS

The following report documents the U.S. policy of systematically denying water to the residents of Iraqi cities during battle. Such collective
punishment against civilian populations is strictly forbidden by the
Geneva Conventions, which state: "Starvation of civilians as a method
of battle is prohibited. It is therefore prohibited to attack, destroy, remove or render useless for that purpose, objects indispensable to the
survival of the civilian population such as . . . drinking water installations
and supplies."[1] Unable to access fresh water, Iraqi children have already
died in vast numbers from diarrhea, respiratory infections, and other
causes as a result of being forced to depend on unsafe drinking water.[2]
The report, based on a wide range of sources, was prepared in late
2004 by two researchers at the Cambridge Solidarity with Iraq Center
at the University of Cambridge, England. This center is an NGO dedicated to providing information about the humanitarian situation in Iraq.

INTRODUCTION

Water supplies to Tal Afar, Samarra, and Fallujah have been cut off
during U.S. attacks in the past two months, affecting up to 750,000
civilians. This appears to form part of a deliberate U.S. policy of
denying water to the residents of cities under attack. If so, it has
been adopted without a public debate, and without consulting Coalition partners. It is a serious breach of international humanitarian
law, and is deepening Iraqi opposition to the United States, other
coalition members, and the Iraqi government.

SOURCE: Full report available at http://www.casi.org.uk/briefing/041110denialofwater.pdf.
Copyright © 2005 by Daniel O'Huiginn and Alison Klevnas. For citation purposes, the
authors note that "except where otherwise noted, the extracts from the Iraqi press and
broadcast media are taken from the BBC news monitoring service."

[1] Article 54 of the Additional Protocol to the Geneva Conventions of 12 August 1949
and Relating to the Protection of Victims of International Armed Conflicts (Protocol
I), 8 June 1977. See Roy Gutman and David Reiff, eds., *Crimes of War* (New York:
Norton, 1999), p. 377.

[2] Jeffrey Sachs, *Daily Star*, December 2, 2004.

EVIDENCE FOR THE DENIAL OF WATER

Tal Afar

On 19 September 2004, the *Washington Post* reported that U.S. forces "had turned off" water supplies to Tal Afar "for at least three days."[3] Turkish television reported a statement from the Iraqi Turkoman Front that "Tal Afar is completely surrounded. Entries and exits are banned. The water shortage is very serious."[4] Al-Manar television in Lebanon interviewed an aid worker who stated that "the main problem facing the people of Tal Afar and adjacent areas is shortage of water."[5] Moreover, the *Washington Post* reports that the U.S. army failed to offer water to those fleeing Tal Afar, including children and pregnant women.[6]

Samarra

"Water and electricity [were] cut off" during the assault on Samarra on Friday 1 October 2004, according to Knight Ridder Newspapers[7] and the *Independent*.[8] The *Washington Post* explicitly blames "U.S. forces" for this.[9] Al-Jazeera interviewed an aid worker who confirmed that "the city is experiencing a crisis in which power and water are cut off,"[10] as well as the commander of the Samarra Police, who reported that "there is no electricity and no water."[11]

3. Steve Fainaru, "After Recapturing N. Iraqi City, Rebuilding Starts from Scratch," *Washington Post*, September 19, 2004.
4. Comments by Faruq Abd-al-Rahman (leader of the Iraqi Turkoman Front) on TRT 2 television, Ankara, September 12, 2004.
5. Al-Manar television, Beirut, September 14, 2004.
6. Fainaru, "After Recapturing N. Iraqi City."
7. Nancy A. Youssef and Patrick Kerkstra, "U.S., Iraqi Forces Take Control of Samarra," October 1, 2004, http://www.kentucky.com/mld/kentucky/news/world/9813499.htm.
8. Ken Sengupta, "Onslaught in Samarra Escalates in 'Dress Rehearsal' for Major U.S. Assault on Rebels," *Independent*, October 3, 2004.
9. *Washington Post*, October 16, 2004.
10. Al-Jazeera television, October 1, 2004.
11. Al-Jazeera television, October 2, 2004.

Fallujah

On 16 October the *Washington Post* reported that: "Electricity and water were cut off to the city [Fallujah] just as a fresh wave of strikes began Thursday night, an action that U.S. forces also took at the start of assaults on Najaf and Samarra."[12] Residents of Fallujah have told the UN's Integrated Regional Information Networks that "they had no food or clean water and did not have time to store enough to hold out through the impending battle."[13] The water shortage has been confirmed by other civilians fleeing Fallujah.[14] In light of the shortage of water and other supplies, the Red Cross has attempted to deliver water to Fallujah. However the U.S. has refused to allow shipments of water into Fallujah until it has taken control of the city.[15]

JUSTIFICATIONS FOR THE DENIAL OF WATER

Some military analysts have attempted to justify the denial of water on tactical or humanitarian grounds. Ian Kemp, editor of military journal *Jane's Defense Weekly*, argues that "The longer the city [Fallujah] is sealed off with the insurgents inside, the more difficult it is going to be for them. Eventually, their supplies of food and water are going to dwindle."[16]

Barak Salmoni, assistant professor in National Security Affairs at the U.S. Naval Postgraduate School in Monterey, told the *San Francisco Chronicle* that civilians would probably be encouraged to leave Fallujah "by cutting off water and other supplies."[17] These arguments are deeply flawed on legal, humanitarian and political

[12] *Washington Post*, October 16, 2004.
[13] "Iraq: Thousands of Residents Have Fled Fallujah," Integrated Regional Information Networks, November 8, 2004.
[14] Comment by Shirin, http://justworldnews.org/MT/mt-comments.cgi?entry_id=966.
[15] "Iraq: Thousands of Residents Have Fled Fallujah."
[16] "Iraq: U.S. Troops Surround al-Fallujah as Offensive Preparations Continue," Radio Free Europe/Radio Liberty feature, November 8, 2004.
[17] *San Francisco Chronicle*, November 6, 2004.

grounds. The majority of the population of Fallujah fled before the American attack. Those who have not already fled Fallujah are forced to remain, since roads out of the city have been blocked,[18] including by British troops.[19] Not only are those remaining unable to leave, but they are likely to consist largely of those too old, weak, or ill to flee—precisely the groups which will be most severely affected by a shortage of water.

LEGAL IMPLICATIONS

The denial of water to civilians is illegal both under Iraqi and international law. Article 12 of the Transitional Administrative Law, which serves as a constitution during the interim period, states that: "Everyone has the right to life, liberty, and the security of his person."[20] International law specifically forbids the denial of water to civilians during conflict. Under article 14 of the second protocol of the Geneva Conventions, "Starvation of civilians as a method of combat is prohibited. It is therefore prohibited to attack, destroy, remove or render useless for that purpose, objects indispensable to the survival of the civilian population such as food-stuffs, agricultural areas for the production of food-stuffs, crops, livestock, drinking water installations and supplies and irrigation works."[21]

[18.] http://www.news.independent.co.uk/world/middle_east/story.jsp?story=580548.
[19.] http://www.news.bbc.co.uk/1/hi/scotland/3989815.stm.
[20.] Law of administration for the state of Iraq for the transitional period.
[21.] http://www.icrc.org/ihl.nsf/7c4d08d9b287a42141256739003e636b/d67c3971bcffic10c12 5641e0052b54.

U.S. Violations of Occupation Law in Iraq

Center for Economic and Social Rights

In order to protect people of an occupied country, the Geneva Conventions provide detailed rules about the responsibilities of occupying powers. The following June 2004 report documents that U.S. violations of these rules—including collective punishment and failure to provide essential services such as health services and safe drinking water—is not an occasional lapse but a systematic result of the policies of the Bush administration. The Center for Economic and Social Rights is an international human rights organization based in New York, and holds consultative status with the United Nations.

The Bush Administration is committing war crimes and other serious violations of international law in Iraq as a matter of routine policy. Beyond the now-infamous examples of torture, rape, and murder at Abu Ghraib prison, the United States has ignored international law governing military occupation and violated the full range of Iraqis' national and human rights—economic, social, civil and political rights.

The laws of occupation derive from both humanitarian law, including the Hague Regulations and Geneva Conventions, and human rights law, including the International Bill of Rights. Under well-established legal principles, Occupying Powers are required, first and foremost, to end the occupation and, in the interim: 1) to protect civilians and their property; 2) to ensure the well-being of the occupied population by respecting their human rights, including rights to life, health, food, education, and employment; and 3) to refrain from changing the country's legal and economic systems.

This report presents categories of U.S. violations of the laws of occupation, documented by human rights groups, journalists, eyewitnesses, and, at times, the U.S. military itself. This list, which is by no

SOURCE: Available at http://www.cesr.org/low/node/view/227. Copyright © 2005 by Roger Norman and the Center for Economic and Social Rights.

means comprehensive, demonstrates how U.S. practices violate the full range of laws meant to safeguard the rights of the Iraqi people.

VIOLATION: FAILURE TO PROVIDE PUBLIC ORDER AND SAFETY

In the three weeks following the U.S. takeover, unchecked looting effectively gutted every important public institution in the city—with the notable exception of the Oil Ministry.
> —Peter Galbraith, former U.S. Ambassador to Croatia[1]

Stuff happens . . . Freedom's untidy, and free people are free to make mistakes and commit crimes and do bad things.
> —Defense Secretary Donald Rumsfeld, on the looting in Iraq[2]

Occupation law clearly requires an Occupying Power to safeguard property, and particularly institutions dedicated to religion, charity and education, the arts and sciences, and health and public welfare. In effect, the Occupying Power steps into the shoes of the previous government and assumes full responsibility for preventing looting and maintaining public order. U.S. occupation forces have utterly failed to fulfill this duty.

In the first two weeks of April 2003, every aspect of Iraq's vital infrastructure was ransacked, including ministries, museums, libraries, hospitals, electric plants, schools and universities.[3] Despite advance warnings from NGOs, UN agencies, and even internal government reports,[4] U.S. forces failed to protect these properties even when physically present at the scene.[5] There are documented re-

---

[1] Quoted in James Fallows, "Blind into Baghdad," *Atlantic Monthly*, January–February 2004.

[2] Quoted in Sean Loughlin, "Rumsfeld on Looting in Iraq: 'Stuff Happens,'" CNN, April 12, 2003.

[3] Amnesty International, *Iraq: Looting, Lawlessness and Humanitarian Consequences* (April 11, 2003). AI Index: MDE14/085/2003.

[4] Fallows, "Blind into Bagdad."

[5] Amnesty International, *Iraq.*

ports of occupation troops actually encouraging looters.[6] Losses were extensive, including irreplaceable cultural heritage, vital public records, and physical infrastructure necessary to maintain life-saving services.[7] The entire affair was experienced by many Iraqis as a public humiliation that also set back efforts to rebuild the country. The looting of essential infrastructure continues even today, with water, electrical, and other facilities being stripped and their parts transported to Jordan to be sold as scrap.[8]

The Occupying Power is also responsible for ensuring public safety on a daily basis. Yet the U.S. created the conditions for increased crime and lawlessness by summarily dismissing the entire Iraqi army, police, and security forces shortly after the war—without a back-up plan for maintaining order.[9] The predictable and well-documented result has been a sharp rise in violent crime, including revenge killing, rape, kidnapping, theft, and sexual crime.[10] Women are most at risk, with little hope of obtaining justice when victimized.[11] The breakdown in public safety was entirely foreseeable. One can imagine what would happen in any American city if all governing authorities, including law enforcement, were suddenly eliminated, at a time when most of the population was experiencing desperate poverty.

VIOLATION: UNLAWFUL ATTACKS

> [We will] use a sledgehammer to crush a walnut.
>   —U.S. major general Charles H. Swannack Jr.[12]

[6] David Enders, "Getting Back on the Grid," *Baghdad Bulletin*, June 10, 2003.

[7] Ken Guggenheim, "Iraq's Looting Appears More Serious Year after War," Associated Press, March 14, 2004.

[8] James Glanz, "In the Scrapyards of Jordan, Signs of a Looted Iraq," *New York Times*, May 28, 2004.

[9] Richard Norton-Taylor, "Violence Blamed on U.S. Decision to Disband Iraq Army," *Guardian*, April 7, 2004.

[10] Human Rights Watch, *Sidelined: Human Rights in Postwar Iraq* (January 26, 2004).

[11] Human Rights Watch, *Climate of Fear: Sexual Violence and Abduction of Women and Girls in Baghdad* (July 16, 2003).

[12] Major General Charles H. Swannack Jr., special operational briefing from Baghdad, November 18, 2003. Available at http://www.cpa-iraq.org/transcripts/20031118a_Nov-18-Gen-Swannack-Briefing-post.htm.

It is a war crime either to target protected persons and property or to conduct indiscriminate attacks in civilian areas. Yet it is well documented that U.S. forces routinely conduct indiscriminate attacks in populated areas, causing unnecessary and disproportionate civilian casualties. Numerous eyewitnesses have reported incidents in which U.S. forces kill and injure civilians through random fire during military operations or in response to attacks by resistance forces.[13] The reported killing of over 40 people at a wedding party near Al Qaim,[14] and over 600 people in Fallujah, half of them women and children,[15] appear to be particular egregious examples of indiscriminate killing. Even top commanders of British occupation forces in Iraq have condemned the unrestrained use of U.S. firepower.[16]

The Geneva Conventions also guarantee special protections to medical staff and facilities in order to ensure the functioning of health services even during war. These norms have been regularly violated by U.S. forces. There are widespread and consistent reports of U.S. attacks against well-marked medical personnel, ambulances, and hospitals, including attacks by snipers situated near hospitals.[17] These war crimes have prevented injured persons from accessing life-saving treatment.[18]

VIOLATION: COLLECTIVE PUNISHMENT

Many routine practices of the U.S. occupation violate the prohibition against imposing collective punishment on the civilian population. In addition to mass arrests and detention, mass lay-offs, and failure to provide public safety, the U.S. has prevented freedom of

---

[13.] Eyewitness testimony is available on the Web site of the World Tribunal for Iraq, New York session.

[14.] Scheherezade Faramarzi, "U.S. Aircraft Reportedly Kills 40 Iraqis," Associated Press, May 19, 2004.

[15.] Abdul Qader-Saadi, "Fallujah Death Toll for Week More than 600," Associated Press, April 12, 2004.

[16.] Sean Rayment, "U.S. Tactics Condemned by British Officers," *Telegraph*, April 11, 2004.

[17.] Dahr Jamail, "Sarajevo on the Euphrates," *Nation*, April 12, 2004. Jo Wilding, "Getting Aid Past U.S. Snipers Is Impossible," *Guardian*, April 17, 2004.

[18.] Eyewitness testimony is available on the Web site of the World Tribunal for Iraq, New York session, http://www.worldtribunal-nyc.org.

movement through checkpoints and road closures, demolished civilian homes, and sealed off entire towns and villages. After U.S. forces were attacked on the road skirting Abu Hishma on November 2003, the entire village was encircled with razor wire and residents prevented from entering or leaving without U.S.-issued identification cards.[19] Human rights groups have also documented numerous examples of home demolitions being used as collective punishment. As Human Rights Watch has pointed out, "destroying civilian property as a reprisal or as a deterrent amounts to collective punishment, a violation of the 1949 Geneva Conventions."[20]

VIOLATION: FAILURE TO ENSURE VITAL SERVICES

The Occupying Power is under an explicit duty to meet the population's basic needs by maintaining electricity, water, transportation, and other vital services. These services—upon which many Iraqis depend to work, eat, and survive—were already badly damaged due to 12 years of war and sanctions.[21] Yet despite the lifting of sanctions and the awarding of billions of dollars in reconstruction contracts to (mostly) U.S. companies,[22] vital services remain in disrepair, often worse than before the occupation. Iraqi companies and experts with ability to repair these facilities at low cost have been excluded from the reconstruction process.[23] Although Russian, German and French companies built much of Iraq's infrastructure, the U.S. refuses to import spare parts from these countries, instead contracting with American companies to rebuild entire facilities.[24]

[19.] Dexter Filkins, "Key U.S. Officer Tied to Cover-Up of Iraqi Death," New York Times, June 25, 2004.

[20.] Human Rights Watch, Sidelined.

[21.] Center for Economic and Social Rights, The Human Cost of War in Iraq (February 2003).

[22.] See http://www.publicintegrity.org/wow/resources.aspx?act=resources and http://www.iraqrevenuewatch.org/.

[23.] Ariana Eunjung Cha, "Iraqi Experts Tossed with the Water Workers Ineligible to Fix Polluted Systems," Washington Post, February 27, 2004.

[24.] Antonia Juhasz, "The Economic Colonization of Iraq: Illegal and Immoral," testimony before the World Tribunal on Iraq, May 8, 2004. Available at http://www.worldtribunal-nyc.org/Document/Case_3_Juhasz.pdf.

According to the UN, at the current rate of repair it will take another four to five years before 90% of the population has electricity.[25] Lack of electricity damages health and sanitation systems and undermines overall economic development. The failure of U.S. occupation authorities to respect the legal obligation to maintain public services stands in stark contrast to the successful rebuilding effort undertaken with very limited resources by the Iraqi government after the 1991 Gulf War.

VIOLATION: FAILURE TO PROTECT THE RIGHTS TO HEALTH AND LIFE

Hepatitis is everywhere. It's unbelievable that standing water still causes such outbreaks, a year after the U.S.-led invasion of Iraq.

—Omar Mekki, medical officer for WHO-Iraq[26]

The Occupying Power is obligated to respect the right to health, to ensure access to health care, and to prevent the spread of contagious disease. Yet even the U.S.-appointed Ministry of Health official who oversees Iraq's public hospitals reports that health services are currently in worse shape than during the war or under sanctions.[27] Unsanitary conditions are common in hospitals.[28] There has been a consistent decline in available medicines, drugs,[29] and basic supplies, such as gloves, painkillers, syringes, gauze, and oxygen.[30] Basic health

[25.] "In Pictures: Living Conditions and Reconstruction in Iraq," BBC News, April 10, 2004.
[26.] "Inadequate Sewage Disposal Blamed for Hepatitis Outbreak," Integrated Regional Information Networks, June 1, 2004.
[27.] Jeffrey Gettleman, "Chaos and War Leave Iraq's Hospitals in Ruins," *New York Times*, February 14, 2004.
[28.] Ibid.
[29.] "Pénurie generalisée de médicaments—Le Comité d'Aide Médicale dénonce une situation inquiétante," April 19, 2004. "Patients Complain of Medicine Shortage," Integrated Regional Information Networks, January 22, 2004.
[30.] Geert Van Morter, M.D., *One Year After the Fall of Baghdad: How Healthy Is Iraq?* (April 28, 2004). Available at http://www.healthnow.org/site/article.php?articleId= 193&menuId=1.

infrastructure remains broken and in disrepair. Bechtel's failure to fulfill a contract to repair the Rustamiya sewage treatment plant in Baghdad means that one and a half tons of raw sewage are being dumped into the Tigris River every day.[31] One third of the population still lacks clean drinking water,[32] and bottled water is too expensive for most Iraqis. A World Health Organization–supported sentinel disease surveillance in the summer of 2003 found that diarrhea had increased threefold from the previous year.[33] UN officials report that unsanitary conditions throughout Iraq are causing outbreaks of water-borne disease like hepatitis and cholera.[34]

U.S. failure to protect Iraqis' right to health inevitably results in widespread violations of the right to life.[35] Deaths due to diarrhea and acute respiratory infections already accounted for 70 percent of childhood mortality in 2002.[36] This figure is certainly higher today due to deteriorated health services and increased poverty throughout occupied Iraq. It is worth bearing in mind that over 500,000 children under the age of five died during the sanctions period, largely as a result of unsafe water, inadequate health care services, shortages of medical supplies, and simple poverty.

VIOLATION: FAILURE TO PROTECT THE RIGHTS TO FOOD AND EDUCATION

The Occupying Power must ensure that the population has access—physical and financial—to adequate food and education. Yet more Iraqis are hungry now than before the occupation. The UN Food and Agricultural Organization classifies approximately eleven million Iraqis as food insecure,[37] mainly due to unemploy-

[31.] "Patients Complain of Medicine Shortage," Integrated Regional Information Networks.
[32.] *USA Today*/CNN/Gallup Poll, April 28, 2004.
[33.] UN Humanitarian Briefing, July 10, 2003.
[34.] "Patients Complain of Medicine Shortage," Integrated Regional Information Networks.
[35.] The UN Human Rights Committee has interpreted the right to life to protect against government failure to provide adequate health care.
[36.] Food and Agricultural Organization, *Crop, Food Supply, and Nutrition Assessment Mission to Iraq* (September 23, 2003).
[37.] Ibid.

ment and the rising price of food and other basic necessities since the introduction of "free market" measures. Things could get even worse—the CPA [Coalition Provisional Authority] is considering "monetizing" and phasing out the national food rationing system upon which 60% of Iraqi families completely depend for basic nutrition, despite predictions that this will lead to inflation and make basic necessities unaffordable.[38]

Similarly, the education system is in shambles throughout Iraq. Already crippled by 12 years of sanctions, educational opportunities have been reduced even further under the occupation. Up to two-thirds of school-age children in Baghdad do not attend school full time because of inadequate numbers of teachers, dilapidated school buildings, and poverty.[39] Girls are particularly unlikely to attend, due to well-founded fears of insecurity and kidnapping.[40] An internal U.S. Army audit of schools supposed to be repaired by Bechtel as part of its nearly-three billion dollar contract found that "the work was horrible," with dangerous debris left in playgrounds, crumbling walls, sloppy paint jobs, and broken toilets.[41]

CONCLUSIONS

While the U.S. is clearly obligated to comply with occupation law, the primary conclusion to be drawn is that the occupation itself is the root cause of ongoing war crimes and rights violations documented in this report. The violations will not end until the occupation ends and Iraqis are allowed to exercise genuine self-determination.

[38.] "Briefing Paper on Food Security," Integrated Regional Information Networks, May 26, 2004. See also Nathaniel Hurd, "Iraqi Food Security in Hands of Occupying Powers," *Middle East Report*, December 2, 2003.

[39.] Christian Aid, "Life 'Worse' for Many of Iraq's Poor, Survey Reveals," April 16, 2004, http://www.alertnet.org/thenews/fromthefield/108237842520.htm.

[40.] "School Attendance Falling Due to Fear of Abduction," Integrated Regional Information Networks, October 7, 2003.

[41.] Larry Kaplow, "Bechtel Criticized over School Project in Iraq," *Palm Beach Post-Cox News Service*, December 14, 2003.

TANTAMOUNT TO TORTURE

Torture is illegal in all forms, in all places, and at all times. It is defined as "any act by which severe pain or suffering, whether physical or mental, is intentionally inflicted on a person for such purposes as obtaining from him or a third person information or a confession."[1] The Geneva Conventions recognize no circumstances, whether in a state of war or public emergency, which may be invoked in defense of such abuse.[2] Indeed, international law refuses even the "compelling state interest" doctrine applied by the U.S. Supreme Court to restrict the freedoms of speech and press.[3]

Allegations of American torture began in December 2002 with an internal investigation by the Department of Defense into the death of an Afghan farmer and taxi driver who died of "blunt force injuries to lower extremities complicating coronary artery disease."[4] In April 2004, almost a year and a half after this initial investigation, Americans first learned of prisoner abuse from the television program *60 Minutes* and from an article by Seymour Hersh in the *New Yorker*, which revealed shocking photographs from the Abu Ghraib prison in Iraq. Some pictures showed American men and women in uniform smiling in front of piles of naked Iraqi prisoners being sexually humiliated. Others showed military personnel watching as dogs attacked prisoners. In another a hooded man stood alone on a box with electrical wires attached to his limbs. Americans were shocked.

---

[1] The definition of *torture* has been codified in the 1984 Convention for the Prevention of Torture and Inhuman or Degrading Treatment or Punishment. Available at http://www.yale.edu/lawweb/avalon/diana/undocs/33198-5.html.

[2] Likewise article 3 of all four Geneva Conventions clarifies that "violence to life and person, in particular murder of all kinds, mutilation, cruel treatment and torture . . . outrages upon personal dignity, in particular humiliating and degrading treatment" are banned under all circumstances. See also Convention for the Prevention of Torture and Inhuman or Degrading Treatment or Punishment.

[3] See Sanford Levinson, "Contemplating Torture," in *Torture: A Collection*, ed. Sanford Levinson (New York: Oxford University Press, 2004), p. 23.

[4] Carlotta Gall, "U.S. Military Investigating Death of Afghan in Custody," *New York Times*, March 4, 2003.

The Bush administration reacted to the Abu Ghraib scandal by arguing that a "few rotten apples" were to blame for the torture. But reporters at the *Washington Post* and *Newsweek*, followed by freedom-of-information lawsuits by the American Civil Liberties Union, soon uncovered a paper trail of legal memorandums, FBI e-mails, and other government documents indicating a common plan on the part of the Administration to violate the laws of war. These included White House Counsel Alberto Gonzales's memo to President Bush stating that a "new paradigm renders obsolete Geneva's strict limitations on questioning of enemy prisoners" and made other Geneva Convention provisions "quaint."

Meanwhile, reports of torture, deaths, and "extraordinary rendition"—the CIA practice of spiriting people away to countries that may practice torture—began to seep out of Guantánamo, Afghanistan, and Iraq. This section begins with one of these accounts in the form of a letter addressed to the U.S. Armed Services Committee written by two British citizens who were held and tortured in Guantánamo for more than two years. This letter provided some of the first information about conditions at the detention center. It also openly contradicted claims by Secretary of Defense Donald Rumsfeld that Abu Ghraib remained an isolated incident.

By early 2005 the instances of publicly documented torture had become almost innumerable. These endless crimes have been followed by a constant flow of government reports, newspaper and human rights investigations, court documents, and victim statements. Instead of presenting an exhaustive and confusing catalog of these materials, this section offers a selection of documents that trace the parameters of the Administration's crimes, and ends with a report providing readers a context and chronology for the torture scandals.

The letter from Guantánamo prisoners that begins this section is followed by classified government documents largely corroborating many of their claims. The first is a leaked excerpt of a report prepared by Major General Antonio M. Taguba *(Taguba Report)*, which was commissioned by the Department of Defense to investigate the abuse revealed by the Abu Ghraib photographs. Internal FBI e-mails follow, obtained by the ACLU under court order, indicating FBI officials' concern about "serious physical abuse" and subsequent "cover-up." Both of these documents detail beatings, rape, and other abuses at the hands of the U.S. military.

Following the government documents are three individual accounts of torture. They are excerpted from a legal brief filed by the Center for Constitutional Rights on behalf of multiple torture victims.

Next is an Associated Press article on the death of an Iraqi man while under interrogation by the CIA. The prisoner, al-Jamadi, was one of the CIA's "ghost detainees," known to the world through the release of the photo showing "Abu Ghraib guards giving a thumbs-up over his bruised and puffy-faced corpse, which had been packed on ice."

Finally, this compilation of evidence is placed in context by the Human Rights Watch report *The Road to Abu Ghraib*, which tracks the decision-making process and policy decisions that led to war crimes at Abu Ghraib and Guantánamo. It addresses the question we all are left with after reviewing the evidence: how did our country ever end up here?

Letter to Members of the Senate Armed Services Committee

SHAFIQ RASUL AND ASIF IQBAL

As the Bush administration worked to contain the Abu Ghraib abuse scandal by claiming it an isolated incident, the accounts of two released British citizens, Shafiq Rasul and Asif Iqbal, provided the outside world with the first detailed account of similar abuses at Guantánamo. These men, who relate their experience in the following letter to the U.S. Armed Services Committee, were held captive for more than two years and never charged with a crime. Their personal accounts of torture, initially regarded as dubious by many in the government and media, were later supported by the release of classified FBI e-mails and other government documents.

Shafiq Rasul was born in Dudley, a small town in England's West Midlands. Asif Iqbal is a native of West Bromwich, a small town in England's West Midlands, the area where he has lived all of his life.

May 13, 2004

Dear Committee Member:

We were kept captive, unlawfully, by U.S. Forces in Guantánamo Bay for more than two years until the 8th March of this year. We are now back in the United Kingdom.

The legality of our detention was due to be considered by the Supreme Court when we were suddenly pulled out of Guantánamo Bay and taken to England, where we were released within 24 hours.

During the past week, we have seen with disgust the photographs of men detained and tortured in [Abu Ghraib] Iraq. At the same time we are reading with astonishment in the newspapers here, official statements made by the United States Government about "interrogation techniques" used at Guantánamo Bay that are completely untrue.

For instance, we read that these techniques "are meant to wear down detainees but the rules forbid the kind of tortures coming to light in Iraq." The techniques, it is said, are "designed to cause

SOURCE: Available at http://www.ccr-ny.org/vz/reports/docs/ltr%20to%20Sentate%2012 mayo4v2.pdf.

disorientation, fatigue and stress," "but there is no stripping detainees naked." There is "no physical contact at all . . . our procedures prohibit us from disrobing a prisoner for any reason at all" (Army Colonel David McWilliams).

Our own experience, and our close knowledge of the experience of other men detained beside us, demonstrates that each of these claims is completely untrue.

From the moment of our arrival in Guantánamo Bay (and indeed from long before) we were deliberately humiliated and degraded by the use of methods that we now read U.S. officials denying.

At Kandahar, we were questioned by U.S. soldiers on our knees, in chains, with guns held to our heads, and we were kicked and beaten. They kept us in "three-piece suits" made up of a body belt with a chain down to leg irons and hand shackles attached. Before we boarded the plane to Guantánamo, they dressed us in earmuffs, painted-out goggles and surgical masks so we were completely disoriented. On the plane, they chained us to the floor without access to a toilet for the 22-hour flight.

Our interrogations in Guantánamo, too, were conducted with us chained to the floor for hours on end in circumstances so prolonged that it was practice to have plastic chairs for the interrogators that could be easily hosed off because prisoners would be forced to urinate during the course of them and were not allowed to go to the toilet. One practice that was introduced specifically under the regime of General [Geoffrey] Miller was "short shackling" where we were forced to squat without a chair with our hands chained between our legs and chained to the floor. We would be left in this position for hours before an interrogation, during the interrogations (which could last as long as 12 hours), and sometimes for hours while the interrogators left the room. The air conditioning was turned up so high that within minutes we would be freezing. There was strobe lighting and loud music played that was itself a form of torture. Sometimes dogs were brought in to frighten us.

We were not fed all the time that we were there, and when we were returned to our cells, we would not be fed that day.

We should point out that there were and no doubt still are

cameras everywhere in the interrogation areas. We are aware that evidence that could contradict what is being said officially is in existence.

They recorded the interrogations in which we were driven to make false confessions: they insisted we were the other men in a video they showed us from August 2000 with Osama bin Laden and Mohamed Atta, but we had been in England at that time. After three months in solitary confinement under harsh conditions and repeated interrogations, we finally agreed to confess. Last September an agent from MI5 came to Guantánamo with documentary evidence that proved we could not have been in Afghanistan at the time the video was made. In the end we could prove our alibis, but we worry about people from countries where records are not as available.

Soldiers told us personally of going into cells and conducting beatings with metal bars which they did not report. Soldiers told us "we can do anything we want." We ourselves witnessed a number of brutal assaults upon prisoners. One, in April 2002, was of Jummah Al-Dousari from Bahrain, a man who had become psychiatrically disturbed, who was lying on the floor of his cage immediately near to us when a group of eight or nine guards known as the ERF Team (Extreme Reaction Force) entered his cage. We saw them severely assault him. They stamped on his neck, kicked him in the stomach even though he had metal rods there as a result of an operation, and they picked up his head and smashed his face into the floor. One female officer was ordered to go into the cell and kick him and beat him which she did, in his stomach. This is known as "ERFing." Another detainee, from Yemen, was beaten up so badly that we understand he is still in hospital eighteen months later. It was suggested that he was trying to commit suicide. This was not the case.

We wish to make it clear that all of these and other incidents and all of the brutality, humiliation and degradation were clearly taking place as a result of official policies and orders.

Sometimes detainees would be taken to the interrogation room day after day and kept short-shackled without interrogation ever happening, sometimes for weeks on end. We received distressed reports from other detainees of their being taken to the interrogation room, left naked and chained to the floor, and of women being brought into the room who would inappropriately provoke and indeed molest them. It was completely clear to all the detainees that this was happening to particularly vulnerable prisoners, especially those who had come from the strictest of Islamic backgrounds.

Shortly before we left, a new practice was started. People would be taken to what was called the "Romeo" block where they would be stripped completely. After three days they would be given underwear. After another three days they would be given a top, and then after another three days given trouser bottoms. Some people only ever got underwear. This was said to be for "misbehaving."

We are completely sure that the International Red Cross has all of these complaints recorded and must undoubtedly have drawn all of them to the attention of the Administration. We therefore find it extraordinary that such lies are being told publicly today by senior officials as to the conditions and methods used at Guantánamo Bay. We are confident that records and pictures must exist and that these should all now be provided to the public in your country as well as ours at the earliest opportunity so that they can form their own judgment.

We look forward to an immediate response in view of the misinformation that is being put into the public domain worldwide and which we know to be untrue.

Yours sincerely,
Shafiq Rasul and Asif Iqbal

The Taguba Report on Treatment of Abu Ghraib Prisoners in Iraq

MAJOR GENERAL ANTONIO M. TAGUBA

Triggered by the release of the shocking Abu Ghraib torture photographs, the Department of Defense commissioned Major General Antonio M. Taguba to investigate. The following excerpts of the classified
Taguba Report, leaked to CBS and the *New Yorker* in May 2004, document rape, beatings, simulated electric shock treatment, as well as the
illegal hiding of "ghost detainees" from the International Committee of
the Red Cross, the organization charged with monitoring prisoner conditions during wartime under the Geneva Conventions.

　　Major General Taguba, the second highest-ranking Filipino-
American in the army, served as acting director of the army staff during
the Iraq war under General Eric K. Shinseki. He is also a graduate of the
U.S. College of Naval Command and Staff and the U.S. Army War
College.

Between October and December 2003, at the Abu Ghraib Confinement Facility (BCCF), numerous incidents of sadistic, blatant, and
wanton criminal abuses were inflicted on several detainees. This
systemic and illegal abuse of detainees was intentionally perpetrated by several members of the military police guard force in Tier
1-A of the Abu Ghraib Prison (BCCF).

　　[S]everal detainees described the following acts of abuse,
which under the circumstances, I find credible based on the clar-
ity of their statements and supporting evidence provided by other
witnesses

　　a. Breaking chemical lights and pouring the phosphoric liquid
　　　 on detainees;
　　b. Threatening detainees with a charged 9mm pistol;
　　c. Pouring cold water on naked detainees;

SOURCE: The full Taguba report, entitled *Article 15-6 Investigation of the 800th Military
Police Brigade,* is available at http://www.humanrightsfirst.org/US_paw/800th_MP_
Brigade_Master 14_Mar_04-dc.pdf.

d. Beating detainees with a broom handle and a chair;

e. Threatening male detainees with rape;

f. Allowing a military police guard to stitch the wound of a detainee who was injured after being slammed against the wall in his cell;

g. Sodomizing a detainee with a chemical light and perhaps a broom stick;

h. Using military working dogs to frighten and intimidate detainees with threats of attack, and in one instance actually biting a detainee.

[T]he intentional abuse of detainees by military police personnel included the following acts:

a. Punching, slapping, and kicking detainees; jumping on their naked feet;

b. Videotaping and photographing naked male and female detainees;

c. Forcibly arranging detainees in various sexually explicit positions for photographing;

d. Forcing detainees to remove their clothing and keeping them naked for several days at a time;

e. Forcing naked male detainees to wear women's underwear;

f. Forcing groups of male detainees to masturbate themselves while being photographed and videotaped;

g. Arranging naked male detainees in a pile and then jumping on them;

h. Positioning a naked detainee on a MRE Box, with a sandbag on his head, and attaching wires to his fingers, toes, and penis to simulate electric torture;

i. Writing "I am a Rapest" (sic) on the leg of a detainee alleged to have forcibly raped a 15-year-old fellow detainee, and then photographing him naked;

j. Placing a dog chain or strap around a naked detainee's neck and having a female soldier pose for a picture;

k. A male MP guard having sex with a female detainee;

l. Using military working dogs (without muzzles) to intimidate and frighten detainees, and in at least one case biting and severely injuring a detainee;

m. Taking photographs of dead Iraqi detainees.

These findings are amply supported by written confessions provided by several of the suspects, written statements provided by detainees, and witness statements.

The various detention facilities operated by the 800th MP Brigade have routinely held persons brought to them by Other Government Agencies (OGAs) without accounting for them, knowing their identities, or even the reason for their detention. The Joint Interrogation and Debriefing Center (JIDC) at Abu Ghraib called these detainees "ghost detainees." On at least one occasion, the 320th MP Battalion at Abu Ghraib held a handful of "ghost detainees" (6–8) for OGAs that they moved around within the facility to hide them from a visiting International Committee of the Red Cross (ICRC) survey team. This maneuver was deceptive, contrary to Army Doctrine, and in violation of international law.

Torture E-mails

FEDERAL BUREAU OF INVESTIGATION

The ACLU obtained the following classified FBI e-mails, one of which is addressed directly to the FBI director, under court order. They discuss in graphic detail reports of strangulation, use of cigarettes to burn detainees, and the explicit cover-up of the crimes at Guantánamo. The contents of the FBI documents show that the abuse reached far beyond Iraq. The dates of these e-mails establish that torture continued at Guantánamo months after the U.S. Army launched its January 14, 2004, criminal investigation at Abu Ghraib.

Date: June 25, 2004
From: Sacramento Division
To: THE DIRECTOR [FBI]
Re: Urgent Report
The following information provides initial details from an individual REDACTED who observed serious physical abuses of civilian detainees in REDACTED Iraq during the period of REDACTED . . . REDACTED observed numerous physical abuse incidents of Iraqi civilian detainees conducted in REDACTED Iraq. He described that such abuses included strangulation, beatings, placement of lit cigarettes into the detainees ear openings, and unauthorized interrogations. REDACTED was providing this information to the FBI based on his knowledge that REDACTED cover-up of these abuses. He stated these cover-up efforts included REDACTED.[1]

Date: August 2, 2004
From: REDACTED
To: REDACTED
Subject: RE GTMO
Here is a brief summary of what I observed at GTMO. On a couple of occasions, I entered interview rooms to find a detainee chained hand and foot in a fetal position to the floor, with no chair,

[1.] Available at http://www.aclu.org/torturefoia/released/FBI.121504.4910_4912.pdf.

food, or water. Most times they had urinated or defecated on them-selves and had been left there for 18 [to] 24 hours or more. On one occasion, the air conditioning had been turned down so far and the temperature was so cold in the room, that the barefooted detainee was shaking with cold . . . On another occasion, the A/C had been turned off, making the temperature in the unventilated room prob-ably well over 100 degrees. The detainee was almost unconscious on the floor with a pile of hair next to him. He had apparently been literally pulling his own hair out throughout the night.[2]

---

[2] Available at http://www.aclu.org/torturefoia/released/FBI.121504.5053.pdf.

Individual Accounts of Torture

CENTER FOR CONSTITUTIONAL RIGHTS

In 2004, the Center for Constitutional Rights brought a criminal complaint against Bush administration officials on behalf of four Iraqi nationals who were victims of torture. Facing the systematic refusal of
U.S. Justice Department officials to investigate the Iraqi prisoner
abuses, CCR filed the complaint in Germany under a law that grants
German prosecutors the right to hear charges of international war
crimes.[1] The following excerpt presents three of these plaintiffs' abuse
accounts. CCR has been at the forefront of human rights litigation, successfully arguing before the Supreme Court for the due process rights
of Guantánamo detainees.

AHMED SHEHAB AHMED

Ahmed Shehab Ahmed is an Iraqi citizen from Baghdad born on
January 1, 1968. He is a trader by profession and described himself as
a politically independent Muslim. He was arrested in his home by
personnel of the U.S. Armed Forces. At this time his 80-year-old
handicapped father was shot and killed and valuables were stolen
from the house. He was at first held at Baghdad International Airport and then brought to Rehidwaniya, an old property of Saddam
Hussein. There he was beaten and stripped. He was deprived of
sleep and food, and had to survive three days without sanitary facilities. During his detention he was threatened with rape, beaten until
unconscious, and forbidden to pray. He was doused with cold water.
Soldiers injected his genitalia with unidentified substances. An
American officer held a loudspeaker to his ears and shouted at him,
so that the plaintiff lost his hearing. During an interrogation with a
female translator he was naked and only his head was hooded. In

SOURCE: Available at http://www.ccr-ny.org/v2/legal/september_11th/docs/German_
COMPLAINT_English_Version.pdf. Copyright © 2005 by the Center for Constitutional Rights.

[1.] At least six investigations have been conducted by various branches of the U.S. military. However, as Mark Danner points out in an interview with National Public Radio, reprinted in part II of this book, there has been "no real report that assesses
broadly the responsibility of policy-makers."

the course of this interrogation the interrogator and interpreter attempted sexual acts with him. As a consequence of this sexual abuse he has become impotent. He was threatened with the rape of his family and children. Upon his release, he was told that they were sorry that they had false information about him and [his] father.

AHMED HASSAN MAHAWIS DERWEESH

Ahmed Hassan Mahawis Derweesh is an Iraqi citizen from the town of Balad born on July 1, 1956. He is a retired officer, was Baathist but is now an independent Muslim. He was arrested at 2:30 in the morning along with his brothers by CIA and military personnel. The brothers were hooded, beaten, tied up and insulted, while the American army personnel destroyed and stole several objects in the house, including money and documents. At his first interrogation, an Iraqi-Turcoman interpreter, Mohammed Al-Trucomani, was present. The latter accused him falsely and let the American interrogator hit him. He was insulted, pushed, shouted at and threatened with rape. During his detention in Balad, the plaintiff was threatened with dogs, sexually harassed and threatened with rape. He was deprived of sleep, doused with cold water and exposed to extreme heat. He was given electrical shocks, was forced to behave like a dog and was kept in stress positions. While nude in cold weather, he had cold water poured on him. As a result he contracted a severe flu, and his extremities became dry and numb. Nevertheless for an entire month he received no medical treatment. During the night he heard female prisoners taken and raped by army personnel. He heard that these women were later killed by their families. The plaintiff spoke with another prisoner who had been repeatedly raped and whose genitalia were subjected to electric shocks. He had lost all feeling in his genitalia. The plaintiff was never formally charged.

FAISAL ABDULLA ABDULLATIF

Faisal Abdulla Abdullatif is an Iraqi citizen from Baghdad born on September 7, 1958. He was a teacher at a technical institute and a member of the Neighborhood Council in Hay Al-Shaik-Maroof.

He is a member of the Iraqi Islamic Party and a Muslim. He was arrested by the U.S. Armed Forces during a meeting of the Neighborhood Council. From there he was brought to his house where soldiers stole money, a computer and equipment. He was then brought to the former Al-Muthana Airport in Baghdad, later transported to the former presidential palace, then to Abu Ghraib and finally to Camp Bucca. During his detention [he] was poorly fed and was denied sleep and sufficient water. He was cursed at and physically mistreated. He was threatened with transfer to Guantánamo. He was exposed to cold temperatures. His genitals were squeezed while he was searched. Several times he was held at gunpoint, hooded, and exposed to cold water. He was prevented from cleansing himself for prayer ceremonies. He was hung up by his tied hands. [He] further witnessed the torture and death of other prison inmates, and heard dogs attacking other detainees. He saw grave physical mistreatment by soldiers of other detainees. From other detainees he heard that they were stripped, physically severely abused, humiliated and raped. In one such instance, a naked male prisoner was forced to serve food to female prisoners. When he tried to cover himself, he was beaten. The plaintiff was never charged with a crime or indicted.

Iraqi Died While Hanging by His Wrists

Seth Hettena

By May 2004, thirty-seven deaths at American detention centers were being formally investigated by the Department of Defense. In the following Associated Press story from February 18, 2005, the reporter documents the death of a "ghost detainee"—prisoner held secretly—at the hands of the CIA. The victim was wrapped in cellophane, packed in ice to "preserve the detainee's body in an attempt to spirit it out of the prison, [and] connected to an intravenous drip to make it appear the dead man was simply ill."[1]

An Iraqi whose corpse was photographed with grinning U.S. soldiers at Abu Ghraib died under CIA interrogation while in a position condemned by human rights groups as torture—suspended by his wrists, with his hands cuffed behind his back, according to reports reviewed by the Associated Press.

The prisoner died in a position known as "Palestinian hanging," the documents reviewed by the AP show. It is unclear whether that position was approved by the Bush administration for use in CIA interrogations.

Al-Jamadi was one of the CIA's "ghost" detainees at Abu Ghraib—prisoners being held secretly by the agency.

His death in November 2003 became public with the release of photos of Abu Ghraib guards giving a thumbs-up over his bruised and puffy-faced corpse, which had been packed in ice.

Al-Jamadi died in a prison shower room during about a half-hour of questioning, before interrogators could extract any information, according to the documents, which consist of statements from Army prison guards to investigators with the military and the CIA's Inspector General's office.

[1.] Dexter Filkins, "Key U.S. Officer Tied to Cover-Up of Iraqi Death," *New York Times*, June 25, 2004.

One Army guard, Sgt. Jeffery Frost, said the prisoner's arms were stretched behind him in a way he had never before seen. Frost told investigators he was surprised al-Jamadi's arms "didn't pop out of their sockets."

Frost and other guards had been summoned to reposition al-Jamadi, who an interrogator said was not cooperating. As the guards released the shackles and lowered al-Jamadi, blood gushed from his mouth "as if a faucet had been turned on."

The Road to Abu Ghraib

Human Rights Watch

Human Rights Watch (HRW), a leading human rights organization in the United States, specializes in investigations of concealed human rights violations in countries around the world. In the following document, HRW applies this established methodology to the U.S. torture scandal, providing the context for understanding the accumulating war crimes evidence.

INTRODUCTION

Since late April 2004, when the first photographs appeared of U.S. military personnel humiliating, torturing, and otherwise mistreating detainees at Abu Ghraib prison in Iraq, the United States government has repeatedly sought to portray the abuse as an isolated incident, the work of a few "bad apples" acting without orders. On May 4, U.S. Secretary of Defense Donald H. Rumsfeld, in a formulation that would be used over and over again by U.S. officials, described the abuses at Abu Ghraib as "an exceptional, isolated" case.

In fact, the only exceptional aspect of the abuse at Abu Ghraib may have been that it was photographed. Detainees in U.S. custody in Afghanistan have testified that they experienced treatment similar to what happened in Abu Ghraib—from beatings to prolonged sleep and sensory deprivation to being held naked—as early as 2002. Comparable—and, indeed, more extreme—cases of torture and inhuman treatment have been extensively documented by the International Committee of the Red Cross and by journalists at numerous locations in Iraq outside Abu Ghraib.

This pattern of abuse did not result from the acts of individual soldiers who broke the rules. It resulted from decisions made by the Bush administration to bend, ignore, or cast rules aside. Administration policies created the climate for Abu Ghraib in three fundamental ways.

SOURCE: Available at http://www.hrw.org/reports/2004/usa0604/. Copyright © 2005 by Human Rights Watch.

First, in the aftermath of the September 11 attacks on the United States, the Bush administration seemingly determined that winning the war on terror required that the United States circumvent international law. Senior administration lawyers in a series of internal memos argued over the objections of career military and State Department counsel that the new war against terrorism rendered "obsolete" long-standing legal restrictions on the treatment and interrogation of detainees.

The administration effectively sought to re-write the Geneva Conventions of 1949 to eviscerate many of their most important protections. These include the rights of all detainees in an armed conflict to be free from humiliating and degrading treatment, as well as from torture and other forms of coercive interrogation. The Pentagon and the Justice Department developed the breathtaking legal argument that the president, as commander-in-chief of the armed forces, was not bound by U.S. or international laws prohibiting torture when acting to protect national security, and that such laws might even be unconstitutional if they hampered the war on terror. The United States began to create offshore, off-limits, prisons such as Guantánamo Bay, Cuba, maintained other detainees in "undisclosed locations," and sent terrorism suspects without legal process to countries where information was beaten out of them.

Second, the United States began to employ coercive methods designed to "soften up" detainees for interrogation. These methods included holding detainees in painful stress positions, depriving them of sleep and light for prolonged periods, exposing them to extremes of heat, cold, noise and light, hooding, and depriving them of all clothing. News reports describe a case where U.S. personnel with official approval tortured a detainee held in an "undisclosed location" by submerging him in water until he believed he would drown. These techniques, familiar to victims of torture in many of the world's most repressive dictatorships, are forbidden by prohibitions against torture and other cruel, inhuman or degrading treatment not only by the Geneva Conventions, but by other international instruments to which the U.S. is a party and by the U.S. military's own long-standing regulations.

Third, until the publication of the Abu Ghraib photographs

forced action, Bush administration officials took at best a "see no evil, hear no evil" approach to all reports of detainee mistreatment. From the earliest days of the war in Afghanistan and the occupation of Iraq, the U.S. government has been aware of allegations of abuse. Yet high-level pledges of humane treatment were never implemented with specific orders or guidelines to forbid coercive methods of interrogation. Investigations of deaths in custody languished; soldiers and intelligence personnel accused of abuse, including all cases involving the killing of detainees, escaped judicial punishment. When, in the midst of the worst abuses, the International Committee of the Red Cross complained to Coalition forces, Army officials apparently responded by trying to curtail the ICRC's access.

The severest abuses at Abu Ghraib occurred in the immediate aftermath of a decision by Secretary Rumsfeld to step up the hunt for "actionable intelligence" among Iraqi prisoners. The officer who oversaw intelligence gathering at Guantánamo was brought in to overhaul interrogation practices in Iraq, and teams of interrogators from Guantánamo were sent to Abu Ghraib. The commanding general in Iraq issued orders to "manipulate an internee's emotions and weaknesses." Military police were ordered by military intelligence to "set physical and mental conditions for favorable interrogation of witnesses." The captain who oversaw interrogations at the Afghan detention center where two prisoners died in detention posted "Interrogation Rules of Engagement" at Abu Ghraib, authorizing coercive methods (with prior written approval of the military commander)— such as the use of military guard dogs to instill fear—that violate the Geneva Conventions and the Convention against Torture and Other Cruel, Inhuman Degrading Treatment or Punishment.

A POLICY TO EVADE INTERNATIONAL LAW

The first public manifestation of a policy to circumvent normal detention rules came in January 2002, when the United States began sending persons picked up during the armed conflict in Afghanistan to its naval base at Guantánamo Bay, Cuba. Ultimately Guantánamo would hold more than 700 detainees from forty-four countries, many apprehended far from any conflict zone. Guantánamo was deliberately chosen in an attempt to put the detainees beyond the jurisdiction of the U.S. courts. Indeed, in response to a legal challenge by several detainees, the U.S. government later argued that U.S. courts would not have jurisdiction over these detainees even if they were being tortured or summarily executed.[1]

CIRCUMVENTING THE GENEVA CONVENTIONS

Ignoring the deeply rooted U.S. military practice of applying the Geneva Conventions broadly, U.S. Defense Secretary Donald H. Rumsfeld labeled the first detainees to arrive at Guantánamo on January 11, 2002 as "unlawful combatants," automatically denying them possible status as prisoners of war (POWs). "Unlawful combatants do not have any rights under the Geneva Convention," Mr. Rumsfeld said, overlooking that the Geneva Conventions provide explicit protections to all persons captured in an international armed conflict, even if they are not entitled to POW status.

At the same time, a series of legal memoranda written in late 2001 and early 2002 by the Justice Department helped build the framework for circumventing international law restraints on prisoner interrogation. These memos argued that the Geneva Conventions did not apply to detainees from the Afghanistan war.

Alberto R. Gonzales, the White House counsel, in a January 25, 2002 memorandum to President Bush, endorsed the Justice Department's (and Rumsfeld's) approach and urged the president to declare the Taliban forces in Afghanistan as well as al-Qaeda outside the coverage of the Geneva Conventions. This, he said, would preserve the U.S.'s "flexibility" in the war against terrorism. Mr. Gonzales wrote that the war against terrorism, "in my judgment renders obsolete Geneva's strict limitations on questioning of enemy prisoners."

The Gonzales memorandum drew a strong objection the next day from Secretary of State Colin L. Powell. Powell argued that declaring the conventions inapplicable would "reverse over a century of U.S. policy and practice in supporting the Geneva Conventions

[1.] See *Gherebi v. Bush*, Ninth Circuit, December 18, 2003.

and undermine the protections of the law of war for our troops, both in this specific conflict and in general."[2]

On February 7, 2002, in the face of growing international criticism,[3] President Bush announced that the U.S. government would apply the "principles of the Third Geneva Convention" to captured members of the Taliban, but would not consider any of them to be POWs because, in the U.S. view, they did not meet the requirements of an armed force under that Convention. As for captured members of al-Qaeda, he said that the U.S. government considered the Geneva Conventions inapplicable but would nonetheless treat the detainees "humanely."

These decisions essentially reinterpreted the Geneva Conventions to suit the administration's purposes. Belligerents captured in the conflict in Afghanistan should have been treated as POWs unless and until a competent tribunal individually determined that they were not eligible for POW status. Taliban soldiers should have been accorded POW status because they openly fought for the armed forces of a state party to the Convention. Al-Qaeda detainees would likely not be accorded POW status, but the Conventions still provide explicit protections to all persons held in an international armed conflict, even if they are not entitled to POW status. Such protections include the right to be free from coercive interrogation, to receive a fair trial if charged with a criminal offense, and, in the case of detained civilians, to be able to appeal periodically the security rationale for continued detention.

UNDERMINING THE RULES AGAINST TORTURE

While the administration was publicly rejecting the use of torture or cruel, inhuman, or degrading treatment, it was apparently laying the legal groundwork for the use of just such tactics. The *Washington Post* has reported that in August 2002, the Justice Department advised Gonzales, in response to a CIA request for guidance, that torturing al-

---

[2] Memorandum from Colin L. Powell to Counsel to the President, January 26, 2002.
[3] See, e.g., Statement of High Commissioner for Human Rights on Detention of Taliban and al-Qaeda.

Qaeda detainees in captivity abroad "may be justified," and that international laws against torture "may be unconstitutional if applied to
interrogations" conducted in the war on terrorism.[4] The memo added
the doctrines of "necessity and self-defense could provide justifications that would eliminate any criminal liability" on the part of officials who tortured al-Qaeda detainees. The memo also took an
extremely narrow view of which acts might constitute torture. It referred to seven practices that U.S. courts have ruled to constitute torture: severe beatings with truncheons and clubs, threats of imminent
death, burning with cigarettes, electric shocks to genitalia, rape or sexual assault, and forcing a prisoner to watch the torture of another person. It then advised that "interrogation techniques would have to be
similar to these in their extreme nature and in the type of harm
caused to violate law." The memo suggested that "mental torture"
only included acts that resulted in "significant psychological harm of
significant duration, e.g., lasting for months or even years."

The legal reasoning of the Justice Department memo re-
appeared in an April 2003 memorandum from a working group appointed by Pentagon legal counsel [William J.] Haynes that was
headed by Air Force General Counsel Mary Walker and included
senior civilian and uniformed lawyers from each military branch,
and which consulted the Justice Department, the Joint Chiefs
of Staff, the Defense Intelligence Agency and other intelligence
agencies, according to the *Wall Street Journal*.[5] They contended
that the president was not bound by the laws banning torture. According to a draft of the classified memo, the lawyers argued that
the president had the authority as commander in chief of the
armed forces to approve almost any physical or psychological actions during interrogation, up to and including torture, in order to
obtain "intelligence vital to the protection of untold thousands of
American citizens." The memo presented a number of legal doctrines, including the principles of "necessity" and "self-defense,"
and the inherent powers of the president which could be used to

4. Dana Priest and R. Jeffrey Smith, "Memo Offered Justification for Use of Torture,"
Washington Post, June 8, 2004.
5. Jess Bravin, "Pentagon Report Set Framework for Use of Torture," *Wall Street Journal*, June 7, 2004.

evade the prohibition on torture. The memo advised that the president issue a "presidential directive or other writing" that subordinates charged with torture could use as evidence that their actions were authorized, since authority to set aside the laws in wartime is "inherent in the president."

The Convention Against Torture provides, however, that "[n]o exceptional circumstances whatsoever, whether a state of war or a threat of war, internal political instability or any other public emergency, may be invoked as a justification of torture."[6] The International Covenant on Civil and Political Rights, which also bans torture and other mistreatment, considers the right to be free from torture and other cruel, inhuman or degrading treatment as nonderogable, meaning that it can never be suspended by a state, including during periods of public emergency.

According to media accounts and Human Rights Watch interviews, senior officials in the Defense and Justice Departments and the Central Intelligence Agency approved a set of coercive interrogation techniques for use in Afghanistan and Iraq that violate the prohibition of cruel, inhuman, or degrading treatment and can amount to torture.[7] These techniques apparently include stripping detainees naked during interrogation, subjecting them to extremes of heat, cold, noise, and light, hooding them, depriving them of sleep, and keeping them in painful positions.[8]

[6.] Convention Against Torture and Other Cruel, Inhuman or Degrading Treatment or Punishment, adopted and open for signature, ratification, and accession by General Assembly resolution 39/46 of December 10, 1984, article 16.

[7.] The *Washington Post* reported that a "list of about 20 techniques was approved at the highest levels of the Pentagon and the Justice Department," techniques for use at the Guantánamo Bay prison. Dana Priest and Joe Stephens, "Pentagon Approved Tougher Interrogations," *Washington Post*, May 9, 2004. Senior government officials had earlier told Human Rights Watch of the approval of a "72-point matrix." It is possible that this seventy-two-point list was reduced to twenty in the approval process.

[8.] According to Physicians for Human Rights: "Prolonged periods of sleep deprivation can result in confusion and psychosis, physical symptoms including headaches and dizziness, and chronic disruption of normal sleep patterns." Also, "deprivations or normal sensory stimulation (e.g., sound, light, sense of time, isolation, restrictions of sleep, food, water, toilet facilities, bathing, motor activity, medical care, and social contacts) serve to disorient victims, to induce exhaustion and debility, difficulty concentrating, impair memory and instill fear, helplessness, despair, and, in

The *New York Times*, citing current and former counterterrorism officials, reported that in one case CIA interrogators used graduated levels of force against Khalid Sheikh Mohammed, a detainee held in an "undisclosed location" (see *infra*), including a technique known as "water boarding," in which a prisoner is strapped down, forcibly pushed under water and made to believe he might drown. According to the *Times*, "these techniques were authorized by a set of secret rules for the interrogation of some 12 to 20 high-level al-Qaeda prisoners that were endorsed by the Justice Department and the CIA."[9]

RENDITIONS

The Bush administration facilitated or participated directly in the transfer of an unknown number of persons without extradition proceedings, a practice known as "irregular rendition," to countries in the Middle East known to practice torture routinely. The *Washington Post* in December 2002 described the rendition of captured al-Qaeda suspects from U.S. custody to other countries, such as Syria, Uzbekistan, Pakistan, Egypt, Jordan, Saudi Arabia, and Morocco, where they were tortured or otherwise mistreated. Unnamed U.S. officials suggested that detainees were deliberately moved to countries known for their use of torture to ease constraints on their interrogations. One official was quoted as saying, "We don't kick the [expletive] out of them. We send them to other countries so they can kick the [expletive] out of them." An official who had supervised the capture and transfer of accused terrorists said "If you don't violate someone's human rights some of the time, you probably aren't doing your job . . . I don't think we want to be promoting a view of zero tolerance on this."[10]

---

some cases, can result in severe anxiety and hallucinations and other psychotic reactions." Physicians for Human Rights, *Interrogations, Torture and Ill Treatment: Legal Requirements and Health Consequences* (May 14, 2004), pp. 7–8.

[9.] James Risen, David Johnston, and Neil A. Lewis, "Scrutiny Worries CIA Interrogators," *New York Times*, May 13, 2004.

[10.] Dana Priest and Barton Gellman, "U.S. Decries Abuse but Defends Interrogations," *Washington Post*, December 26, 2002.

Tarek Dergoul, a Briton released from Guantánamo in March 2004, said that during interrogation there he was threatened with being sent to Morocco or Egypt, "where I would be tortured."

In one case, Maher Arar, a Syrian-born Canadian in transit from a family vacation through John F. Kennedy Airport in New York, was detained by U.S. authorities. After holding him for nearly two weeks, U.S. authorities flew him to Jordan, where he was driven across the border and handed over to Syrian authorities, despite his repeated statements to U.S. officials that he would be tortured in Syria and his repeated requests to be sent home to Canada. Mr. Arar, whom the United States asserts has links to al-Qaeda, was released without charge from Syrian custody ten months later and has described repeated torture, often with cables and electrical cords, during his confinement in a Syrian prison.

In another case, Swedish television reported in May 2004 that in December 2001 a U.S. government–leased Gulfstream 5 jet airplane transported two Egyptian terrorism suspects who were blindfolded, hooded, drugged, and diapered by hooded operatives, from Sweden to Egypt. There the two men were tortured, including in Cairo's notorious Tora prison.[11] The plane was apparently the same one that had allegedly been used two months earlier to transport a Yemeni suspect from Pakistan to Jordan.

In a third case, U.S. operatives reportedly managed the capture and transfer of Mohammed Haydar Zammar, a top al-Qaeda suspect and dual German-Syrian national, to Syria in June 2002, over the protests of the German government. The United States has reportedly provided questions to Syrian interrogators.[12]

---

[11] Swedish TV4 Kalla Fakta Program: "The Broken Promise," May 17, 2004. See English transcript at http://www.hrw.org/english/docs/2004/05/17/sweden8620.htm.

[12] Murhaf Jouejati, Adjunct Professor at George Washington University, and an expert on Syria, told the National Commission on Terrorist Attacks Upon the United States that "although US officials have not been able to interrogate Zammar, Americans have submitted questions to the Syrians." Statement of Murhaf Jouejati to the National Commission on Terrorist Attacks Upon the United States, July 9, 2003.

"DISAPPEARANCES"

Among the most disturbing cases, perhaps unprecedented in U.S. history, are the detainees who have simply been "disappeared."[13] Perhaps out of concern that Guantánamo will eventually be monitored by the U.S. courts, certainly to ensure even greater secrecy, the Bush administration does not appear to hold its most sensitive and high-profile detainees there. Terrorism suspects are detained by the United States instead in "undisclosed locations," presumably outside the United States, with no access to the ICRC, no notification to families, no oversight of any sort of their treatment, and in most cases no acknowledgement that they are even being held. Human Rights Watch has pieced together information on 13 such detainees, apprehended in places such as Pakistan, Indonesia, Thailand, Morocco, and the United Arab Emirates, who have "disappeared" in U.S. custody.

GUANTÁNAMO: AMERICA'S "BLACK HOLE"

The United States has carefully controlled information about the detainees at Guantánamo, barring them from most contact with the outside world.[14] As a result, little is publicly known about the more than 700 detainees from forty-four countries, including children

---

[13.] According to the preamble of the Declaration on the Protection of all Persons from Enforced Disappearance, "enforced disappearances occur, in the sense that persons are arrested, detained or abducted against their will or otherwise deprived of their liberty by officials of different branches or levels of Government, . . . followed by a refusal to disclose the fate or whereabouts of the persons concerned or a refusal to acknowledge the deprivation of their liberty, which places such persons outside the protection of the law." General Assembly resolution 47/133 of December 18, 1992. *Enforced disappearance* has been defined by the Rome Statute of the International Criminal Court as the "arrest, detention or abduction of persons by, or with the authorization, support or acquiescence of, a State or a political organization, followed by a refusal to acknowledge that deprivation of freedom or to give information on the fate or whereabouts of those persons, with the intention of removing them from the protection of the law for a prolonged period of time." Article 7 (2) (1).

[14.] Guantánamo detainees are visited by the ICRC, which does not report publicly, and some have been interviewed by representatives of their home governments.

as young as 13, who have been held at Guantánamo.[15] Guantánamo has been described as a "legal black hole" by Lord Johan Steyn, a judicial member of Britain's House of Lords.[16]

Statements by U.S. officials that the Geneva Conventions do not apply to al-Qaeda detainees—indeed, the Bush administration's refusal to acknowledge that any law applies to them—and that harsher methods of interrogation are therefore permissible, only heighten this concern. In his January 2002 memo to the president, for instance, White House counsel Gonzales endorsed not applying the Conventions to Guantánamo to avoid "Geneva's strict limitations on questioning of enemy prisoners."[17]

It was the failure to obtain sufficient information using non-coercive methods on Guantánamo detainees which reportedly led to the creation of the working group which informed Secretary Rumsfeld in April 2003 that the president, as commander in chief, could authorize torture notwithstanding domestic and international legal prohibitions.[18] According to the *Wall Street Journal*, a U.S. official who helped prepare the report said "We'd been at this for a year-plus and got nothing out of them [certain Guantánamo detainees] . . . we need to have a less-cramped view of what torture is and is not." According to the official, interrogation techniques including drawing on prisoners' bodies, putting women's underwear on their heads, and threatening imminent harm to their families had not borne fruit and there was a need to "ratchet up the pressure."[19]

The *Washington Post* reported that in April 2003, officials at the highest levels of the Defense and Justice Departments approved a list

[15.] On January 29, 2004, the United States released three children believed to be between thirteen and fifteen years of age, but continued to hold an unspecified number of older children. For a more detailed discussion of the special risks to children held at Guantánamo, see Human Rights Watch, "Despite Releases, Children Still Held at Guantánamo" (January 29, 2004); and Human Rights Watch, letter to Secretary Rumsfeld on child detainees at Guantánamo, April 24, 2003.

[16.] Johan Steyn, "Guantánamo: A Monstrous Failure of Justice," *International Herald Tribune*, November 28, 2003.

[17.] See, e.g., John Yoo, "Terrorists Have No Geneva Rights," *Wall Street Journal*, May 26, 2004.

[18.] Jess Bravin, "Pentagon Report Set Framework for Use of Torture," *Wall Street Journal*, June 7, 2004.

[19.] Ibid.

of about twenty interrogation techniques for use at Guantánamo Bay that permit, among other things, reversing the normal sleep patterns of detainees and exposing them to heat, cold and "sensory assault," including loud music and bright lights, according to defense officials.

Human Rights Watch has examined the accounts of people released from Guantánamo concerning their incarceration there. These include persons directly interviewed by Human Rights Watch in Afghanistan and Pakistan, a sworn statement by a British former detainee provided to Human Rights Watch by his legal representative, and comments to media sources by several others.

[For example] Afghan former detainee A. told Human Rights Watch: "I saw some other prisoners who were beaten and blood was running from their heads. Specifically I saw two Arabs who were acting obstinately who were beaten."[20] Mohammad Saghir, from Pakistan, says he witnessed the beating by seven guards of an Arab prisoner for spitting at a guard: "They all went into the cell and were beating him and kicking him."[21]

Briton Tarek Dergoul alleges that he was himself beaten, and had a chemical spray administered when he refused to comply with cell searches. He also said the cell searches were sometimes staged when prisoners were praying. He has stated: "If I refused a cell search MPs would call the Extreme Reaction Force who came in riot gear with plastic shields and pepper spray. The Extreme Reaction Force entered the cell, ran in and pinned me down after spraying me with pepper spray and attacked me. The pepper spray caused me to vomit on several occasions. They poked their fingers in my eyes, banged my head on the floor and kicked and punched me and tied me up like a beast. They often forced my head into the toilet."[22]

IRAQ: APPLYING COUNTER-TERRORISM TACTICS DURING A MILITARY OCCUPATION

Since President Bush declared the end of major combat in Iraq in May 2003, more than 12,000 Iraqis have been taken into custody by

[20.] Human Rights Watch, interview with A. [name withheld], February 6, 2004.
[21.] Human Rights Watch, interview with Mohammad Saghir, January 17, 2004.
[22.] Statement by Tarek Dergoul made available to Human Rights Watch.

U.S. forces and detained for weeks or months. In its February 2004 report to Coalition forces, the International Committee of the Red Cross reported that military intelligence officers told the ICRC that 70 to 90 percent of those in custody in Iraq last year had been arrested by mistake.[23]

The U.S.'s treatment of detainees in Iraq was shrouded in secrecy from the beginning of the occupation. What is clear is that abusive treatment used after September 11 on suspects in the "war on terror" came to be considered permissible. Procedures used in Afghanistan and Guantánamo were imported to Iraq, including the use of "stress and duress" tactics and the use of prison guards to set the conditions for the interrogation of detainees.[24]

In its February 2004 report, the ICRC found that "methods of physical and psychological coercion were used by the military intelligence in *a systematic way* to gain confessions and extract information" (emphasis added). The methods cited by the ICRC included:

- hooding to disorient and prevent detainees from breathing freely
- being forced to remain for prolonged periods in painful stress positions
- being attached repeatedly over several days, for several hours each time, to the bars of cell doors naked or in positions causing physical pain
- being held naked in dark cells for several days and paraded naked, sometimes hooded or with women's underwear over their heads
- sleep, food, and water deprivation
- prolonged exposure while hooded to the sun during the hottest time of day

[23.] *Report of the International Committee of the Red Cross (ICRC) on the Treatment by the Coalition Forces of Prisoners of War and Other Protected Persons by the Geneva Conventions in Iraq During Arrest, Internment and Interrogation* (February 2004). Hereafter [referred to in the text as] "ICRC report."

[24.] As Major General Antonio Taguba noted in his report, recent intelligence collection in support of Operation Enduring Freedom [the war in Afghanistan] posited a template whereby military police actively set favorable conditions for subsequent interviews. Investigative report, on alleged abuses at U.S. military prisons in Abu Ghraib and Camp Bucca, Iraq, by Major General Antonio M. Taguba: *Article 15-6 Investigation of the 800th Military Police Brigade* [2004].

REPORTS OF ABUSE IGNORED

Prior to the publication of the Abu Ghraib photos, the U.S. government had multiple opportunities to take all necessary action to address what officials should have recognized was a serious and widespread problem. In fact, the ICRC report states that it alerted U.S. authorities to abuses orally and in writing throughout 2003. In May 2003, the ICRC sent a memorandum based on over 200 allegations of ill-treatment of prisoners of war during capture and interrogation at collecting points, battle group stations and temporary holding areas. That same month, the Special Representative of the United Nations Secretary-General, Mr. Sergio Vieira de Mello, raised concerns about the treatment of detainees with the Coalition Administrator, Ambassador Paul Bremer.[25] In early July 2003, the ICRC presented a paper detailing approximately 50 allegations of ill-treatment in the military intelligence section of Camp Cropper, at Baghdad International Airport.

According to the ICRC these incidents included:

> violence aimed at securing the co-operation of the persons deprived of their liberty with their interrogators; threats . . . against members of their families (in particular wives and daughters); hooding; tight handcuffing; use of stress positions . . .; taking aim at individuals with rifles, striking them with rifle butts, slaps, punches, prolonged exposure to the sun, and isolation in dark cells. ICRC delegates witnessed marks on the bodies of several persons deprived of their liberty consistent with their allegations.

In one case, a detainee:

> alleged that he had been hooded and cuffed with flexi-cuffs, threatened to be tortured and killed, urinated on, kicked in the head, lower back and groin, force-fed a baseball which was tied into the mouth using a scarf and deprived of sleep for four

[25.] See *Report of the Secretary-General to the U.N. Security Council* (July 17, 2003), S/2003/715, para. 47.

consecutive days. Interrogators would allegedly take turns ill-treating him. When he said he would complain to the ICRC he was allegedly beaten more. An ICRC medical examination revealed haematoma in the lower back, blood in urine, sensory loss in the right hand due to tight handcuffing with flexi-cuffs, and a broken rib.

During a visit to Abu Ghraib prison in October 2003, ICRC delegates witnessed "the practice of keeping persons deprived of their liberty completely naked in totally empty concrete cells and in total darkness," the report said. "Upon witnessing such cases, the ICRC interrupted its visits and requested an explanation from the authorities. The military intelligence officer in charge of the interrogation explained that this practice was 'part of the process.' "[26]

Rather than responding to these warning signals, however, according to one senior U.S. Army officer who served in Iraq, Army officials responded to the report of abuses at Abu Ghraib prison by trying to curtail the ICRC's spot inspections, insisting that the ICRC should make appointments before visiting the cellblock.[27]

GUANTÁNAMO MEETS AFGHANISTAN AT ABU GHRAIB

What is clear is that U.S. military personnel at Abu Ghraib felt empowered to abuse the detainees. The brazenness with which the soldiers at the center of the scandal conducted themselves, snapping photographs and flashing the "thumbs-up" sign as they abused prisoners, suggests they felt they had nothing to hide from their superiors. The abuse was so widely known and accepted that a picture of

[26.] Red Cross: Iraq Abuse 'Tantamount to Torture': Agency Says U.S. Was Repeatedly Given Details of Mistreatment," MSNBC News, May 11, 2004.

[27.] Douglas Jehl and Eric Schmitt, "Army Tried to Limit Abu Ghraib Access," *New York Times*, May 20, 2004. The article also quotes Brigadier General Janis Karpinski, commander of the 800th Military Police Brigade, whose soldiers guarded the prisoners, as saying that senior officers in Baghdad had treated the ICRC report in "a lighthearted manner."

naked detainees forced into a human pyramid was reportedly used as a screen saver on a computer in the interrogation room.[28]

According to Maj. Gen. Taguba, "interrogators actively requested that MP guards set physical and mental conditions for favorable interrogation of witnesses . . . [The] MP Brigade [was] directed to change facility procedures to 'set the conditions' for military intelligence interrogations." Taguba cited the testimony of several military police: "One said the orders were 'Loosen this guy up for us. Make sure he has a bad night. Make sure he gets the treatment.'" Another stated that "the prison wing belongs to [Military Intelligence] and it appeared that MI personnel approved the abuse." That MP also noted that "[t]he MI staffs, to my understanding, have been giving Graner [an MP in charge of night shifts at Abu Ghraib] compliments on the way he has been handling the MI [detainees]. Example being statements like 'Good job, they're breaking down real fast.'"

28. Kate Zernike, "Only a Few Spoke Up on Abuse as Many Soldiers Stayed Silent," *New York Times*, May 22, 2004.

Part II

Who's Culpable: Accountability and the Chain of Command

INTRODUCTION

Who bears the ultimate responsibility for an illegal invasion and occupation, dropping cluster bombs onto residential neighborhoods, attacking hospitals, and torturing prisoners?

The U.S. Supreme Court affirmatively answered this question in 1945 by upholding the conviction and death sentence of the Japanese commander Yamashita for his failure to halt the crimes of his troops. According to the court's majority opinion, the law of war "presupposes that its violation is to be avoided through the control of the operation of war by its commanders."[1] Fifty years later, this theory of *command responsibility* was the basis for The Hague Tribunal indictments of the Serbian civilian leader, Radovan Karadzic, and the commander of the army, Ratko Mladic. These courts understood that meaningful enforcement of international law depends on holding those in power accountable for both the effects of their policy decisions and the conduct of their troops.

Clearly the decisions about whether to invade Iraq and the conduct and character of the occupation are the responsibility of the political leadership in Washington. At minimum, the doctrine of command responsibility implicates military and civilian leaders— including Paul Bremer, General Tommy Franks, Paul Wolfowitz, Condoleezza Rice, and others—for their policy-making roles in war crimes such as the use of cluster bombs and napalm, denial of water to civilians, and waging an illegal war.[2] Part II includes Mark LeVine's article "The War Crimes of the Occupation" as one portrayal of these policies and crimes.

In the Yamashita case, the U.S. Supreme Court took the doctrine of command responsibility even farther to include the principle that "a person in a position of superior authority . . . should also be held responsible for failure to deter the unlawful behavior of

[1.] *The Matter of Yamashita*, 327 US I, 15 (1946).

[2.] The doctrine of command responsibility has been extended to civilian authorities exercising control over military forces. The International Criminal Tribunal for the Former Yugoslavia (ICTY) and the International Criminal Tribunal for Rwanda (ICTR) have held civilians criminally liable for the actions of militarized forces under their control. The term *command responsibility* is increasingly being replaced by *superior responsibility*.

subordinates."[3] Such standards, combined with the evidence of the crimes in part I on the conduct of the Iraq war, fully establish the culpability of the Bush administration. As a result, the culpability issues in part II focus primarily on crimes for which the Administration's responsibility is less self-evident, namely the war crimes of torture and prisoner abuse.

With the criminal conviction of Corporal Charles Graner and other low-level individuals for prisoner abuse at Abu Ghraib, the Bush administration insists justice has been served, as these "bad apples" acted alone, without orders. But the *Washington Post* editorial "War Crimes," included in this part, finds that subsequent congressional hearings, internal investigations, and the release of thousands of pages of confidential documents under court order "establish beyond any doubt that every part of this cover story is false."

According to a Department of Defense report prepared by former U.S. Defense Secretary James Schlesinger, "The abuses were not just the failure of some individuals to follow known standards, and they are more than the failure of a few leaders to enforce proper discipline. There is both institutional and personal responsibility at higher levels."[4] Eerily, Scott Horton, International Law Committee Chair of the Association of the Bar of the City of New York, in his article "A Nuremberg Lesson," details how U.S. Nuremberg prosecutors rejected the "rotten apples" defense and held German Nazi officials accountable for the consequences of their policy decisions.

How high up the chain of command does the evidence lead? The various documents and articles in part II follow the trail: Gonzales's leaked memo advising the President that the Geneva Conventions are "quaint" and "obsolete"; FBI e-mails indicating that new interrogation techniques were mandated by "an Executive order signed by President Bush" and "approved by the Dep. Sec. Def."; and the "Hard Facts Timeline" prepared by the ACLU to track the policy decisions of Defense Secretary Rumsfeld that led to the torture of detainees. All this evidence points to the top.

[3] *The Matter of Yamashita*, 327 US I, 15 (1946).
[4] James Schlesinger, *Final Report of the Independent Panel to Review DoD Detention Operations* (August 24, 2004), p. 5. Hereafter cited as *Schlesinger Report*.

Administration officials are well aware they risk being charged with war crimes. In his memo of January 25, 2002, then–White House counsel Alberto Gonzales warned President Bush that his circumvention of the Geneva Conventions exposed Administration officials to war crimes prosecution, since it "was difficult to predict with confidence" how prosecutors might apply the Conventions' limitations on "inhuman treatment" in the future. Marjorie Cohn's "The Gonzales Indictment" may cause the President's new Attorney General more sleepless nights.

If equivalent evidence pointed to those accused of murder or burglary, our justice system would have opened a criminal investigation long ago. According to the U.S. Attorney General's office, investigations of crime may be initiated where facts or circumstance merely "reasonably indicate" that a crime has been committed.[5] Thus, the burden of this section is not to prove that Secretary Rumsfeld ordered the torture of prisoners at Abu Ghraib or the binding of doctors and patients in Fallujah. Its requirement is to "reasonably indicate" that top officials, not just lowly grunts, bear the responsibility for these crimes. The documents in part II meet this burden and more. As former Nixon Counsel John Dean concludes in his article "The Torture Memo by Judge Jay S. Bybee," this is "damning evidence suggesting a common plan on the part of the Administration to violate the laws of war," and "[s]trikingly, such a 'common plan,' or conspiracy, is itself a war crime."

While the burden of "reasonable indication" of a criminal conspiracy is met in the following pages, there is little chance that the Bush administration will prosecute itself. Mark Danner finds that despite more than a half-dozen investigations by the Department of Defense, not one addresses the central question of how the decisions of policy makers affected what soldiers and officers did to detainees. This is little surprise to Scott Horton, who states in his affidavit supporting the "Criminal Indictment Against the United States Secretary of Defense Rumsfeld et al.," brought before a court in Germany, that

[5] According to FBI guidelines, the "reasonable indication" threshold is substantially lower than probable cause. See "The Attorney General's Guidelines on General Crimes, Racketeering Enterprise and Terrorism Enterprise Investigation." Available at http://www.usdoj.gov/olp/generalcrimes2.pdf.

"no such criminal investigation or prosecution would occur in the United States for the reason that the criminal investigation and prosecutorial functions are currently controlled by individuals who are involved in the conspiracy to commit war crimes."[6] This failure to conduct a formal and proper investigation is itself a crime, meeting the requirements for a misprision of a felony.

The Bush administration is engaged in a massive cover-up, ranging from refusal to cooperate with congressional committees to hiding detainees from international authorities. The actions of Administration officials indicate their fear of the basic mandates of legal procedure, including questioning by authorities, documentation of witness testimony and physical evidence, and requirements for a fair and impartial hearing. They fear objective prosecutors and independent counsels, as well as the laws of command responsibility and the ramifications of the Nuremberg trials. For they are running from the law. In the words of one U.S. federal appellate judge, in the post-Nuremberg era "the torturer, like the pirate of old, has become *hostis humanis generis*, the enemy of mankind."[7]

[6.] Scott Horton, *Expert Report by Scott Horton* (January 28, 2005). Available at http://www.ccr-ny.org/v2/legal/september_11th/docs/ScottHortonGermany013105.pdf.

[7.] *Filartiga v. Pena-Irala*, 630 F.2d 876, 577 F.Supp. 860.

Federal Bureau of Investigation E-mails

The following classified FBI e-mails, obtained under court order by the American Civil Liberties Union, are widely considered Abu Ghraib's "smoking gun," indicating Executive branch approval of illegal interrogation techniques. These e-mails, sent between January and December of 2004 with most of the personal information redacted, identify President Bush ("Executive Order") and Defense Secretary Rumsfeld ("Dep. Sec. Def.") as personally authorizing interrogation techniques "beyond the bounds of standard FBI practice." They also show the FBI's growing concern that the "impersonation" of FBI agents by military officials would leave the FBI "holding the bag before the public" if these "torture techniques" became known.

From: REDACTED
To: Briese MC
Re: Request for Guidance
Date: 05/22/04

We have also instructed our personnel not to participate in interrogations by military personnel which might include techniques authorized by Executive Order but beyond the bounds of standard FBI practice . . . We are aware that prior to a revision in policy last week, an Executive order signed by President Bush authorized the following interrogation techniques among others[:] sleep "management," use of MWDs (military working dogs), "stress positions" such as half squats, "environmental manipulation" such as the use of loud music, sensory deprivation through the use of hoods, etc.

SOURCE: The e-mail of May 22, 2004, is available at http://www.aclu.org/torturefoia/released/FBI.121504.4940_4941.pdf; the e-mail of January 21, 2004, at http://www.aclu.org/torturefoia/released/FBI.121504.4631.pdf; and the e-mail of December 5, 2004, at http://www.aclu.org/torturefoia/released/FBI.121504.3977.pdf.

From: REDACTED
To: REDACTED
Date: 01/21/04 5:15PM
Subject: Fwd: Re: Impersonating FBI

Regarding the "impersonation," [i]t's fairly clear to me that the "FBI Agent" wasn't successful in gaining the detainees cooperation . . . Once again, this technique, and all of those used in these scenarios, was approved by the Dep Sec. Def.

From: REDACTED
To: Bald, Gary, Battle, Frankie, Cummings, Arthur . . .
Date: 12/05/04 9:53AM
Subject: Fwd: Impersonating FBI at GTMO

If this detainee is ever released or his story made public in any way, DOD interrogators will not be held accountable because these torture techniques were done [by] "FBI" interrogators. The FBI will be left holding the bag before the public.

War Crimes

WASHINGTON POST EDITORIAL

Published on December 27, 2004, just days after the release of highly incriminating FBI e-mails, this editorial in the *Washington Post,* a paper that had enthusiastically supported the war in Iraq, represented one of the first steps by a member of the mainstream media to directly accuse the Bush administration of war crimes.

Thanks to a lawsuit by the American Civil Liberties Union and other human rights groups, thousands of pages of government documents released this month have confirmed some of the painful truths about the abuse of foreign detainees by the U.S. military and the CIA— truths the Bush administration implacably has refused to acknowledge. Since the publication of photographs of abuse at Iraq's Abu Ghraib prison in the spring the administration's whitewashers—led by Defense Secretary Donald H. Rumsfeld—have contended that the crimes were carried out by a few low-ranking reservists, that they were limited to the night shift during a few chaotic months at Abu Ghraib in 2003, that they were unrelated to the interrogation of prisoners and that no torture occurred at the Guantánamo Bay prison where hundreds of terrorism suspects are held. The new documents establish beyond any doubt that every part of this cover story is false.

Though they represent only part of the record that lies in government files, the documents show that the abuse of prisoners was already occurring at Guantánamo in 2002 and continued in Iraq even after the outcry over the Abu Ghraib photographs. FBI agents reported in internal e-mails and memos about systematic abuses by military interrogators at the base in Cuba, including beatings, chokings, prolonged sleep deprivation and humiliations such as being wrapped in an Israeli flag. "On a couple of occasions I entered interview rooms to find a detainee chained hand and foot in a fetal position to the floor, with no chair, food, or water," an unidentified FBI agent wrote on Aug. 2, 2004. "Most times they had urinated or defecated on themselves and had been left there for 18 to 24 hours or more." Two defense intelligence officials reported seeing prisoners severely beaten in Baghdad by members of a special operations unit, Task Force 6-26, in June. When they protested they were threatened and pictures they took were confiscated.

Other documents detail abuses by Marines in Iraq, including mock executions and the torture of detainees by burning and electric shock. Several dozen detainees have died in U.S. custody. In many cases, Army investigations of these crimes were shockingly shoddy: Officials lost records, failed to conduct autopsies after suspicious deaths and allowed evidence to be contaminated. Soldiers found to have committed war crimes were excused with noncriminal punishments. The summary of one suspicious death of a detainee at the Abu Ghraib prison reads: "No crime scene exam was conducted, no autopsy conducted, no copy of medical file obtained for investigation because copy machine broken in medical office."

Some of the abuses can be attributed to lack of discipline in some military units—though the broad extent of the problem suggests, at best, that senior commanders made little effort to prevent or control wrongdoing. But the documents also confirm that interrogators at Guantánamo believed they were following orders from Mr. Rumsfeld. One FBI agent reported on May 10 about a conversation he had with Guantánamo's commander, Maj. Gen. Geoffrey D. Miller, who defended the use of interrogation techniques the FBI regarded as illegal on the grounds that the military "has their marching orders from the Sec Def." Gen. Miller has testified under oath that dogs were never used to intimidate prisoners at Guantánamo, as authorized by Mr. Rumsfeld in December 2002; the FBI papers show otherwise.

The Bush administration refused to release these records to the human rights groups under the Freedom of Information Act until it was ordered to do so by a judge. Now it has responded to their publication with bland promises by spokesmen that any wrongdoing will be investigated. The record of the past few months suggests that the administration will neither hold any senior official accountable nor change the policies that have produced this shameful record. Congress, too, has abdicated its responsibility under its Republican leadership: It has been nearly four months since the last hearing on prisoner abuse. Perhaps intervention by the courts will eventually stem the violations of human rights that appear to be ongoing in Guantánamo, Iraq and Afghanistan. For now the appalling truth is that there has been no remedy for the documented torture and killing of foreign prisoners by this American government.

A Nuremberg Lesson:
Torture Scandal Began Far Above
"Rotten Apples"

Scott Horton

In the following op-ed, Scott Horton, Chair of the International Law Committee of the Association of the Bar of the City of New York, explains why Americans should reject the Bush administration's defense that only a few "rotten apples" were to blame for the torture scandal. Writing during the trial of Corporal Charles Graner and other low-ranking military figures for their role in the abuse of prisoners at Abu Ghraib, Horton provides both historical and legal rationale for holding U.S. policy makers responsible for war crimes.

Scott Horton is a partner at the law firm Patterson, Belknap, Webb & Tyler, based in New York and Moscow, where he has worked since 1985. He chaired the Committee on International Human Rights from 2000 to 2003.

"This so-called ill treatment and torture in detention centers, stories of which were spread everywhere among the people, and later by the prisoners who were freed . . . were not, as some assumed, inflicted methodically, but were excesses committed by individual prison guards, their deputies, and men who laid violent hands on the detainees."

Most people who hear this quote today assume it was uttered by a senior officer of the Bush administration. Instead, it comes from one of history's greatest mass murderers, Rudolf Hess, the SS commandant at Auschwitz. Such a confusion demonstrates the depth of the United States' moral dilemma in its treatment of detainees in the war on terror.

In past weeks, we have been treated to a show trial of sorts at Ft. Hood, Texas, starring Cpl. Charles Graner and other low-ranking

SOURCE: Originally appeared in the *Los Angeles Times*, January 20, 2005. Available at http://www.pqasb.pqarchiver.com/latimes/781093651.html?did=781093651&FMT=ABS &FMTS=FT&date=Jan+20%2C+2005&author=Scott+Horton&desc=Commentary% 3B+A+Nuremberg+Lesson%3B+Torture+scandal+began+far+above+%27rotten+apples .%27. Copyright © 2005 by Scott Horton.

military figures. The Graner court-martial and the upcoming trial of Pfc. Lynndie England are being hyped as proof of Defense Secretary Donald Rumsfeld's explanation for the Abu Ghraib prison tortures: A few "rotten apples"—not U.S. policy or those who created it—are to blame.

Graner entered a "Nuremberg defense"—arguing that he was acting on orders of his superiors. This defense was rejected in Ft. Hood as it was in Nuremberg 60 years ago, when Nazi war criminals were found guilty of crimes against humanity. A misled American public can choose to see in the Graner verdict the proof of the "rotten apples" theory and of the notion that Graner and the others acted on their own initiative. But what it should see is a larger Nuremberg lesson: Those who craft immoral policy deserve the harshest punishment.

Consider the memorandum written by Alberto Gonzales—then the president's attorney, now his nominee for attorney general. He wrote that the Geneva Convention was "obsolete" when it came to the war on terror. Gonzales reasoned that our adversaries were not parties to the convention and that the Geneva concept was ill suited to anti-terrorist warfare. In 1941, General-Field Marshal Wilhelm Keitel, the head of Hitler's *Wehrmacht*, mustered identical arguments against recognizing the Geneva rights of Soviet soldiers fighting on the Eastern Front. Keitel even called Geneva "obsolete," a remark noted by U.S. prosecutors at Nuremberg, who cited it as an aggravating circumstance in seeking, and obtaining, the death penalty. Keitel was executed in 1946.

Rumsfeld and the White House would have us believe that there is no connection between policy documents exploring torture and evasion of the Geneva Convention and the misconduct on the ground in Guantánamo Bay, Iraq and Afghanistan—misconduct that has produced at least 30 deaths in detention associated with "extreme" interrogation techniques. But the Nuremberg tradition contradicts such a contention.

At Nuremberg, U.S. prosecutors held German officials accountable for the consequences of their policy decisions without offering proof that these decisions were implemented with the knowledge of the policymakers. The existence of the policies and evidence that the conduct contemplated in them occurred was taken as proof enough.

There is no doubt that individuals like Graner and England should be held to account. But where is justice—and where are the principles the U.S. proudly advanced at Nuremberg—if those in the administration and the military who seem most culpable for the tragedy not only escape punishment but in some cases are slated for promotion?

Next week, the world will commemorate the liberation of Auschwitz. A memorial prayer for the death camp victims will be read at the United Nations. German Foreign Minister Joschka Fischer will attend to acknowledge that the depravities at Auschwitz were not the work of a few "rotten apples" but the responsibility of a nation. Such a courageous assumption of responsibility should provide a model for the United States, which can still act to salvage its tradition and its honor.

The War Crimes of the Occupation

MARK LEVINE

The Bush administration's culpability for war crimes encompasses its refusal to protect and provide for Iraqi civilians. Mark LeVine argues in the following article that the United States, as an occupying power, has violated international humanitarian law by its deliberate prevention of medical care, as well as its failure to supply goods and services essential to the survival of the Iraqi population. Since providing medical care, food, electricity, and other resources remain a matter of U.S. government policy, the refusal or failure to do so goes directly to the culpability of top U.S. military and civilian policy makers.

Mark LeVine is an assistant professor of history at the University of California, Irvine. He is the coeditor, with Pilar Perez and Viggo Mortensen, of *Twilight of Empire: Responses to Occupation* and the author of *Why They Don't Hate Us: Islam and the World in the Age of Globalization.*

Following the revelations of prisoner abuse and torture at the Abu Ghraib prison, the swirl of apologia, controversy, and debate has managed to avoid a basic truth: the occupation is essentially one giant war crime.

As the internationally recognized occupying power in Iraq, the United States and other members of the coalition are obligated under UN Security Council Resolution 1483 of May 22, 2003 to "promote the welfare of the Iraqi people through the effective administration of the territory." More broadly, the resolution calls upon the coalition to "comply fully with their obligations under international law." What this means is that the coalition must assure humane treatment for the civilian population (under Article 27 of the 4th Geneva Convention) and permit life in Iraq to continue as unaffected by its presence as possible.[1]

At the same time it must ensure the public order, safety and welfare of the Iraqi people. This includes using all the means at its

SOURCE: Originally appeared in *TomDispatch*, May 11, 2004. Available at http://www.tomdispatch.com/index.mhtml?pid=1434. Copyright © 2004 by Mark LeVine.

[1.] "IV Geneva Convention Relative to the Protection of Civilian Persons in Time of War. Geneva, 12 August 1949." Available at http://www.icrc.org/ihl.nsf/ 7c4d08d9b287a4214 1256739003e636b/6756482d86146898c125641e004aa3c5.

disposal to meet the basic food (Article 50), health (Articles 20, 50, 55, 56 and 59, among others), and education needs (Article 50) of the population.[2] Moreover, Articles 68 and 69 of Protocol 1 of the Geneva Conventions (which is accepted as customary international law by the U.S. even though it hasn't signed the Protocol) reaffirm as a central obligation the provision of medical care while adding the requirement to provide "clothing, bedding, means of shelter and other supplies essential to the survival of the civilian population."[3]

The problem of possibly systematic U.S. and coalition war crimes has been an issue in the foreign press over the past year and has resulted in direct accusations by normally cautious human rights organizations like Amnesty International and Human Rights Watch. As, speaking of the occupiers, a March 2004 report by Amnesty on the human rights situation in Iraq makes clear, "Under international humanitarian law, as occupying powers it was their duty to maintain and restore public order, and provide food, medical care and relief assistance. They failed in this duty, with the result that millions of Iraqis faced grave threats to their health and safety."[4] More recently, groups like the Center for Constitutional Rights, Human Rights First and the American Civil Liberties Union have sued the U.S. government in American and European courts to force it to stop practices involving torture and the "rendition" of detainees from the war on terror to countries with documented records of torturing prisoners.

As international law professor and author Victor Conde explains, with each death due to a decrepit health care system that could have been fixed with modest inputs of money, supplies, and effort, the purposeful targeting of ambulances, or the prevention of or delay in the receiving of medical care, as happened during the fighting in Fallujah and on numerous other occasions, the U.S. crosses the line between "merely" violating international

---

[2] Ibid.

[3] "Protocol Additional to the Geneva Conventions of 12 August 1949, and Relating to the Protection of Victims of International Armed Conflicts (Protocol I), 8 June 1977."

[4] Amnesty International, *Iraq: One Year on the Human Rights Situation Remains Dire* (March 18, 2004).

humanitarian law and the commission of actual war crimes. These are defined as grave breaches of the 4th Geneva Convention as described in article 147, including "willful killing, torture or inhuman treatment, including . . . willfully causing great suffering or serious injury to body or health, unlawful deportation or transfer or unlawful confinement of a protected person . . . or willfully depriving a protected person of the rights of fair and regular trial . . . taking of hostages and extensive destruction and appropriation of property, not justified by military necessity and carried out unlawfully and wantonly."[5]

This is not an issue of soldiers exceeding their authority. It's an issue of the commander-in-chief of the United States armed forces, along with his top commanders and civilian officials, being responsible for a military system that, once unleashed, cannot but commit systematic violations of humanitarian law. Without making ludicrous comparisons between President Bush and Slobodan Milosevic or Saddam Hussein, the same logic and international laws that led the U.S. to support their captures and trials could leave President Bush open to prosecution for the systematic commission of war crimes by the military forces and civilian personnel under his command.

Indeed, well before the circulation of the torture photos, evidence of war crimes was in the morning newspaper. To take but one example, in the midst of cease-fire negotiations in the city of Fallujah, an extemporaneous remark by American commanders might have alerted Americans to the commission of war crimes by their troops. In explaining to reporters that they would start "letting in medical and relief supplies" after two weeks in which the main hospital was also closed and medical personnel were prohibited from entering the city, Marine commanders implicitly admitted that they had, in fact, prevented those supplies from reaching the city and so, to that moment, were in "grave breach" of Articles 55 and 147 of the 4th Geneva Convention. These articles, so crucial to the protection of civilians in wartime, insist that "to the fullest extent of the means available to it, the Occupying Power has the duty of ensuring the

5. "IV Geneva Convention."

118 ■ In the Name of Democracy

food and medical supplies of the population; it should, in particular, bring in the necessary foodstuffs, medical stores and other articles if the resources of the occupied territory are inadequate."[6] Not only is the prevention of medical care prohibited, but any deaths resulting from such an action are considered war crimes.

And so to Iraqis and much of the rest of the world the torture photos did not reveal an isolated phenomenon; they reflected a larger well-known structural problem. The situation had, in fact, become so bad that UN special envoy to Iraq Lakdar Brahimi alluded to the problem of war crimes when speaking of the situation in Fallujah. He asked ABC News' George Stephanopoulos, "When you surround a city, you bomb the city, when people cannot go to hospital, what name do you have for that?" Indeed, only weeks after the occupation began a group of Belgian doctors who had spent the last year in Baghdad explained that, whatever crimes might be committed by Iraqis, as the internationally recognized belligerent occupiers "the current humanitarian catastrophe is entirely and solely the responsibility of the US and British authorities."

When I'm outside the U.S., whether in the Muslim world, Europe or almost anywhere else, people invariably ask me why Americans don't care that their country is violating the very principles of international law the U.S. helped design.

[6.] Ibid.

Criminal Indictment Against the United States Secretary of Defense Donald Rumsfeld et al.

CENTER FOR CONSTITUTIONAL RIGHTS

U.S. Justice Department officials and Congress have systematically re-fused to investigate the Bush administration's role in the torture at Abu Ghraib and Guantánamo. In response to this inaction, the Center for Constitutional Rights brought an indictment, excerpted here, against Defense Secretary Donald Rumsfeld on behalf of four Iraqi nationals who were victims of torture. CCR filed the complaint in Germany un-der a law granting German prosecutors the right to hear and investi-gate international war crimes cases. CCR is a nonprofit legal and educational organization dedicated to protecting and advancing the rights guaranteed by the U.S. Constitution and the Universal Declara-tion of Human Rights.

SECTION 4.1. COMMAND RESPONSIBILITY

The responsibility of military and civilian superiors has been recog-nized according to international law since the Nuremberg and Tokyo war crimes trials as well as the work of the United Nations War Crimes Commission. The doctrine of superior responsibility, formerly designated as "command responsibility," originated in the decision "in re Yamashita." Yamashita was a Japanese commander in the Philippines, who in 1945 was sentenced to death by a U.S. mil-itary commission, because he did not intervene to stop numerous crimes committed by his troops. The sentence was affirmed at the time by the U.S. Supreme Court. The principle of superior respon-sibility has accordingly been affirmed by the international criminal tribunals for Rwanda and former Yugoslavia in numerous cases.

In the Rome Statute of the International Criminal Court, this matter is treated as follows in article 28:

SOURCE: Available at http://www.ccr-ny.org. Copyright © 2005 by the Center for Con-stitutional Rights. Many legal citations, footnotes, and German code references have been eliminated in this excerpt for the benefit of readers outside the legal community. See the original document for precise legal references.

(a) A military commander or person effectively acting as a military commander shall be criminally responsible for crimes within the jurisdiction of the Court committed by forces under his or her effective command and control, or effective authority and control as the case may be, as a result of his or her failure to exercise control properly over such forces, where:

(i) That military commander or person either knew or, owing to the circumstances at the time, should have known that the forces were committing or about to commit such crimes; and

(ii) That military commander or person failed to take all necessary and reasonable measures within his or her power to prevent or repress their commission or to submit the matter to the competent authorities for investigation and prosecution.

In the Additional Protocol of the Geneva Convention of August 12, 1949 on the protection of victims of international armed conflicts (Protocol I), the criminal or disciplinary responsibility of a superior is provided for, in Art. 86, Para. 2, when such persons "knew, or had information which should have enabled him to conclude in the circumstances at the time, that he was committing or was going to commit such a breach and if they did not take all feasible measures within their power to prevent or repress the breach."

It is therefore according to international customary law completely unambiguous that superiors make themselves culpable under the above-mentioned conditions, when their subordinates commit war crimes.

Secretary Donald Rumsfeld

Donald Rumsfeld is currently the Secretary of Defense under President George W. Bush. Secretary Rumsfeld was authorized by Presidential Military Order entitled "Detention, Treatment and Trial of Certain Non-Citizens in the War Against Terrorism" to "detain individuals under such conditions he may prescribe and to issue related orders and regulations as necessary."[1]

[1.] Fay/Jones Report: *The Investigation of Intelligence Activities at Abu Ghraib* (August 9, 2004), pp. 29–30.

Secretary Rumsfeld is directly responsible for violations of [the Code of Crimes Against International Law] as he ordered, solicited, induced, aided and abetted war crimes. He is also liable as a civilian commander over the military for his control over individuals accused of war crimes in Afghanistan, Guantánamo, and Iraq, as Secretary of Defense he is ultimately responsible for military policy.

Secretary Rumsfeld Is Directly Responsible for War Crimes

Secretary Rumsfeld created an environment conducive to abuse by demanding "more actionable" intelligence, by creating a confusing and misleading set of standards for interrogation and detention practices relative to the treatment of detainees. The severest abuses at Abu Ghraib occurred in the immediate aftermath of a decision by Rumsfeld to step up the hunt for "actionable intelligence" among Iraqi prisoners.[2]

Secretary Rumsfeld Ordered War Crimes

Army Field Manual 34-52, with its list of 17 authorized interrogation methods, has long been the standard source of interrogation doctrine within the Department of Defense. In October 2002, authorities at Guantánamo requested approval of stronger interrogation techniques to counter tenacious resistance by detainees. Secretary Rumsfeld responded with a December 2, 2002 decision authorizing the use of 16 additional techniques at Guantánamo, such as hooding, removal of clothing, use of dogs, and mild, non-injurious contact. At the bottom of this memo authorizing the additional techniques, Rumsfeld included a handwritten note, referring to the use of standing as a "stress position" for up to 4 hours, remarking "However, I stand for 8–10 hours a day. Why is standing limited to 4 hours?"[3]

On April 16, 2003 Secretary Rumsfeld promulgated a list of approved techniques for use at Guantánamo. This policy remains

[2.] Human Rights Watch, *The Road to Abu Ghraib*, p. 3.
[3.] Memorandum from William J. Haynes II, General Counsel of the Department of Defense, to Defense Secretary Donald Rumsfeld on counterresistance techniques, December 2, 2002.

in force at Guantánamo. Former U.S. Secretary of Defense Schlesinger noted "It is clear that pressures for additional intelligence and the more aggressive methods sanctioned by the Secretary of Defense memorandum, resulted in stronger interrogation techniques that were believed to be needed and appropriate in the treatment of detainees defined as 'unlawful combatants.'"[4]

In August 2003, Secretary Rumsfeld instructed his top intelligence aide, Stephen A. Cambone, to send MG [Major General] Miller (who oversaw the interrogation efforts at the U.S. military base at Guantánamo Bay, Cuba) to "review current Iraqi Theater ability to rapidly exploit internees for actionable intelligence."[5] MG Miller was tasked with "Gitmo-izing" interrogation practices in Iraq, which directly contributed to confusion about interrogation practices.

BG [Brigadier General Janis] Karpinski stated in September 2003 that the classification "security detainee" was created in response to Secretary Rumsfeld's order to categorize detainees, and that a security detainee had fewer rights than an enemy prisoner of war.[6]

Secretary Rumsfeld "[o]rdered military officials in Iraq, in November 2003, to hold a detainee off the prison rolls in order to prevent the International Committee of the Red Cross from monitoring his treatment, in violation of international law. Additionally, prisoners reportedly are being held in at least a dozen facilities which operate in secret, hidden from Red Cross monitoring."[7] The Pentagon itself has acknowledged that Secretary Rumsfeld personally ordered at least one detainee kept from the ICRC and the Schlesinger report noted that Secretary Rumsfeld publicly declared he directed one detainee be held secretly at the request of the Director of Central Intelligence.[8]

---

[4] *Schlesinger Report*, August 24, 2004, pp. 7–8, 35; see *Fay-Jones Report*, p. 23, for a list of some of the techniques that required approval; memorandum from Defense Secretary Donald Rumsfeld to the commander of U.S. Southern Command, April 16, 2003.

[5] *Taguba Report Investigating the Treatment of Iraqi Prisoners at Abu Ghraib Prison* (March 2004), p. 7.

[6] Human Rights First, *Getting to Ground Truth: Investigating US Abuses in the "War on Terror"* (September 2004), fn 21.

[7] Eric Schmitt and Tom Shanker, "Rumsfeld Issued an Order to Hide Detainee in Iraq," *New York Times*, June 17, 2004; "Rumsfeld, at Tenet's Request, Secretly Held Suspect in Iraq," *Wall Street Journal*, June 17, 2004.

[8] Human Rights First, *Getting to Ground Truth*, p. 12; *Schlesinger Report*, p. 87.

The above facts show Secretary Rumsfeld's direct participation in the commission of war crimes: as head of the Department of Defense, he authorized or ordered techniques and actions which amounted to war crimes.

Rumsfeld Induced, Aided and Abetted War Crimes

Secretary Rumsfeld labeled the first detainees to arrive at Guantá-namo on January 11, 2002 "unlawful combatants," automatically denying them possible status as prisoners of war (POWs). Rumsfeld stated that "Unlawful combatants do not have any rights under the Geneva Convention," overlooking that the Geneva Conventions provide explicit protections to all persons captured in an international armed conflict, even if they are not entitled to POW status.

Secretary Rumsfeld directed Department of Defense General Counsel, William J. Haynes, to establish a working group to study interrogation techniques.[9] The working group played a significant role in relaxing the definition of torture, enabling Rumsfeld to authorize techniques viewed as impermissible by both military manuals and international law.[10]

According to Representative [Neil] Abercrombie during the House Armed Services Committee Hearing on military intelligence at Abu Ghraib prison, "the plain fact is, it was well known in the secretary's office and elsewhere that this [memo indicating that the more aggressive interrogation techniques are approved for Guantánamo] was circulating all over the place, and the Schlesinger report says so." MG Fay confirmed that this was indeed the case.[11]

Secretary Rumsfeld himself admitted in his testimony before the House Armed Services Committee on May 7, 2004 that he "failed to recognize how important it was to elevate a matter of such gravity to the highest levels, including the president and the leaders in Congress."[12] On May 5, 2004, he told a television interviewer the

9. *Schlesinger Report*, p. 8.
10. Human Rights First, *Getting to Ground Truth*, p. 7.
11. House Armed Services Committee Hearing, September 9, 2004, p. 28.
12. Available at http://www.dod.gov/speeches/2004/sp20040507- secdef0421.html.

Geneva Conventions "did not apply precisely" in Iraq but were "basic rules" for handling prisoners.[13]

Rumsfeld's failure to establish clear policies, his pressure on his subordinates to produce actionable intelligence, and his well-known [view about] the Geneva Conventions created an understanding within the military and intelligence community that "anything goes." His actions and attitude towards detainees encouraged and allowed war crimes to take place.

Secretary Rumsfeld Had Knowledge War Crimes Were Being Committed

Secretary Rumsfeld directly approved unlawful interrogation techniques and was aware that they were being used on detainees.

There were numerous complaints in the press by human rights organizations over conditions at Guantánamo, and the ICRC made repeated efforts to have the administration address these concerns before more abuses occurred. Rumsfeld was clearly aware of the possibility of abuses going beyond those he specifically approved due to these reports, yet he failed to take action to prevent this from happening.

Rumsfeld Has Responsibility as a Civilian Commander for War Crimes

As Secretary of Defense, Rumsfeld is the penultimate civilian commander over the military, except for President Bush. There is no doubt Rumsfeld had control over the individuals who committed war crimes, indeed, he ordered the commission of some war crimes, and set the conditions [that made] possible the commission of others.

Secretary Rumsfeld knew of the crimes being committed, as he had specifically authorized certain crimes. He set the conditions favorable for more crimes to occur, and in fact failed to take action to prevent more crimes from occurring. He is therefore directly liable for war crimes.

[13.] Human Rights Watch, *The Road to Abu Ghraib*, p. 7.

As one of the highest civilian commanders of U.S. Forces, it is Rumsfeld's responsibility to ensure all military and civilian personnel act within the confines of the law. Rumsfeld was aware of the possibility that more crimes beyond those he approved would be committed, and failed to take action to prevent this from happening. The above facts show Rumsfeld must be held liable for war crimes as civilian commander.

Additionally, Secretary Rumsfeld failed to properly ensure troops were adequately trained. In addition, his failure to take appropriate action when he first learned of the abuses allowed the crimes to continue. His admitted failure to recognize the magnitude of the scandal does not excuse him from his duty to remain informed, thus rendering him liable for his failure in his duty of supervision.

The Case Against Rumsfeld: Hard Facts Timeline

AMERICAN CIVIL LIBERTIES UNION AND
HUMAN RIGHTS FIRST

The following "Hard Facts Timeline" tracks the policy decisions, actions, and omissions of Secretary of Defense Rumsfeld that led to the torture of detainees in Iraq, Afghanistan, and Guantánamo. The American Civil Liberties Union (ACLU) and Human Rights First prepared the timeline in support of their 2005 complaint on behalf of eight torture victims filed in Illinois federal district court. The lawsuit charges Secretary Rumsfeld with violations of the U.S. Constitution and international law prohibiting torture and cruel, inhuman, or degrading punishment. The lawsuit seeks compensatory damages for the harms suffered as a result of torture and other abuse.

According to the complaint, Secretary Rumsfeld "authorized an abandonment of our nation's inviolable and deep-rooted prohibition against torture or other cruel, inhuman or degrading treatment or punishment of detainees in U.S. military custody." The complaint further charges that Secretary Rumsfeld personally approved brutal and illegal interrogation techniques in December 2002.

The ACLU is one of the oldest and most respected civil liberties organizations in the United States. Human Rights First is a legal organization working in the United States and abroad to enforce human rights laws. The groups are joined as co-counsel in the lawsuit by Rear Admiral John D. Hutson (Ret. USN), former Judge Advocate General of the Navy; Brigadier General James Cullen (Ret. USA), former Chief Judge (IMA) of the U.S. Army Court of Criminal Appeals; and Bill Lann Lee, Chair of the Human Rights Practice Group at Lieff, Cabraser, Heimann & Bernstein, LLP, and former Assistant Attorney General for Civil Rights at the Department of Justice.

SOURCE: Copyright © 2005 by the American Civil Liberties Union and Human Rights First. "Hard Facts Timeline" available at http://www.aclu.org/rumsfeld/timeline.pdf.

The Case Against Rumsfeld:
HARD FACTS TIMELINE

October 11, 2002
Guantanamo officials "request that additional techniques beyond those in the field manual be approved for use."

December 2, 2002
Rumsfeld prescribes new interrogation policy for Guantanamo, authorizing "stress positions," hooding, 20-hour interrogations, removal of clothing, exploiting phobias to induce stress (e.g., fear of dogs), prolonged isolation, sensory deprivation, and forced grooming. These techniques soon spread to Afghanistan and later to Iraq.

December 2002
FBI officials complain to Defense Department of abuses at Guantanamo. Afghan detainees killed during interrogation in U.S. custody at Bagram Air Force Base, Afghanistan.

December 26, 2002
Washington Post reports regular, systemic abuses at Bagram, including "stress and duress" techniques during interrogation.

January 2003
Judge Advocates repeatedly object to aggressive interrogation techniques at Guantanamo but "Pentagon officials 'didn't think this was a big deal, so they just ignored the JAGs.'"

January 15, 2003
Rumsfeld rescinds blanket approval of some techniques but indicates techniques may continue based on his individual case approval.

Rumsfeld designates "Working Group" to assess legal, policy and operational issues for detainee interrogation in the "war on terrorism."

January 24, 2003
Afghanistan Commander forwards list of techniques being used in Afghanistan, including some inconsistent with Army Field Manual, to inform Rumsfeld's Working Group, including the use of dogs to induce fear, the use of stress positions, and sensory deprivation.

April 4, 2003
Working Group issues final report; recommends 35 interrogation techniques to Rumsfeld, including techniques from Afghanistan inconsistent with Army Field Manual.

April 16, 2003
Rumsfeld approves 24 of the recommended techniques for use at Guantanamo, including dietary and environmental manipulation, sleep adjustment, false flag and isolation.

September 2003
Lt. Gen. Sanchez authorizes 29 interrogation techniques for use in Iraq, including the use of dogs, stress positions, sensory deprivation, loud music and light control, based on Rumsfeld's April 16 techniques and suggestions from captain of military unit formerly in Afghanistan.

October 12, 2003
Iraqi interrogation techniques modified but still authorize officers to "control" the lighting, heat, food, shelter, and clothing given to detainees and permit the use of dogs in interrogations with prior authorization.

November 12, 2003
Human Rights First writes Rumsfeld as well as Afghan field commander requesting status of investigations into the deaths of detainees in U.S. custody in Afghanistan in 2002.

December 2003
U.S. Army report details abuses committed against detainees in Iraq by task force of military Special Operations and CIA officers, known as Task Force 121.

January 13, 2004
Joseph Darby gives Army criminal investigators CD containing the Abu Ghraib photographs depicting detainee torture and abuses. Rumsfeld informed.

February 24, 2004
Red Cross issues confidential report to Coalition Provisional Authority documenting widespread abuse and command failures to take corrective action.

August 31 – September 9, 2003
Guantanamo commander brings policies to Abu Ghraib; uses techniques as "baseline" for recommending new, harsher interrogation techniques at Abu Ghraib.

August 2003
Iraqi citizens Arkan Mohammed Ali Al-Hasnawi, Dahi Mohammed Sabbar, Sherzad Kamal Khalid Al-Barwari and Ali H. detained and abused at various U.S. detention facilities in Iraq, including Abu Ghraib.

July/August 2003 – June 2004

October – December 2003
Torture and serious abuses of detainees take place at Abu Ghraib.

UNDER LAW: THE COMMANDER IS RESPONSIBLE FOR CRIMES DIRECTLY ORDERED, AS WELL AS FOR CRIMES COMMITTED BY OFFICERS WHEN THE COMMANDER KNEW OR SHOULD HAVE KNOWN THEY WERE GOING ON BUT FAILED TO PREVENT OR PUNISH THEM.

May 2004
Abuse of detainees continues in Iraq.

April 28, 2004
60 Minutes II airs segment showing Abu Ghraib photos.

February 26, 2004
Maj. Gen. Taguba completes investigation; reports of "systematic" and "sadistic, blatant and wanton criminal abuses" at Abu Ghraib.

August 2003
Rumsfeld sends Guantanamo commander to Iraq to "gitmo-ize" Iraqi detention facilities, promoting wide-scale deployment of more aggressive interrogation methods in Iraq.

July 2003
Captain of unit responsible for killing two detainees in Afghanistan proposes interrogation techniques for Abu Ghraib, including stress positions, removal of clothing, lengthy isolation, sensory and sleep deprivation and use of dogs. Lt. Gen. Sanchez approves techniques.

June 2003 – June 2004
Afghan citizens Mehboob Ahmad, Said Nabi Siddiqi, Mohammed Karim Shirulah and Haji Abdul Rahman detained and abused at U.S.-held Kandahar and Bagram facilities.

May 30, 2004
FBI reasserts its objections to Guantanamo interrogation techniques to Guantanamo commander.

May 2003
Red Cross reports 200 cases of alleged detainee abuse in U.S. custody in Iraq to U.S. Central Command.

March 2005
Pending investigative reports on detainee and interrogation operations (promised for delivery in summer 2004) still incomplete.
April 16, 2003 interrogation policy still in effect.
No U.S. official above the rank of Major has been prosecuted. Rumsfeld still not held accountable.

August 24, 2004
Rumsfeld-appointed panel reports Rumsfeld interrogation policy led to confusion in the field as to what techniques were authorized; also reports that civilian Defense Department leaders failed in their interrogation and detention duties.

The Torture Memo
by Judge Jay S. Bybee

JOHN W. DEAN

In the following article published on the heels of Alberto Gonzales's confirmation hearing, John Dean traces how a declassified memo by Assistant Attorney General Jay S. Bybee to Gonzales is direct evidence of a conspiracy to commit war crimes. According to Dean, "This document is the most alarming bit of classified information to surface during wartime since the 1971 leak of the Pentagon Papers relating to the war in Vietnam." As former counsel to President Nixon, Dean was a key figure in revealing executive branch wrongdoing during Watergate, leading to Nixon's resignation and the imprisonment of key administration figures. Dean is a columnist for FindLaw.com and the author of six books.

Former Assistant Attorney General Jay S. Bybee, as the head of the Office of Legal Counsel—an office once known as the conscience of the U.S. Department of Justice—issued a formal legal opinion in 2002 interpreting the Convention Against Torture and a related law enacted by Congress prohibiting torture. Bybee's memo is incredible, a damning document showing the depravity to which the Bush administration has taken the United States in dealing with terrorism—exactly what the terrorist, of course, hoped would occur.

Bybee's so-called legal interpretations guided the Bush administration for some twenty-two months. A powerful case has been made, however, that Bybee's extraordinary reading of the law led Americans to engage in torture at Abu Ghraib and elsewhere. Not surprisingly, Bybee's memo outraged many in the legal community, particularly those concerned with humanitarianism and the laws of war. But Bybee's work also distressed countless active-duty military officers, who realized that he had opened the door for our enemies to claim justification for torturing American soldiers.

Bybee's memo defines torture so narrowly that only activities

SOURCE: Adapted by the author based on his January 14, 2005, column at FindLaw .com. Available at http://www.writ.findlaw.com/dean.20050114.html. Copyright © 2005 by John W. Dean.

resulting in "death, organ failure or the permanent impairment of a significant body function" qualify. The memo also asserts that the criminal law prohibiting torture "may be unconstitutional if applied to interrogations undertaken of enemy combatants pursuant to the President's Commander-in-Chief powers." According to Bybee, when acting as commander-in-chief, the president is above the law. (Richard Nixon could have used Jay Bybee, and survived Watergate.)

EXPERTS HAVE MADE CLEAR THAT THE BYBEE MEMO EVIDENCES WAR CRIMES

Following the appearance of Alberto Gonzales before the Senate Judiciary Committee for his confirmation as attorney general, a panel of experts testified. The panel included Harold Koh, a former Assistant Secretary for Human Rights, who worked in the Office of Legal Counsel during the Reagan Administration. Koh, an expert in international human rights, is now the Dean of Yale Law School.

According to Dean Koh, Bybee's blatantly flawed memo simply ignores the government's long existing "zero tolerance policy" on torture, not to mention that it defines torture so loosely that it would tolerate "the things that Saddam Hussein's forces did" such as "beating, pulling out a fingernail, burning with hot irons, suspension from ceiling fans"—to name a few. In addition, Koh testified, the memo so "grossly overreads the president's constitutional power" that, under its logic, the president could "order genocide or other kinds of acts" and neither Congress nor the courts could stop him.

Additionally, the memo's advice that "executive officials can escape prosecution if they are carrying out the president's orders as commander in chief" is, Koh explained, the same I-was-following-orders "defense which was rejected in Nuremberg"—a rejection that is "the very basis of our international criminal law." Finally, Koh noted, Bybee's memo would tolerate "cruel, inhuman or degrading treatment," which is clearly contrary to the existing law. Although Dean Koh did not say it, the subtext of his testimony was that no self-respecting lawyer would have ever written the legal opinion that Bybee issued.

I have written, at some length, in a new chapter for the paperback edition of *Worse Than Watergate: The Secret Presidency of George W. Bush,* about how other international law, and law of war, experts have told me that Bybee's memo (not to mention a few others) is evidence showing a common plan on the part of the Administration to violate the laws of war. Strikingly, such a "common plan," or conspiracy, is not less than a war crime itself.

IS A WAR CRIME AN IMPEACHABLE OFFENSE? WHY BYBEE SHOULD NOT BE ON THE BENCH

A war crime must surely be a "high crime or misdemeanor" under our Constitution. Accordingly, I wondered during the Gonzales hearings if the future attorney general would be asked if the House of Representatives should initiate impeachment proceedings against Jay Bybee, who had recently been confirmed to be a federal judge. Bybee had slipped through the confirmation process with the world unaware of his secret legal opinions. The question, however, was never raised. And even if it had been, it would doubtless have elicited from Gonzales nothing more than another non-answer which, by then, he had become practiced at providing.

Nonetheless, the question still lingers. Even the Bush administration, for which Bybee once worked, has repudiated his work, saying, in essence, that they were wrongfully counseled that cruel illegalities were perfectly legal. Experts in the law of war say that Bybee's memo is clear and convincing evidence suggesting he participated in a war crime. In light of these facts, there are several unavoidable questions: Why no outrage? Should a putative war criminal remain on the federal bench? Why no impeachment proceedings to resolve this matter?

Memorandum from
Alberto R. Gonzales to the President

ALBERTO GONZALES

This now infamous memo by former White House counsel Alberto Gonzales to President Bush demonstrates the Bush administration's deliberate plans to evade the Geneva Conventions. It also expresses concern about "future prosecutors and independent counsels who may in the future decide to pursue" war crimes charges.

1/25/2002, 3:30pm
MEMORANDUM FOR THE PRESIDENT
FROM: ALBERTO R. GONZALES
SUBJECT: DECISION RE APPLICATION OF THE GENEVA
CONVENTION . . .

Ramifications of Determination that [Geneva Convention on the Treatment of Prisoners of War] does not apply . . .

◆ Positive:
  • Preserves flexibility . . . this new paradigm renders obsolete Geneva's strict limitations on questioning of enemy prisoners and renders quaint some of its provisions . . .
◆ Substantially reduced the threat of domestic criminal prosecution under the War Crimes Act (18 U.S.C. 2441).
  • That Statute, enacted in 1996, prohibits the commission of a "war crime" by or against a U.S. official. "War crime" for these purposes is defined to include any grave breach of [Geneva Convention on the Treatment of Prisoners of War] . . .
  • . . it is difficult to predict the motives of prosecutors and independent counsels who may in the future decide to pursue unwarranted charges based on Section 2441. Your determination [to not apply the Geneva Conventions] would create a reasonable basis in law that Section 2441 does not apply, which would provide a solid defense to any future prosecution.

Senate Judiciary Committee Attorney General Confirmation Hearing for Alberto Gonzales

The following are excerpts taken from Alberto Gonzales's Senate confirmation hearings held on January 7, 2005. Here Gonzales affirms his support for relaxing the definition of *torture* and his confusion as to whether the federal War Crimes Act applies to U.S. personnel.

SENATOR PATRICK LEAHY: I'd like to ask you a few questions about the torture memo that is dated back in August 1st, 2002 . . . addressed to you, it was written at your request, and it . . . says for an act to violate the torture statute, it must be equivalent in intensity to the pain accompanying serious physical injury, such as organ failure, impairment of bodily function or even death. In August 2002 did you agree with that conclusion?

MR. GONZALES: Senator, in connection with that opinion, I did my job as counsel to the president to ask the question.

SEN. LEAHY: I just want to know: Did you agree—I mean, we could spend an hour with that answer, but I'm trying to keep it very simple. Did you agree with that interpretation of the torture statute back in August 2002?

MR. GONZALES: . . . I don't recall today whether or not I was in agreement with all of the analysis, but I don't have a disagreement with the conclusions then reached by the department . . .

SEN. RICHARD DURBIN: . . . Do you believe there are circumstances where other legal restrictions, like the War Crimes Act, would not apply to U.S. personnel? (Pause.)

MR. GONZALES: Senator, I don't believe that that would be the case. But I would like the opportunity—I know I want to be very candid with you and obviously thorough in my response to that question. It is sort of a legal conclusion, and I would like to have the opportunity to get back to you on that.

The Gonzales Indictment

MARJORIE COHN

The following excerpt of the war crime indictment of Alberto Gonzales clearly establishes the legal grounds for opening an independent counsel investigation. Marjorie Cohn is a professor at Thomas Jefferson School of Law, executive vice president of the National Lawyers Guild, and the U.S. representative to the executive committee of the American Association of Jurists.

Alberto Gonzales should not be the Attorney General of the United States. He should be considered a war criminal and indicted by the Attorney General. This is a suggested indictment of Alberto Gonzales for war crimes under Title 18 U.S.C. section 2441, the War Crimes Act.

APPLICATION OF GENEVA CONVENTIONS; DEFINITION OF TORTURE

On or about January 25, 2002 through January 16, 2005, Defendant ALBERTO GONZALES, Counsel to George W. Bush, the President of the United States of America, did write, commission and concur in memoranda that advocated conduct by United States military forces, amounting to war crimes under Title 18 U.S.C. section 2441 (the War Crimes Act).

The War Crimes Act defines as war crimes: grave breaches of the Geneva Conventions, and violations of Article 3 common to the Geneva Conventions.

Section 130 of the Geneva Convention Relative to the Treatment of Prisoners of War (Third Geneva Convention) defines as grave breaches of that Convention: "willful killing, torture or inhuman treatment," and "willfully causing great suffering or serious injury to body or health."

SOURCE: Originally appeared on the Web site, www.truthout.org, January 10, 2005. Available at http://www.truthout.org/docs_05/011905A.shtml. Copyright © 2005 by Marjorie Cohn.

It is well-established that Article 3 common applies to international as well as internal armed conflicts. Article 3 common provides that "persons taking no active part in the hostilities, including members of armed forces who have laid down their arms . . . shall in all circumstances be treated humanely, without any adverse distinction founded on race, colour, religion or faith, sex, birth or wealth, or any other similar criteria."

The following acts constitute violations of Article 3 common: "Violence to life and person, in particular murder of all kinds, mutilation, cruel treatment and torture"; "outrages upon personal dignity, in particular, humiliating and degrading treatment"; and "the passing of sentences and the carrying out of executions without previous judgment pronounced by a regularly constituted court affording all the judicial guarantees which are recognized as indispensable by civilized peoples."

Article 5 of the Third Geneva Convention provides: "Should any doubt arise as to whether persons, having committed a belligerent act and having fallen into the hands of the enemy [are prisoners of war under this Convention], such persons shall enjoy the protection of the present Convention until such time as their status has been determined by a competent tribunal."

Defendant ALBERTO GONZALES wrote, in a memorandum to President George W. Bush dated January 25, 2002, that the war against terrorism is a "new paradigm" that "renders obsolete Geneva's strict limitations on questioning of enemy prisoners and renders quaint some of its provisions."

Defendant GONZALES wrote that the Third Geneva Convention should not apply to members of the Taliban and Al Qaeda who were captured after the United States invaded Afghanistan in October 2001. Defendant GONZALES also advised President Bush in that memorandum that he could avoid allegations of war crimes under the War Crimes Act by simply declaring that the Geneva Convention does not apply to members of the Taliban and Al Qaeda. Defendant GONZALES wrote that a determination of the inapplicability of the Third Geneva Convention would insulate against prosecution by future "prosecutors and independent counsels."

In apparent reliance on the advice in Defendant GONZALES'

memorandum, and notwithstanding the requirement of Article 5 of the Third Geneva Convention that a "competent tribunal" determine the status of prisoners, President George W. Bush issued an order on February 7, 2002, specifying that the United States would not apply the Third Geneva Convention to members of Al Qaeda, and that as commander-in-chief of the United States, he had the power to suspend the Geneva Conventions regarding the conflict in Afghanistan, although he declined to suspend them at that time.

Defendant ALBERTO GONZALES commissioned the Office of Legal Counsel of the Department of Justice's memorandum dated August 1, 2002, which required that, in order to constitute "torture," the pain caused by an interrogation must include "injury such as death, organ failure, or serious impairment of body functions." This definition is contrary to the War Crimes Act and the Convention Against Torture and Other Cruel, Unusual or Degrading Treatment or Punishment, a treaty ratified by the United States.

The January 25, 2002 and August 1, 2002 memoranda, and the February 7, 2002 order set forth policies that led to the willful killing, torture or inhuman treatment; and great suffering or serious injury to body or health of prisoners in United States custody in Afghanistan, Iraq, Guantánamo Bay, Cuba.

Defendant ALBERTO GONZALES knew or should have known that, pursuant to memoranda written by, commissioned or concurred in by him, prisoners in United States custody would be subjected to willful killing, torture or inhuman treatment; and great suffering or serious injury to body or health, in violation of the War Crimes Act.

PENALTIES UNDER THE WAR CRIMES ACT

Title 18 U.S.C. sec. 2441 provides that any national of the United States who commits a war crime "shall be fined under this title or imprisoned for life or any term of years, or both, and if death results to the victim, shall also be subject to the penalty of death."

Flawed Investigations

NATIONAL PUBLIC RADIO INTERVIEW
WITH MARK DANNER

In the following National Public Radio interview, Mark Danner argues that the Department of Defense's investigations into prisoner abuse are designed in a way that protects Bush administration officials from scrutiny. Each investigation refuses to "address the question how the decisions of policy-makers affected what soldiers and officers did to detainees." Danner, a staff writer at the *New Yorker* and a regular contributor to the *New York Review of Books,* is the author of several books including *Torture and Truth: America, Abu Ghraib and the War on Terror.* He is a professor of journalism at the University of California at Berkeley and Henry R. Luce Professor of Human Rights and Journalism at Bard College.

MARK DANNER (AUTHOR): When you have these military reports that are commissioned by the government, they can only look down the chain of command. They can't look up it. So we've had no real report that assesses broadly the responsibility of policy-makers, that tries to connect decisions that were made by Alberto Gonzales, who was then the White House counsel, Secretary of Defense Rumsfeld and other high officials, including the president.

[RENEE] MONTAGNE (HOST): What are the most important things that we know now?

DANNER: What we know now can be compared to a jigsaw puzzle that's two-thirds of the way filled in. So we can see the shape of the image the puzzle detects, although there's still significant gaps. We know that there was systematic abuse at Abu Ghraib. We know that a good deal of this abuse was witnessed by interrogators. It was carried out over a number of days; it included sustained beatings, beating prisoners into unconsciousness connected to interrogation. It was not simply sadistic activity carried out by a few individuals. All

SOURCE: National Public Radio, "Author Mark Danner Talks About the Church report," *Morning Edition,* March 11, 2005. Copyright © 2005 by National Public Radio.

of that we know because the investigations have showed it, including by the Army's own Major General Antonio Taguba. What we don't yet know, because we haven't had a thorough investigation—how the decisions made by policy-makers precisely affected decisions that were made by interrogators.

MONTAGNE: Well, the administration would argue that there is no evidence linking torture as policy, no evidence linking these activities with higher-ups.

DANNER: Well, the best way to show a connection between policy-makers and what actually happened on the ground is to simply follow the migration of interrogation techniques that were approved by Donald Rumsfeld for Guantánamo that then were used in Abu Ghraib prison in Iraq. While prisoners in Guantánamo were not accorded the protection of the Geneva Convention, prisoners in Iraq were, indeed, accorded protection. The problem is that you had some of the same interrogators moving from Guantánamo to Iraq, and this led to violations. And you can chart a straight line from Rumsfeld's decisions to Abu Ghraib. And this is something we can chart using the documents that we already have. The problem is, of course, that we lack a lot of documents because the government hasn't released them and because there has been no thorough investigation. What we've had is a half dozen or more partial investigations that look down the chain of command and that in large part do not address the question how the decisions of policy-makers affected what soldiers and officers did to detainees.

MONTAGNE: What is out there that might, in fact, bring blame higher up?

DANNER: In the absence of a broader investigation, an investigation that would either be commissioned by Congress and would have subpoena power or a specially appointed commission that would also have subpoena power—in the absence of that, we have to look to private lawsuits, one of which was just filed by the American Civil Liberties Union and Human Rights First and are essentially suing Secretary of Defense Donald Rumsfeld on behalf of eight former prisoners. And as these suits go forward, one can expect that many documents will be pried out of the various bureaucracies by the court. But at least, in the absence of a broader investigation, the ACLU–Human Rights First lawsuit will bring us as close as we're likely to get in the near term to a full accounting of what actually happened.

Part III

Beyond Iraq:
The Future of U.S. War Crimes

INTRODUCTION

The Bush administration gives every indication that it intends to continue the criminal activities described in part 1 of this book as long as it is allowed to do so. It has predicted that the war on terror will last for decades or generations, and that the "new paradigm" that authorizes what would otherwise be war crimes will prevail indefinitely. Administration officials, far from showing remorse, have refused even to say that any of their acts were mistakes. Meanwhile, many of those most directly implicated, like Alberto Gonzales and Condoleezza Rice, have been promoted to positions of still greater authority.

The basic intentions of the Bush administration were set out in 2002 in *The National Security Strategy of the United States*. This extraordinary document declared a war against terrorists "of uncertain duration." It enunciated a doctrine of preventive war in which "the United States will act against such emerging threats before they are fully formed." The United States "will not hesitate to act alone, if necessary, to exercise our right of self defense by acting preemptively."

That such policies were not empty words was demonstrated by U.S. attacks on Afghanistan and Iraq and the train of massacres and torture that has followed them. And evidence indicates that further war crimes are currently being planned.

Officials in the Bush administration have made threats against countries all over the world, ranging from "Axis of Evil" members North Korea and Iran to Cuba to Syria, among others. Are these all empty threats? Evidence suggests otherwise. Seymour Hersh, the journalist who did so much to open the realities of Abu Ghraib to public scrutiny, revealed that President Bush had signed "a series of findings and executive orders authorizing secret commando groups and other Special Forces units to conduct covert operations against suspected terrorist targets in as many as ten nations in the Middle East and South Asia." Hersh's "The Coming Wars" describes these plans. According to Bob Herbert of the *New York Times*, the Pentagon is even proposing "commencing combat operations" whose purpose is "chiefly to obtain intelligence" —a war crime on its face.

Meanwhile, according to numerous press reports, the Pentagon is considering the use of teams of assassins—what are generally known as death squads—to attack those they allege to be the leadership of the Iraqi resistance. In "The Salvador Option," three *Newsweek* reporters describe the plans to revive strategies used to terrorize the population of El Salvador during the civil war and Pentagon proposals to use them against the Sunni population in Iraq.

And the Bush administration is preparing to hide its crimes indefinitely into the future. It plans to subject those who have not been eliminated by the "Salvador option" to lifetime "detentions" in secret prisons around the world. According to the *Washington Post*, the Department of Defense, which holds five hundred prisoners at Guantánamo Bay, "plans to ask Congress for $25 million to build a 200-bed prison to hold detainees who are unlikely to ever go through a military tribunal for lack of evidence, according to defense officials." The prison will be designed "for prisoners the government believes have no more intelligence to share." And the CIA "has been scurrying since Sept. 11, 2001, to find secure locations abroad where it could detain and interrogate captives without risk of discovery, and without having to give them access to legal proceedings."[1]

Are such plans really likely to be implemented? Former Reagan administration official and conservative columnist Paul Craig Roberts argues that, with the elimination of more moderate voices in the Bush administration, the military, and the CIA, "there is no one left to stop them."

Since the Bush administration's plans are shrouded in secrecy, who knows what other plans are in the works? Only through leaks and whistle-blowing are the public and even the Congress likely to discover what these leaders have in store for us. The plans already revealed merely hint at the price to be paid in the future for the impunity with which the Bush administration has committed war crimes up till now. They also indicate that their crimes are not just "water over the dam," but rather an ongoing practice that will continue unless and until it is brought to a halt.

[1] Dana Priest, "Long-Term Plan Sought for Terror Suspects," *Washington Post*, January 2, 2005.

The National Security Strategy of the United States of America

PRESIDENT OF THE UNITED STATES

In September 2002, well before the attack on Iraq, a major policy report from President Bush to Congress called *The National Security Strategy of the United States* laid out the basis for the Administration's ongoing disregard of both American and international law. As Senator Robert Byrd observed, "Under this strategy, the President lays claim to an expansive power to use our military to strike other nations first, even if we have not been threatened or provoked. There is no question that the President has the inherent authority to repel attacks against our country, but this *National Security Strategy* is unconstitutional on its face. It takes the checks and balances established in the Constitution that limit the President's ability to use our military at his pleasure, and throws them out the window. This doctrine of preemptive strikes places the sole decision of war and peace in the hands of the President and undermines the Constitutional power of Congress to declare war."

The report's threat of "anticipatory action" even in the event of "uncertainty . . . as to the time and place of the enemy's attack" directly contradicts the UN Charter and international law's established prohibition of "preventive war." *The National Security Strategy of the United States* provided a charter for the Bush administration's war crimes in the past—and it provides a charter for continuing war crimes in the future.

The great struggles of the twentieth century between liberty and totalitarianism ended with a decisive victory for the forces of freedom—and a single sustainable model for national success: freedom, democracy, and free enterprise.

Today, the United States enjoys a position of unparalleled military strength and great economic and political influence. In keeping with our heritage and principles, we do not use our strength to press for unilateral advantage. We seek instead to create a balance of power that favors human freedom: conditions in which all nations

SOURCE: Available at http://www.whitehouse.gov/nsc/nss.html.

and all societies can choose for themselves the rewards and challenges of political and economic liberty.

Defending our Nation against its enemies is the first and fundamental commitment of the Federal Government. Today, that task has changed dramatically. Enemies in the past needed great armies and great industrial capabilities to endanger America. Now, shadowy networks of individuals can bring great chaos and suffering to our shores for less than it costs to purchase a single tank. Terrorists are organized to penetrate open societies and to turn the power of modern technologies against us.

To defeat this threat we must make use of every tool in our arsenal—military power, better homeland defenses, law enforcement, intelligence, and vigorous efforts to cut off terrorist financing. The war against terrorists of global reach is a global enterprise of uncertain duration. America will help nations that need our assistance in combating terror. And America will hold to account nations that are compromised by terror, including those who harbor terrorists— because the allies of terror are the enemies of civilization. The United States and countries cooperating with us must not allow the terrorists to develop new home bases. Together, we will seek to deny them sanctuary at every turn.

The gravest danger our Nation faces lies at the crossroads of radicalism and technology. Our enemies have openly declared that they are seeking weapons of mass destruction, and evidence indicates that they are doing so with determination. The United States will not allow these efforts to succeed. We will build defenses against ballistic missiles and other means of delivery. We will cooperate with other nations to deny, contain, and curtail our enemies' efforts to acquire dangerous technologies. And, as a matter of common sense and self-defense, America will act against such emerging threats before they are fully formed.

As we defend the peace, we will also take advantage of an historic opportunity to preserve the peace. Today, the international community has the best chance since the rise of the nation-state in the seventeenth century to build a world where great powers compete in peace instead of continually prepare for war. Today, the world's great powers find ourselves on the same side—united by common dangers of terrorist violence and chaos.

In building a balance of power that favors freedom, the United States is guided by the conviction that all nations have important responsibilities. Nations that enjoy freedom must actively fight terror. Nations that depend on international stability must help prevent the spread of weapons of mass destruction. Nations that seek international aid must govern themselves wisely, so that aid is well spent. For freedom to thrive, accountability must be expected and required.

The United States of America is fighting a war against terrorists of global reach. The enemy is not a single political regime or person or religion or ideology. The enemy is terrorism—premeditated, politically motivated violence perpetrated against innocents.

In many regions, legitimate grievances prevent the emergence of a lasting peace. Such grievances deserve to be, and must be, addressed within a political process. But no cause justifies terror. The United States will make no concessions to terrorist demands and strike no deals with them. We make no distinction between terrorists and those who knowingly harbor or provide aid to them.

The struggle against global terrorism is different from any other war in our history. It will be fought on many fronts against a particularly elusive enemy over an extended period of time. Progress will come through the persistent accumulation of successes—some seen, some unseen.

Today our enemies have seen the results of what civilized nations can, and will, do against regimes that harbor, support, and use terrorism to achieve their political goals. Afghanistan has been liberated; coalition forces continue to hunt down the Taliban and al-Qaida. But it is not only this battlefield on which we will engage terrorists.

Thousands of trained terrorists remain at large with cells in North America, South America, Europe, Africa, the Middle East, and across Asia. Our priority will be first to disrupt and destroy terrorist organizations of global reach and attack their leadership; command, control, and communications; material support; and finances.

This will have a disabling effect upon the terrorists' ability to plan and operate.

While the United States will constantly strive to enlist the support of the international community, we will not hesitate to act alone, if necessary, to exercise our right of self defense by acting preemptively against such terrorists, to prevent them from doing harm against our people and our country; and denying further sponsorship, support, and sanctuary to terrorists by convincing or compelling states to accept their sovereign responsibilities.

We must be prepared to stop rogue states and their terrorist clients before they are able to threaten or use weapons of mass destruction against the United States and our allies and friends. Our response must take full advantage of strengthened alliances, the establishment of new partnerships with former adversaries, innovation in the use of military forces, modern technologies, including the development of an effective missile defense system, and increased emphasis on intelligence collection and analysis.

Traditional concepts of deterrence will not work against a terrorist enemy whose avowed tactics are wanton destruction and the targeting of innocents; whose so-called soldiers seek martyrdom in death and whose most potent protection is statelessness. The overlap between states that sponsor terror and those that pursue WMD compels us to action.

For centuries, international law recognized that nations need not suffer an attack before they can lawfully take action to defend themselves against forces that present an imminent danger of attack. Legal scholars and international jurists often conditioned the legitimacy of preemption on the existence of an imminent threat— most often a visible mobilization of armies, navies, and air forces preparing to attack. We must adapt the concept of imminent threat to the capabilities and objectives of today's adversaries.

Rogue states and terrorists do not seek to attack us using conventional means.

They know such attacks would fail. Instead, they rely on acts of terror and, potentially, the use of weapons of mass destruction— weapons that can be easily concealed, delivered covertly, and used without warning. The targets of these attacks are our military forces and our civilian population, in direct violation of one of the principal norms of the law of warfare. As was demonstrated by the losses on September 11, 2001, mass civilian casualties is the specific objective of terrorists and these losses would be exponentially more severe if terrorists acquired and used weapons of mass destruction.

The United States has long maintained the option of preemptive actions to counter a sufficient threat to our national security. The greater the threat, the greater is the risk of inaction—and the more compelling the case for taking anticipatory action to defend ourselves, even if uncertainty remains as to the time and place of the enemy's attack. To forestall or prevent such hostile acts by our adversaries, the United States will, if necessary, act preemptively.

The Coming Wars

SEYMOUR HERSH

In a pair of *New Yorker* articles and his book *Chain of Command,* the investigative journalist Seymour Hersh not only revealed the prisoner abuse in Abu Ghraib but exposed top Bush administration officials' responsibility for it. After President Bush's reelection, Hersh began to investigate the Bush administration's plans for military action against Iran and as many as ten additional countries. Virtually unlimited authority has been given to Defense Secretary Donald Rumsfeld to operate in and against other countries without the consent of their governments, the U.S. Congress, or the international community. Such activity violates both American and international law on its face.

Hersh wrote the first account of the My Lai massacre in South Vietnam in 1969. He has won more than a dozen major journalism prizes, including the 1970 Pulitzer Prize for International Reporting and four George Polk Awards. He is also the author of six books, including *The Price of Power: Kissinger in the Nixon White House,* which won the National Book Critics Circle Award and the *Los Angeles Times* Book Award.

George W. Bush's reelection was not his only victory last fall. The President and his national-security advisers have consolidated control over the military and intelligence communities' strategic analyses and covert operations to a degree unmatched since the rise of the post–Second World War national-security state. Bush has an aggressive and ambitious agenda for using that control — against the mullahs in Iran and against targets in the ongoing war on terrorism — during his second term.

Despite the deteriorating security situation in Iraq, the Bush Administration has not reconsidered its basic long-range policy goal in the Middle East: the establishment of democracy throughout the region. Bush's reelection is regarded within the Administration as evidence of America's support for his decision to go to war. It has reaffirmed the position of the neoconservatives in the Pentagon's civilian leadership who advocated the invasion, including

SOURCE: Originally appeared in the *New Yorker,* January 24 and 31, 2005. Available at http://www.newyorker.com/fact/content/?050124fa_fact. Copyright © 2005 by Seymour Hersh. Reprinted by permission of International Creative Management, Inc.

Paul Wolfowitz, the Deputy Secretary of Defense, and Douglas Feith, the Under-secretary for Policy. According to a former high-level intelligence official, Secretary of Defense Donald Rumsfeld met with the Joint Chiefs of Staff shortly after the election and told them, in essence, that the naysayers had been heard and the American people did not accept their message. Rumsfeld added that America was committed to staying in Iraq and that there would be no second-guessing.

"This is a war against terrorism, and Iraq is just one campaign. The Bush Administration is looking at this as a huge war zone," the former high-level intelligence official told me. "Next, we're going to have the Iranian campaign. We've declared war and the bad guys, wherever they are, are the enemy. This is the last hurrah—we've got four years, and want to come out of this saying we won the war on terrorism."

In interviews with past and present intelligence and military officials, I was told that the agenda had been determined before the Presidential election, and much of it would be Rumsfeld's responsibility. The war on terrorism would be expanded, and effectively placed under the Pentagon's control. The President has signed a series of findings and executive orders authorizing secret commando groups and other Special Forces units to conduct covert operations against suspected terrorist targets in as many as ten nations in the Middle East and South Asia.

The Administration has been conducting secret reconnaissance missions inside Iran at least since last summer. Much of the focus is on the accumulation of intelligence and targeting information on Iranian nuclear, chemical, and missile sites, both declared and suspected. The goal is to identify and isolate three dozen, and perhaps more, such targets that could be destroyed by precision strikes and short-term commando raids. "The civilians in the Pentagon want to go into Iran and destroy as much of the military infrastructure as possible," the government consultant with close ties to the Pentagon told me.

Some of the missions involve extraordinary cooperation. For example, the former high-level intelligence official told me that an American commando task force has been set up in South Asia and is now working closely with a group of Pakistani scientists and technicians who had dealt with Iranian counterparts. (In 2003, the I.A.E.A. [International Atomic Energy Agency] disclosed that Iran had been secretly receiving nuclear technology from Pakistan for more than a decade, and had withheld that information from inspectors.) The American task force, aided by the information from Pakistan, has been penetrating eastern Iran from Afghanistan in a hunt for underground installations. The task-force members, or their locally recruited agents, secreted remote detection devices—known as sniffers—capable of sampling the atmosphere for radioactive emissions and other evidence of nuclear-enrichment programs.

There has also been close, and largely unacknowledged, cooperation with Israel. The government consultant with ties to the Pentagon said that the Defense Department civilians, under the leadership of Douglas Feith, have been working with Israeli planners and consultants to develop and refine potential nuclear, chemical-weapons, and missile targets inside Iran.

The Pentagon's contingency plans for a broader invasion of Iran are also being updated. Strategists at the headquarters of the U.S. Central Command, in Tampa, Florida, have been asked to revise the military's war plan, providing for a maximum ground and air invasion of Iran. Updating the plan makes sense, whether or not the Administration intends to act, because the geopolitics of the region have changed dramatically in the last three years. Previously, an American invasion force would have had to enter Iran by sea, by way of the Persian Gulf or the Gulf of Oman; now troops could move in on the ground, from Afghanistan or Iraq. Commando units and other assets could be introduced through new bases in the Central Asian republics.

It is possible that some of the American officials who talk about the need to eliminate Iran's nuclear infrastructure are doing so as part of a propaganda campaign aimed at pressuring Iran to give up its weapons planning. In my interviews over the past two months, I was given a much harsher view. The hawks in the Administration believe that it will soon become clear that the Europeans' negotiated approach cannot succeed, and that at that time the Administration will act. "We're not dealing with a set of National Security

Council option papers here," the former high-level intelligence official told me. "They've already passed that wicket. It's not *if* we're going to do anything against Iran. They're doing it."

The immediate goals of the attacks would be to destroy, or at least temporarily derail, Iran's ability to go nuclear. But there are other, equally purposeful, motives at work. The government consultant told me that the hawks in the Pentagon, in private discussions, have been urging a limited attack on Iran because they believe it could lead to a toppling of the religious leadership. "Within the soul of Iran there is a struggle between secular nationalists and reformers, on the one hand, and, on the other hand, the fundamentalist Islamic movement," the consultant told me. "The minute the aura of invincibility which the mullahs enjoy is shattered, and with it the ability to hoodwink the West, the Iranian regime will collapse"—like the former Communist regimes in Romania, East Germany, and the Soviet Union. Rumsfeld and Wolfowitz share that belief, he said.

"The idea that an American attack on Iran's nuclear facilities would produce a popular uprising is extremely illinformed," said Flynt Leverett, a Middle East scholar who worked on the National Security Council in the Bush Administration. "You have to understand that the nuclear ambition in Iran is supported across the political spectrum, and Iranians will perceive attacks on these sites as attacks on their ambitions to be a major regional player and a modern nation that's technologically sophisticated." Leverett, who is now a senior fellow at the Saban Center for Middle East Policy, at the Brookings Institution, warned that an American attack, if it takes place, "will produce an Iranian backlash against the United States and a rallying around the regime."

According to a Pentagon consultant, an Execute Order on the Global War on Terrorism (referred to throughout the government as GWOT) was issued at Rumsfeld's direction. The order specifically authorized the military "to find and finish" terrorist targets, the consultant said. It included a target list that cited Al Qaeda network members, Al Qaeda senior leadership, and other high-value targets. The consultant said that the order had been cleared throughout the national-security bureaucracy in Washington.

Two former C.I.A. clandestine officers, Vince Cannistraro and Philip Giraldi, who publish *Intelligence Brief*, a newsletter for their business clients, reported last month on the existence of a broad counter-terrorism Presidential finding that permitted the Pentagon "to operate unilaterally in a number of countries where there is a perception of a clear and evident terrorist threat . . . A number of the countries are friendly to the U.S. and are major trading partners. Most have been cooperating in the war on terrorism." The two former officers listed some of the countries—Algeria, Sudan, Yemen, Syria, and Malaysia. (I was subsequently told by the former high-level intelligence official that Tunisia is also on the list.)

The new rules will enable the Special Forces community to set up what it calls "action teams" in the target countries overseas which can be used to find and eliminate terrorist organizations. "Do you remember the right-wing execution squads in El Salvador?" the former high-level intelligence official asked me, referring to the military-led gangs that committed atrocities in the early nineteen-eighties. "We founded them and we financed them," he said. "The objective now is to recruit locals in any area we want. And we aren't going to tell Congress about it." A former military officer, who has knowledge of the Pentagon's commando capabilities, said, "We're going to be riding with the bad boys."

"It's a finesse to give power to Rumsfeld—giving him the right to act swiftly, decisively, and lethally," the first Pentagon adviser told me. "It's a global free-fire zone."

Shopping for War

BOB HERBERT

In the wake of President Bush's reelection, the Pentagon began to develop new rationales to justify additional military missions in the future. In the context of rivalry among security agencies, news of some of them leaked out. Bob Herbert, an op-ed columnist for the *New York Times* since 1993, provided his reaction to this news in his column of December 27, 2004.

You might think that the debacle in Iraq would be enough for the Pentagon, that it would not be in the mood to seek out new routes to unnecessary wars for the United States to fight. But with Donald Rumsfeld at the apex of the defense establishment, enough is never enough.

So, as detailed in an article in The Times on Dec. 19, Mr. Rumsfeld's minions are concocting yet another grandiose and potentially disastrous scheme. Pentagon officials are putting together a plan that would give the military a more prominent role in intelligence gathering operations that traditionally have been handled by the Central Intelligence Agency. They envision the military doing more spying with humans, as opposed, for example, to surveillance with satellites.

Further encroachment by the military into intelligence matters better handled by civilians is bad enough. Now hold your breath. According to the article, "Among the ideas cited by Defense Department officials is the idea of 'fighting for intelligence,' or commencing combat operations chiefly to obtain intelligence."

That is utter madness. The geniuses in Washington have already launched one bogus war, which has cost tens of thousands of lives and provoked levels of suffering that are impossible to quantify. We don't need to be contemplating new forms of warfare waged for the sole purpose of gathering intelligence.

Part of this plan to further aggrandize Mr. Rumsfeld is being drafted under the direction of Lt. Gen. William Boykin, a deputy under secretary of defense who has already demonstrated that he should not be allowed anywhere near the most serious matters of national security. General Boykin, who once had the job of directing the hunt for Osama bin Laden, is an evangelical Christian who believes God put President Bush in the White House. He has described the fight against Islamic militants as a struggle against Satan and declared that it can be won only "if we come at them in the name of Jesus."

General Boykin asserted his views in speeches that he delivered in his military uniform at religious functions around the country. In one speech, referring to a Muslim fighter in Somalia, the general said: "Well, you know what I knew—that my God was bigger than his. I knew that my God was a real God, and his was an idol."

General Boykin was forced to apologize after media accounts led to widespread criticism. But the Bush administration is still holding him tightly in its embrace. How difficult is it to come to the conclusion that this is not a fellow who should be making decisions on matters involving armed conflict with Muslims?

The war in Iraq was the result of powerful government figures imposing their dangerous fantasies on the world. The fantasies notably included the weapons of mass destruction, the links between Al Qaeda and Saddam Hussein, the throngs of Iraqis hurling kisses and garlands at the invading Americans, and the spread of American-style democracy throughout the Middle East. All voices of caution were ignored and the fantasies were allowed to prevail.

The world is not a video game, although it must seem like it at times to the hubristic, hermetically sealed powerbrokers in Washington who manipulate the forces that affect the lives of so many millions of people in every region of the planet. That kind of power calls for humility, not arrogance, and should be wielded wisely, not thoughtlessly and impulsively.

"The Salvador Option": The Pentagon May Put Special-Forces-Led Assassination or Kidnapping Teams in Iraq

MICHAEL HIRSH AND JOHN BARRY WITH MARK HOSENBALL

Early in 2005, word began to leak out about the Bush administration's new plans to use kidnapping and assassination as weapons in Iraq, violations of both U.S. and international law. In the following *Newsweek* article, a military source involved in Pentagon strategy discussions is quoted as saying that "new offensive operations are needed that would create a fear of aiding the insurgency" on the part of "the Sunni population." Treating a population as a target of military action is a serious violation of the Geneva Conventions.

What to do about the deepening quagmire of Iraq? The Pentagon's latest approach is being called "the Salvador option"—and the fact that it is being discussed at all is a measure of just how worried Donald Rumsfeld really is. "What everyone agrees is that we can't just go on as we are," one senior military officer told NEWSWEEK. "We have to find a way to take the offensive against the insurgents. Right now, we are playing defense. And we are losing." Last November's operation in Fallujah, most analysts agree, succeeded less in breaking "the back" of the insurgency—as Marine Gen. John Sattler optimistically declared at the time—than in spreading it out.

Now, NEWSWEEK has learned, the Pentagon is intensively debating an option that dates back to a still-secret strategy in the Reagan administration's battle against the leftist guerrilla insurgency in El Salvador in the early 1980s. Then, faced with a losing war against Salvadoran rebels, the U.S. government funded or supported "nationalist" forces that allegedly included so-called death squads directed to hunt down and kill rebel leaders and sympathizers. Eventually the insurgency was quelled, and many U.S. conservatives consider the policy to have been a success—despite the deaths of innocent civilians and the subsequent Iran-Contra arms-for-hostages scandal. (Among the current administration officials who dealt with Central America back then is John Negroponte, who is today the U.S. ambassador to Iraq. Under Reagan, he was ambassador to Honduras.)

Following that model, one Pentagon proposal would send Special Forces teams to advise, support and possibly train Iraqi squads, most likely hand-picked Kurdish Peshmerga fighters and Shiite militiamen, to target Sunni insurgents and their sympathizers, even across the border into Syria, according to military insiders familiar with the discussions. It remains unclear, however, whether this would be a policy of assassination or so-called "snatch" operations, in which the targets are sent to secret facilities for interrogation. The current thinking is that while U.S. Special Forces would lead operations in, say, Syria, activities inside Iraq itself would be carried out by Iraqi paramilitaries, officials tell NEWSWEEK.

Meanwhile, intensive discussions are taking place inside the Senate Intelligence Committee over the Defense department's efforts to expand the involvement of U.S. Special Forces personnel in intelligence-gathering missions. Historically, Special Forces' intelligence gathering has been limited to objectives directly related to upcoming military operations—"preparation of the battlefield," in military lingo. But, according to intelligence and defense officials, some Pentagon civilians for years have sought to expand the use of Special Forces for other intelligence missions.

Pentagon civilians and some Special Forces personnel believe CIA civilian managers have traditionally been too conservative in planning and executing the kind of undercover missions that Special Forces soldiers believe they can effectively conduct. CIA traditionalists are believed to be adamantly opposed to ceding any authority to the Pentagon. Until now, Pentagon proposals for a capability to send soldiers out on intelligence missions without direct CIA approval or participation have been shot down. But counterterrorist strike squads, even operating covertly, could be deemed to fall within the Defense department's orbit.

The interim government of Prime Minister Ayad Allawi is said to be among the most forthright proponents of the Salvador option. Maj. Gen. Muhammad Abdallah al-Shahwani, director of Iraq's

National Intelligence Service, said that the U.S. occupation has failed to crack the problem of broad support for the insurgency. He said most Iraqi people do not actively support the insurgents or provide them with material or logistical help, but at the same time they won't turn them in. One military source involved in the Pentagon debate agrees that this is the crux of the problem, and he suggests that new offensive operations are needed that would create a fear of aiding the insurgency. "The Sunni population is paying no price for the support it is giving to the terrorists," he said. "From their point of view, it is cost-free. We have to change that equation."

Long-Term Plan Sought
for Terror Suspects

DANA PRIEST

In the following article Dana Priest, a reporter for the *Washington Post*, discusses the plans being made by Pentagon and CIA officials to hold hundreds of prisoners for the rest of their lives, even though they lack evidence to charge them in court. In many cases they plan to spirit away the captives to other countries—often ones notorious for the practice of torture. This form of disappearance, known by U.S. officials as *rendition*, is strictly prohibited by international law.

Administration officials are preparing long-range plans for indefinitely imprisoning suspected terrorists whom they do not want to set free or turn over to courts in the United States or other countries, according to intelligence, defense and diplomatic officials.

The Pentagon and the CIA have asked the White House to decide on a more permanent approach for potentially lifetime detentions, including for hundreds of people now in military and CIA custody whom the government does not have enough evidence to charge in courts. The outcome of the review, which also involves the State Department, would also affect those expected to be captured in the course of future counterterrorism operations.

One proposal under review is the transfer of large numbers of Afghan, Saudi and Yemeni detainees from the military's Guantánamo Bay, Cuba detention center into new U.S.-built prisons in their home countries.

One approach used by the CIA has been to transfer captives it picks up abroad to third countries willing to hold them indefinitely and without public proceedings. The transfers, called "renditions," depend on arrangements between the United States and other countries, such as Egypt, Jordan and Afghanistan, that have

SOURCE: Originally appeared in the *Washington Post*, January 2, 2005. Available at http://www.washingtonpost.com/wp-dyn/articles/A41475-2005Jan1.html.

agreed to have local security services hold certain terror suspects in their facilities for interrogation by CIA and foreign liaison officers.

"The whole idea has become a corruption of renditions," said one CIA officer who has been involved in the practice. "It's not rendering to justice, it's kidnapping."

There Is No One Left to Stop Them

PAUL CRAIG ROBERTS

The conservative columnist Paul Craig Roberts writes that the Bush administration's neoconservatives will use his reelection as a "mandate for further violence in the Middle East." They intend "to set the U.S. on a course of long and debilitating war." The elimination of more moderate forces in the Administration, the military, and the CIA has removed the constraints that might limit such a course.

Roberts is a senior fellow at the Hoover Institution and John M. Olin Fellow at the Institute for Political Economy. He served as Assistant Secretary of the Treasury for economic policy in the Reagan administration.

The United States is in dire straits. Its government is in the hands of people who connect to events neither rationally nor morally.

If President Bush's neoconservative administration were rational, the U.S. would never have invaded Iraq. If Bush's government were moral, it would be ashamed of the carnage and horror it has unleashed in Iraq.

The Bush administration has no doubts. It knows that it is right and virtuous. Bush and the neocons dismiss factual criticisms as evidence that the critics are "against us."

People who know that they are right cannot avoid sinking deeper into mistakes. The Bush administration led the U.S. into a war on the basis of claims that are now known to be untrue. Yet, President Bush and Vice President Cheney consistently refuse to admit that any mistake has been made. The chances are high, therefore, that the second Bush administration will be more disastrous than the first.

The first Bush administration has cost America 10,000 casualties (dead and wounded). Eight of 10 U.S. divisions are tied down in Iraq by a few thousand lightly armed insurgents. Polls reveal that most Iraqis regard Americans as invaders and occupiers, not as liberators. U.S. prestige in the Muslim world has evaporated. The majority of Muslims who were with us, are now against us. Sooner or later, this change of mind will endanger our puppet regimes in Egypt, Jordan, Pakistan, and Saudi Arabia.

In a futile effort to assert hegemony in Iraq, the U.S. has largely destroyed Fallujah, once a city of 300,000. Hundreds, if not thousands, of civilians have been killed by the indiscriminate use of high explosives.

To cover up the extensive civilian deaths, U.S. authorities count all Iraqi dead as insurgents, delivering a high body count as claim of success for a bloody-minded operation. The human cost for American families is 51 dead and 450 wounded U.S. troops—casualties on par with the worst days of the Vietnam War.

The film of a U.S. Marine shooting a captured, wounded, and unarmed Iraqi prisoner in the head at close range has been shown all over the world. Coming on top of proven acts of torture at U.S. military prisons, this war crime has destroyed what remained of America's image and moral authority.

On Nov. 17, the UN High Commissioner for Human Rights called for investigation of American war crimes in Fallujah. This is a remarkable turn of events, showing how far U.S. prestige and the morale of our armed forces have fallen.

However, for Bush administration partisans, war crimes are no longer something of which to be ashamed. Reflecting the neoconservative mindset that America's monopoly on virtue justifies any and all U.S. actions, Fox "News" talking heads and their Republican Party and retired military guests have arrogantly defended the Marine who murdered the wounded Iraqi prisoner.

Iraqi insurgents are condemned for deaths they inflict on civilians. But when American troops fire indiscriminately upon civilians and U.S. missile and bombing attacks kill Iraqis in their homes, the deaths are dismissed as "collateral damage." This double standard is a further indication that Americans have come to the belief that U.S. ends justify any means.

A number of former top U.S. military leaders and heads of the CIA and National Security Agency have condemned Bush's invasion of Iraq as a "strategic blunder." These are people who gave their lives to the service of our country and can in no way be said to be "against us."

However, the Bush administration and its apologists regard critics as enemies. To accept criticism means to be held accountable, something the Bush administration is determined to avoid. Condoleezza Rice, who failed as National Security Adviser to prevent the Pentagon from using fabricated information to start a Middle East war, is being elevated to secretary of state in Bush's second term.

Indeed, the entire panoply of neoconservatives, who intentionally fabricated the "intelligence" used to justify the U.S. invasion of Iraq, are being rewarded by promotion to higher offices. Stephen Hadley is moving up to National Security Adviser. Hadley is the person who advocates "usable" mini-nukes for the U.S. conquest of the Middle East.

The few officials who are not warmongers, such as Secretary of State Colin Powell and Deputy Secretary of State Richard Armitage, are leaving the Bush administration. Right before our eyes, the CIA is being turned into a neoconservative propaganda organ as numerous senior officials resign and are replaced with yes-men.

With its current troop strength, the Bush administration cannot achieve the Middle East goals it shares with the Israeli government. Either the draft will have to be restored or mini-nukes developed and deployed. As insurgents do not mass in military formations, the mini-nukes would be used as a genocidal weapon to wipe out entire cities that show any resistance to neocon dictates.

Many Bush partisans send me e-mails fiercely advocating "virtuous violence." They do not flinch at the use of nuclear weapons against Muslims who refuse to do as we tell them. These partisans do not doubt for a second that Bush has the right to dictate to Muslims and everyone else (especially the French). Many also express their conviction that all of Bush's critics should be rounded up and sent to the Middle East in time for the first nuke.

These attitudes represent a sharp break from American values and foreign policy. The new conservatives have more in common with the Brownshirt movement that silenced German opposition to Hitler than with America's Founding Fathers.

Bush's reelection, if won fair and square, was won because

20 million Christian evangelicals voted against abortion and homosexuals. However, Bush's neoconservative masters will use his re-election as a mandate for further violence in the Middle East. They intend to set the U.S. on a course of long and debilitating war.

There is no one left in the Bush administration, the CIA, or the military to stop them.

Part IV

Perspectives on American War Crimes

INTRODUCTION

Our country has barely begun to grapple with the facts of American war crimes, let alone with their implications. What does it mean that our actions and those of our leaders have strayed so far out of line with our image of ourselves as a peaceful, ethical, and law-abiding nation? The facts of American war crimes raise questions that go far beyond the narrow legalism of court briefs and judicial rulings.

What are the consequences of rendering null the institutions of international law on which the world's order and security have long been based? What does it mean for democracy at home if the President, as Bush officials claim, has an authority unlimited by Congress or the courts? What will be the long-term effect of open repudiation of international law on American world leadership? What do war crimes say about us as a nation? What should our consciences—individual and national—be telling us about them? Part IV is designed to open a dialogue on those questions.

As Lisa Hajjar points out, "the grimmest lesson" of World War II was that "the most egregious atrocities, perpetrated by modern sovereign states, were not illegal because there were no laws to prohibit them and no authority to prevent them." The Nuremberg war crimes trials and the United Nations established such law and authority. While often given only lip service, they came to life in the 1990s with the UN tribunals for the former Yugoslavia and Rwanda and the creation of the International Criminal Court. But the Bush administration has set out to demolish this hopeful development, for example, by doing everything it can to undermine the International Criminal Court. In place of international law based on "consensus and universalism," the Administration is providing its own unilateral interpretations of international law and attempting to impose them through institutions like the proposed tribunal to try Saddam Hussein that operate under conditions of American domination. "What this risks," Hajjar warns, is "an erosion of the very foundation of international law," an erosion that serves "neither justice nor security."

The questions regarding democratic control of our own government are equally disturbing. The Bush administration has asserted that the rise of international terrorism creates an emergency of "uncertain duration." It maintains that such an emergency requires that the President's powers be unlimited by Congress or the courts. As Sanford Levinson points out, this argument means that the power to declare an emergency is the power to be a "sovereign"—an absolute ruler. If the President exercises the sovereign power of a king or emperor, what is left of America's proud tradition of democracy and government under law?

One resonant voice in the U.S. Senate has demanded to know the answer to that question. In the tradition of Senator William Fulbright, another southern senator who challenged the imperial presidency of Lyndon Johnson during the Vietnam War, Senator Robert Byrd challenges the fundamental constitutionality of the Bush administration's interpretation of the President's war powers. "It takes the checks and balances established in the Constitution that limit the President's ability to use our military at his pleasure, and throws them out the window."

Indeed, as Bruce Shapiro writes, "three years of the war on terror have corrupted public institutions" and brought the failure of "every mechanism which is supposed to keep war crimes from happening." Over many decades, successive presidents and congresses and military leaders embraced "specific laws and procedures designed to prevent atrocity in wartime," such as the Geneva Conventions, the Convention Against Torture, the War Crimes Act of 1996, and the Uniform Code of Military Justice. Shapiro traces a third of a century of struggle over these protections and the way they have been dismantled by the Bush administration. Shapiro notes that a campaign for their restoration would be one in which "hardnosed military and law-enforcement professionals committed to the balance of powers and rule of law could play a prominent part."

Writing on the eve of the U.S. attack on Iraq, Nobel Peace Prize laureate and former President Jimmy Carter warned that "increasingly unilateral and domineering policies have brought international trust in our country to its lowest level in memory." And he raised the question not only of how others see us but of the essential morality of our actions. Reviewing the principles of a just war, he concluded that "a substantially unilateral attack on Iraq does not meet these standards." He pointed out that with few exceptions this was "an almost universal conviction of religious leaders."

Finally, what of the human meaning of war crimes? What about the effect of the devastation documented in part I on its victims? Sister Joan Chittister, a columnist for the *National Catholic Reporter*, describes the impact of an American war crime on one Iraqi family.

War crimes are a scandal, but they are far more than a scandal. They raise complex issues about the future of our world, our democracy, and our own deepest values. Reflection on their significance belongs not only in the courtroom and the halls of Congress but in our schools, colleges, town halls, and religious congregations.

From Nuremberg to Guantánamo: International Law and American Power Politics

LISA HAJJAR

International law has provided a context for both defenders of the Bush administration's policies and for those who denounce these policies as criminal. International law has gone through a significant but little-recognized development in recent years that substantially increases the legal accountability of governments and government officials. The United States contributed to that development, but now is increasingly resisting it. Lisa Hajjar introduces this history and asks whether the Bush administration's approach to international law promotes either justice or security. Hajjar, an editor of *Middle East Report*, teaches in the Law and Society Program at the University of California, Santa Barbara.

All that is needed to achieve total political domination is to kill the juridical in humankind.

—Hannah Arendt, *On the Origins of Totalitarianism*

In the aftermath of the September 11 attacks on the U.S., George W. Bush used terms like "punishment" and "justice" to assert what his administration would make happen and why. Using such legalistic terms was the logical means of legitimizing the American state's planned response to the violence.

Punishment is indeed an appropriate response to crime, and the September 11 attacks were, by any reasoned assessment, crimes against humanity—large-scale and/or systematic attacks against civilians. Crimes against humanity, like genocide, war crimes, torture, apartheid, hijacking and certain kinds of hostage taking, are international crimes because they are defined and prohibited by international laws. The laws criminalizing these practices encode

SOURCE: Originally appeared in *Middle East Report* 229 (Winter 2003) and revised by the author. Available at http://www.merip.org/mer/mer229/229_hajjar.html. Copyright © 2003 by MERIP.

normative principles that reflect a fairly high level of international consensus, and their jurisdiction is international, which means not only that these practices are illegal everywhere, but also that everyone—not just victims—has an interest in their enforcement.

The Bush administration, however, immediately nationalized the international character and consequences of September 11, classifying the attacks as an "act of war" against America and shunning a law enforcement model as the mechanism of punishment. Because the September 11 attacks were perpetrated on American soil and killed thousands of civilians, at the outset there was broad international support for the U.S. decision to respond with military force in Afghanistan. That country was the functional base of al-Qaeda, and the Taliban regime was unwilling to turn over suspected perpetrators of the attacks. That support rapidly eroded as U.S. discretion transformed from hot pursuit rationalized as self-defense into an offensive global war on terror, unrestrained by territory or by law.

Four years on, we can judge the U.S. response to September 11 as a failure on its own terms: the Bush administration has not achieved justice for the victims, nor has the war on terror made the U.S. more secure. The cost of these failures is heightened by what has been destroyed or subverted by U.S. policy and state practices that fall within the ambit of the war on terror. Rather than capitalizing on post–September 11 international sympathy to strengthen multilateral mechanisms of international law enforcement, the U.S. war on terror has put international law—and the norms enshrined therein—at risk, with deleterious ramifications for global security.

THE NUREMBERG PRECEDENT

Until the end of World War II, international laws were oriented primarily to relations among states, excluding, for the most part, the governance and treatment of human beings. State sovereignty constituted a form of supreme power based on principles of political independence, domestic jurisdiction and foreign non-interference. Most human beings had no claim to international rights because they had (virtually) no standing in international law. But World War II took a toll on the legitimacy of this Westphalian order.

The grimmest lesson of the war was that the most egregious atrocities, perpetrated by modern sovereign states, were not illegal because there were no laws to prohibit them and no authority to prevent them.

At the end of the war, tribunals were established in Nuremberg and Tokyo to try Axis leaders. The process of establishing legal codes for the tribunals and the proceedings that took place therein clarified and extended the parameters of "war crimes," laying the ground for the subsequent reform of international humanitarian law ("laws of war") that materialized in the four Geneva Conventions of 1949. The tribunals also articulated a new category of crimes ("crimes against humanity") prohibiting systematic violence against civilians in times of war or peace, and contributed to the establishment of a new category of rights ("human rights"). The United Nations, founded in 1946, first articulated human rights in positive law in 1948 with the Genocide Convention and the Universal Declaration of Human Rights.

These post-war legal developments set new limits on the rights of states, but they did not alter the state-centrism of the international order. Rather, new and reformed international laws changed the norms to which all states would be expected to adhere, while preserving the principle of states' rights as sovereign entities. Human rights obtained their universal character from the fact that people are subjects of states, and states are subject to international law.

But the enforceability of international law was compromised from the outset by *realpolitik* exigencies and Cold War polarizations. Within the UN system, efforts to institute international law enforcement mechanisms were either aborted (no International Criminal Court was created) or subordinated to states' sovereign discretion (the enforcement power of the International Court of Justice was made contingent on the will of states to submit to the court's jurisdiction). Enforcement depended on the willingness of individual states to conform to the laws they signed, and on the system of states to act against those that did not. While some states instituted domestic reforms and pursued foreign policies in keeping with their international obligations, most refused to regard human rights and humanitarian laws as binding, especially if the implications would compromise vested interests or curtail the pursuit of those interests (including through force).

Consequently, from the close of the Nuremberg and Tokyo tribunals to the end of the Cold War, international laws pertaining to the rights of human beings functioned not as law but as moral rhetoric framed in legal language. During these decades, more people were killed and harmed by practices that had come to be characterized as international crimes than in any previous period. The politics of sovereignty held sway over any meaningful commitment to legality, evidenced by active refusal to authorize international action to stop or prevent grotesque abuses. It was an age of impunity.

AMERICAN EXCEPTIONALISM

The U.S. played an important—but decidedly mixed—role in the history of international lawmaking and enforcement. American officials, in cooperation with other victorious Allies, ran the Nuremberg and Tokyo tribunals. These proceedings established a framework for pursuing retribution against the Axis powers. But if horrific violence against civilians could be criminalized and punished, there was a clear double standard in the fact that no similar retributive process was mounted to account for the horrors caused by the bombings of Dresden, Hiroshima and Nagasaki.

The U.S. supported the establishment of the UN to provide for global peace and security, but the organization's structure vested significant power in the Security Council and accorded the U.S. and the other four permanent members with veto power. The combined effects of a lack of political will and the threat of a veto from one or more of these five member states stymied UN intervention on behalf of populations at risk, the most scandalous instance being the genocide in Rwanda in 1993.

The logic of *realpolitik* prevailed through the 1980s. There was a bipartisan American record of perpetration or abetment of practices that constituted international crimes, from Southeast Asia through the Middle East to Latin America. U.S. policy made a mockery of the principles enshrined in international law, while officials opportunistically utilized its moral-legal rhetoric to castigate enemies.

If "American exceptionalism" was invoked to explain (and in some quarters justify) this hypocrisy, there was nothing particularly exceptional about it, in that violations and non-enforcement of international law were the rule around the world throughout the Cold War era.

THE BOOM YEARS

In the late 1980s and early 1990s, the shift from authoritarian to more democratic governments in Latin America, South Africa, and Eastern Europe provided new opportunities to judge the past against standards of international law. Accountability for gross violations became a dominant theme in many countries.

A key turning point was the creation of ad hoc UN tribunals for the former Yugoslavia in 1993 and Rwanda in 1994 to prosecute suspected perpetrators of genocide, war crimes and crimes against humanity. Since then international or mixed tribunals have been established to contend with gross violations perpetrated in other countries. Other major developments of the decade included the indictment of former Chilean dictator Augusto Pinochet and the completion of a treaty to establish a new International Criminal Court (ICC). In 1999, Belgium passed a national universal jurisdiction law, which would make its courts available to prosecute people accused of international crimes like "grave breaches" of the Geneva Conventions, genocide and torture. Together, these developments sought to revive the "Nuremberg precedent" in which individuals could be held accountable and punished for perpetrating or abetting international crimes. Thus, prior to September 11, international law enforcement was on the rise.

The U.S., after shamefully blocking an international response to the genocide in Rwanda, encouraged the establishment of the first UN ad hoc tribunals. Support for this type of international justice could be sold at home because the people subject to the tribunals' jurisdiction did not include American nationals. But where Americans were complicit in gross violations, that support was not forthcoming, clearly evident in the refusal to turn over relevant documents to foreign governments, like Chile and Argentina, seeking to investigate and punish those responsible for gross violations in their "dirty wars."

In the late 1990s, U.S. officials responded to developments in international law enforcement as threats to American interests. The Pinochet case, and the Belgian law which was its progeny, eroded the principle of "sovereign immunity" for crimes of state and boosted the principle of universal jurisdiction. Could the trial of Henry Kissinger be next? Of course, the line of reasoning that perceives universal jurisdiction as threatening conflates the fate of individuals with the fate of states. Moreover, this way of thinking contravenes the legal principle that certain practices are crimes and the individuals responsible for them are punishable, ideally at home but if not, abroad.

The ICC was touted by supporters around the world as a breakthrough in long-thwarted aspirations to globalize the jurisdiction and enforceability of international criminal law. In Rome, where the ICC treaty was negotiated, U.S. officials worked vigorously to limit the court's powers, and many U.S. demands were incorporated into the final text in the hope of gaining American support for the institution—and in acknowledgment that without U.S. support the ICC would be seriously weakened. Not satisfied that the treaty gave the U.S. adequate power to influence the operation of the court or adequately protected American immunity from prosecution for crimes covered by the ICC statute, however, the U.S., along with six other countries, voted against the treaty. When George W. Bush became president in 2000, he removed the U.S. signature from the ICC treaty, which the outgoing Bill Clinton had signed in the very last hours of his presidency. But Clinton was fully aware of domestic opposition to international justice, and even though he signed the treaty he recommended that it not be submitted to Congress for ratification, making it a hollow gesture.

One month after the ICC obtained the needed number of signatures for its establishment in July 2002, Congress passed a law, the American Service Members Protection Act, prohibiting any American cooperation with the ICC, and authorizing the executive to order the use of force to "free" any American citizen or resident who might be taken into ICC custody. This law has been mocked by critics as the "Hague Invasion Act."

DISPUTED FUTURE

The future of international law as a framework for global order has been intensely disputed since September 11. Across the political spectrum, there is a common tendency to characterize the post–September 11 era as a restoration of unbridled *realpolitik* at the expense of international law. Those who embrace this interpretation—especially, but not exclusively, the neo-conservatives—regard the last decade as a dangerously multilateral lapse thankfully reversed by a strong, self-interested U.S. government.

At the start of the war in Iraq, Richard Perle published a eulogy for international law: "What will die is the fantasy of the UN as the foundation of a new world order. As we sift the debris, it will be important to preserve, the better to understand, the intellectual wreckage of the liberal conceit of safety through international law administered by international institutions."[1] Other less cynical but no less skeptical commentators, like Michael Ignatieff and Ronald Dworkin, have pondered whether this era marks the demise of the international legal regime.

The eulogies are premature. The enduring relevance of international law is apparent in the fact that even the unilateralists in the Bush administration continue to seek legal legitimation for their actions—because they need it. The issue is not whether international law will survive the war on terror, but how it will be made, interpreted and used in the future.

U.S. power in a unipolar world is of utmost importance to the future of international law. As Kenneth Anderson aptly points out, the question has become "who owns the laws of war." "Even while there is agreement on the need for fundamental rules governing the conduct of war," he writes, "there is profound disagreement over who has the authority to declare, interpret and enforce those rules, as well as who—and what developments in the so-called art of

---

[1] *Guardian*, March 21, 2003.

war—will shape them now and into the future." Anderson offers an answer to his own question that comports with the neo-conservative American view, which assumes that international law can and should be "domesticated"—that is, interpreted to accommodate and elevate domestic interests over and against international consensus. Anderson writes:

> For the past 20 years, the center of gravity in establishing, interpreting and shaping the law of war has gradually shifted away from the military establishments of leading states and their "state practice." It has even shifted away from the International Committee of the Red Cross (invested by the Geneva Conventions with special authority) and toward more activist and publicly aggressive nongovernmental organizations . . . These NGOs are indispensable in advancing the cause of humanitarianism in war. But the pendulum shift toward them has gone further than is useful and the ownership of the laws of war needs to give much greater weight to the state practices of leading countries . . . NGOs are also wedded far too much to a procedural preference for the international over the national. But that agenda increasingly amounts to internationalism for its own sake, and its specific purpose is to constrain American sovereignty.[2]

The American domestication of international law takes two forms. One entails the use of political arm-twisting to ensure globalized immunity for Americans. To date, the U.S. has signed bilateral ICC immunity agreements with over 90 countries, often using foreign aid as the negative incentive.[3] Indeed, the U.S. is on a quest to sign such agreements with every possible country, including East European states that are not yet members of NATO, thereby heightening tensions with NATO allies, all of whom are ICC signatories. These agreements not only weaken the power of the ICC, which is the declared official U.S. intention, but undermine the global

[2] Kenneth Anderson, "Who Owns the Rules of War?" *New York Times Magazine*, April 13, 2003.

[3] As of December 2004, the U.S. State Department reports over ninety such agreements. For the status of these agreements, see the Web site of the Coalition for the International Criminal Court at http://www.iccnow.org.

jurisdiction of international criminal law. In the spring of 2003, U.S. officials mounted a campaign to force Belgium to discard its universal jurisdiction law. Not satisfied with the "diplomatic filters" that the Belgian parliament instituted, which would have made it quite impossible for any case alleging war crimes against an American to move forward in the Belgian court system, the U.S. threatened to relocate NATO headquarters from Brussels to Warsaw. In August 2003, Belgium overturned the law.

The second form that the American domestication of international law takes is interpretive—using international law selectively, advancing interpretations that defy international consensus and asserting the legality of state practices that foreign governments and international organizations classify as violations. The guiding principle is that absolute security is a legal right of the state. This kind of legal reasoning about the limits of international law for the global "war on terror" became the cornerstone of U.S. policy in the handling of prisoners, as the public learned in the wake of the Abu Ghraib torture scandal when dozens of secret official memos were declassified.[4]

One manifestation of this "domestication" was to characterize prisoners as "unlawful combatants" and to assert that they have no legal rights. This concept encodes the idea that in the war on terror, international humanitarian law does not apply to the treatment of "terrorists," while asserting political (rather than judicial) discretion to determine who falls into this category—for example, in the American prison camp at Guantánamo Bay. The interpretative innovation of a category of "unlawful combatants" has been challenged by international law experts, including representatives of the ICRC, which is the official guardian of the Geneva conventions.[5]

---

[4] Mark Danner, *Torture and Truth: America, Abu Ghraib, and the War on Terror* (New York: New York Review of Books, 2004); Karen J. Greenberg and Joshua L. Dratel, *The Torture Papers: The Road to Abu Ghraib* (Cambridge, England: Cambridge University Press, 2004).

[5] Knut Dormann, "The Legal Situation of 'Unlawful/Unprivileged Combatants,'" *International Review of the Red Cross* 85 (2003).

FREEDOM AND LAW

The concept of freedom has played an important role in the Bush administration's global war on terror. Freedom is constantly invoked by Bush and other officials to explain—and, when criticized, to justify—a variety of practices and goals. Sometimes it is invoked as a right to act unilaterally and to utilize military force in the pursuit of political interests. In these regards, freedom means freedom from international accountability or the backing of international institutions. Sometimes it is invoked as a purpose to which America is committing its resources—"spreading freedom" is the bright side of military intervention.

As a concept, freedom has an indisputable appeal. However, where power is unrestrained and unregulated, freedom can manifest as a Hobbesian "war of all against all." The purpose of law in general, and certainly international law, is both to balance freedom with other interests, not least security, and to establish criteria by which the pursuit of those interests can be regulated and judged. It is the ambiguous legal meaning of freedom that makes it so appealing to the Bush administration.

U.S. interpretations of international law reflect the hypersovereign assertion of states' rights to use force to retaliate against as well as deter anything or anyone officials construe as threats to absolute security. This does not make international law irrelevant, contrary to the claims of eulogists and critics alike. Rather, it appropriates the right of interpretation to the state. The U.S. has made use of law—because this is necessary to legitimize state practices—to explain military preemption, indefinite incommunicado detention, abusive interrogation tactics, assassinations and targeting of areas dense with civilians. But what this risks is an erosion of the very foundation of international law: consensus and universalism. Neither justice nor security is served by these turns.

Torture in Iraq and the Rule of Law in America

SANFORD LEVINSON

Does a threat to national security justify presidential authority to order torture? Does it give the President authority to suspend rights guaranteed in the Constitution? Sanford Levinson examines relevant views of authors of the U.S. Constitution, a Nazi legal theorist, and the Bush administration. He maintains that the debate about torture is only a small part of the debate we should be having about whether "We the People" accept the vision of the American presidency articulated by the Bush administration. Levinson holds the W. St. John Garwood Centennial Chair in Law and teaches international law in the Department of Government at the University of Texas. He is also the author of many books, including *Wrestling with Diversity* and *The Torture Collection*.

In May of 2004 the CBS television program *60 Minutes* and *The New Yorker* released photographs from the Abu Ghraib prison in Iraq. These pictures provoked worldwide outrage and, even more importantly, sparked a long overdue public debate in the United States about torture and the permissible limits of interrogation in the aftermath of the September 11 attacks.

As one might expect in a legalistic culture such as ours, some of this debate has revolved around the definition of torture itself. Common lay understandings of torture are in fact quite different from those articulated by many American lawyers. One reason is that the U.S. Senate, when ratifying in 1994 the United Nations Convention Against Torture and Other Cruel, Inhuman, or Degrading Treatment or Punishment, offered what one might call a more "interrogator-friendly" definition of torture than that adopted by the UN negotiators. Thus the Senate, as is its prerogative, stipulated while consenting to the Convention that the United States understands that, in order to constitute torture, an act must be specifically intended to inflict severe physical or mental pain or suffering and that mental pain or suffering refers to *prolonged* mental

SOURCE: Originally appeared in *Daedalus*, Summer 2004. Available at http://www .mitpress.mit.edu/main/home. Copyright © 2004 by the MIT Press.

harm caused by or resulting from: the intentional infliction or threatened infliction of *severe* physical pain or suffering; the administration or application, or threatened administration or application, of mind-altering substances or other procedures calculated to *disrupt profoundly* the senses or personality; the threat of *imminent death*; or the threat that another person will *imminently* be subjected to death, severe physical pain or suffering, or the administration or application of mind-altering substances or other procedures calculated to *disrupt profoundly* the senses or personality (emphases added).

Each and every term I have italicized here in the 1994 Senate resolution was diligently parsed in the recently disclosed Pentagon "Working Group Report on Detainee Interrogations in the Global War on Terrorism," submitted in March of 2003 to Secretary of Defense Donald Rumsfeld. Given the Senate's highly qualified endorsement of the UN Convention, it is not at all surprising that the report submitted to Rumsfeld appears to have maximized the scope of authority (and power) allowed American interrogators who wish to operate within the law.

The Pentagon report closely followed an analysis submitted to White House Counsel Alberto Gonzales in 2002 by the Office of Legal Counsel (OLC) within the Justice Department. According to the OLC, "acts must be of an extreme nature to rise to the level of torture . . . Physical pain amounting to torture must be equivalent in intensity to the pain accompanying serious physical injury, such as organ failure, impairment of bodily function, or even death." The infliction of anything less intense than such extreme pain, according to Jay Bybee, then head of the OLC (and now a federal judge on the Ninth Circuit Court of Appeals), would not, technically speaking, be torture at all. It would merely be inhuman and degrading treatment, a subject of little apparent concern to the Bush administration's lawyers.

The current debate has sometimes gone beyond terminological quibbles. In the past few months, some experts have forthrightly defended the propriety of torture, however defined, at least in some very limited situations. Harvard Law professor Alan Dershowitz, who has taken such a position, nonetheless is extremely concerned to minimize the use of torture. He has, therefore, vigorously defended the idea that the executive branch should be forced to go to independent judges in order to obtain "torture warrants," which could be issued only after careful examination of executive branch arguments as to the ostensible necessity of torture in a given instance.

Still other experts, including Dershowitz's Harvard colleague Philip Heymann and U.S. federal judge Richard Posner, have disagreed, arguing that such warrants would inevitably prove chimerical as a genuine control and would instead normalize torture as an interrogational tool. Perhaps torture is proper under very restricted circumstances, as Posner in particular agrees, but far better that it be defended *ex post* (after the fact) through specific claims of necessity or self-defense than *ex ante* (before the fact) through the issuing of a warrant.

This debate has been informed both by current events and, for some, by the views of the men who drafted the U.S. Constitution. On the one hand, there is a growing sense (articulated by writers like Philip Bobbitt) that war in the future, at least where the United States is concerned, is unlikely to fit the traditional pattern of threats by states, and is far more likely to involve threats from organizations that have no capitals at which traditional retaliation can be directed.[1] Rules and understandings developed to constrain the conduct of wars between states—where, among other things, mutual self-interest dictates limits on what can be done even to one's enemies—may be inadequate or even, as suggested by White House Counsel Gonzales in a memorandum to the president, "obsolete" in regard to the so-called asymmetric warfare of the twenty-first century. Such new modes of warfare require that we rethink our basic approach to waging war—and also the basic principles of law and morality.

On the other hand, it is equally important to grasp just what the basic principles of law and morality have been in the United States. As recent work on the origins of the U.S. Constitution has demonstrated, the founding fathers hoped to create a government strong enough to defend the fledgling nation against its many potential

---

[1] See Philip Bobbitt's magisterial study, *The Shield of Achilles: War, Peace, and the Course of History* (New York: Knopf, 2002).

enemies, including European powers as well as Indian tribes much closer to home.[2] Among the key provisions of the 1787 Constitution were those authorizing a standing army and effectively unlimited taxing authority to Congress to pay for "the common defense."

James Madison and Alexander Hamilton, for all their notable differences, seemed to be in agreement on the importance of this point. Thus Madison, in Federalist No. 41, asked if it was "necessary to give [the new government] an INDEFINITE POWER of raising TROOPS, as well as providing fleets; and of maintaining both in PEACE as well as in WAR?" He believed that the answer was "so obvious and conclusive as scarcely to justify" any real discussion of anti-Federalist criticisms of the very idea of a standing army. The United States had to structure its own policies by anticipating the likely actions of other states: "The means of security can only be regulated by the means and the danger of attack. They will, in fact, be ever determined by these rules and by no others." Hamilton expressed a related conviction in *Federalist* No. 23: "[I]t must be admitted as a necessary consequence that there *can be no limitation of that authority* which is to provide for the defense and protection of the community in any matter essential to its efficacy—that is, in any matter essential to the *formulation, direction, or support of the* NATIONAL FORCES" (first emphasis added). Thomas Hobbes could have done no better in defending the absolute authority of the sovereign.

The Constitution may proclaim that sovereignty rests with "We the People." But the implication of both Madison's and Hamilton's arguments is that, practically speaking, at least in times of war, sovereignty really rests with a handful of government officials—not with "the People."

Now consider the following maxim: "There exists no norm that is applicable to chaos." It comes not from Madison or Hamilton, but from Carl Schmitt, the leading German philosopher of law during the Nazi period. Schmitt contended that legal norms were only applicable in stable and peaceful situations—and not in times of war,

---

[2.] See particularly David C. Hendrickson, *Peace Pact: The Lost World of the American Founding* (Lawrence: University of Kansas Press, 2003); and Max M. Edling, *A Revolution in Favor of Government: Origins of the U.S. Constitution and the Making of the American State* (Oxford: Oxford University Press, 2003).

when the state confronted "a mortal enemy, with the threat of violent death at the hands of a hostile group." It follows that conventional legal norms are no longer applicable in a state of emergency, when war and chaos pose a standing threat to public safety. To adopt the language of American constitutional law, every norm is subject to limitation when a compelling interest is successfully asserted, and it is hard to think of a more compelling interest than the prevention of violent death at the hands of a hostile group.

But what this means is that one can never have confidence that *any* particular constitutional norm—beyond that of preserving the state itself—will be adhered to. Any attempts within the Constitution to tie the government's hands with regard to defending the nation, then, may be mere "parchment barriers," to use Madison's dismissive term (which he conceived during the period when he doubted the wisdom of adding a Bill of Rights to the Constitution). Both Madison and Schmitt suggest, then, the most likely response to such barriers is a "*necessary* usurpation of power" (as Madison put it in *Federalist* No. 41; emphasis added).

Schmitt, described by Herbert Marcuse as the most brilliant Nazi theorist, may have much to tell us about the legal world within which we live and, even more certainly, seem to be careening. Although some analysts have suggested that the Bush administration has operated under the guidance of the ideas of German émigré Leo Strauss, it seems far more plausible to suggest that the true *éminence grise* of the administration, particularly with regard to issues surrounding the possible propriety of torture, is Schmitt.

September 11, it is said, changed everything. What this means, among other things, is that for many the existing world of "the normal" vanished in an instant, to be replaced by the specter of terrorist groups armed with weapons of mass destruction. And what *this* means is that pre–September 11 norms and expectations are being reconfigured in terms of this new "normality" of endless, frightening threats posed by "a mortal enemy." Ordinary norms—whether the assumption that anyone arrested by American police will have an opportunity to consult with a lawyer, or the assumption that the United States will be faithful to its public pronouncements denouncing torture (as well as to its commitment under the

UN Convention absolutely to refrain from torture whatever the circumstances)—are now up for grabs. "Sovereign is he," wrote Schmitt, "who decides on the state of the exception," or, much the same, who is allowed to redescribe what is "normal."

Administration lawyers whose memoranda have only recently been disclosed seem completely willing to view George W. Bush as the de facto sovereign. Their documents display what can only be called contempt not only for international law, but also for the very idea that any other institution of the American government, whether Congress or the Judiciary, has any role to play. Thus both the Working Group Report submitted to Secretary Rumsfeld and the memorandum prepared earlier by the OLC argued that the Constitution's designation of the president as commander in chief means that "the President enjoys *complete discretion* . . . in conducting operations against hostile forces" (emphasis added). Complete discretion, of course, is a power enjoyed *only* by sovereigns. Non-sovereigns, by definition, are subject to the constraint of some overriding authority. The president, according to administration lawyers, has no authority to which he must answer. Prohibitions of international and domestic law regarding the absolute impropriety of torture simply do not apply to him. "In order to respect the President's inherent constitutional authority to manage a military campaign, [federal laws against torture] must be construed as inapplicable to interrogations undertaken pursuant to his Commander-in-Chief authority," the OLC advised. "Congress lacks authority . . . to set the terms and conditions under which the President may exercise his authority as Commander-in-Chief to control the conduct of operations during a war."

It is impossible to predict whether these quite astonishing arguments (which seem to authorize the president and designated subordinates simply to make disappear those they deem adversaries, as happened in Chile and Argentina in what the Argentines aptly labeled their "dirty war") would prevail before a court of law. We shall know more after the Supreme Court rules in several cases it heard in the spring of 2004 regarding the detention in Guantánamo of foreign combatants and at least one American citizen (Jose Padilla, who has been accorded almost no legal rights since his 2002 arrest at O'Hare International Airport).

Far more important, however, is the articulation, on behalf of the Bush administration, of a view of presidential authority that is all too close to the power that Schmitt was willing to accord his own Fürher.

One temptation is to stop right here, especially if one shares my own doubts about both George W. Bush and the war in Iraq. But that would be too easy, for a number of reasons. One is that there *are* mortal enemies of the United States who *do* threaten violent death. No political leader could suggest that it is not a compelling interest to prevent future replications of September 11. Moreover, as already indicated, one can cite not only the egregious (though brilliant) Schmitt, but also such American icons as Madison and Hamilton for views that are not really so completely different from those enunciated by the Bush administration.

And so we already have many well-credentialed lawyers, several of them distinguished legal academics, who are quick to defend everything that is being done (or proposed) by the Bush administration as passing constitutional muster. They have enlisted in defending a war on terror that is almost certainly of infinite duration. They appear recklessly indifferent to the fact that their arguments, if accepted, would transform the United States into at least a soft version of 1984, where our own version of Big Brother will declare to us who is our enemy *du jour* and assert his own version of a "triumph of the will" to do everything and anything—including torture—in order to prevail.

A final quotation from Carl Schmitt is illuminating: "A normal situation has to be created, and sovereign is he who definitively decides whether this normal state actually obtains. All law is 'situation law.' The sovereign creates and guarantees the situation as a whole in its totality. He has the monopoly on this ultimate decision." This is precisely the argument being made by lawyers within the Bush administration.

The debate about torture is only one relatively small part of a far more profound debate that we should be having. Do "We the People," the ostensible sovereigns within the American system of government, accept the vision of the American president articulated by the Bush administration? And if we do, what, then, is left of the vaunted vision of the rule of law that the United States ostensibly exemplifies?

Standing for the Founding Principles of the Republic

Senator Robert Byrd

Senator Robert Byrd, a longtime student of constitutional history, continued his investigation of the relations among the three branches of government as part of his remarks during the Senate debate on the nomination of Dr. Condoleezza Rice as Secretary of State. Senator Byrd was a member of the U.S. House of Representatives from 1953 through 1959, when he was elected to the Senate. He has served as a senator continuously since that time. His writings include a history of the Senate, as well as a study of Roman constitutionalism, and his latest book is Losing America: Confronting a Reckless and Arrogant Presidency.

[There are] a number of Administration foreign policies which I strongly oppose. These policies have fostered enormous opposition — both at home and abroad — to the White House's view of America's place in the world.

That view of America is one which encourages our Nation to flex its muscles without being bound by any calls for restraint. The most forceful explanation of this idea can be found in *The National Security Strategy of the United States,* a report which was issued by the White House in September 2002. Under this strategy, the President lays claim to an expansive power to use our military to strike other nations first, even if we have not been threatened or provoked.

There is no question that the President has the inherent authority to repel attacks against our country, but this *National Security Strategy* is unconstitutional on its face. It takes the checks and balances established in the Constitution that limit the President's ability to use our military at his pleasure, and throws them out the window.

This doctrine of preemptive strikes places the sole decision of war and peace in the hands of the President and undermines the Constitutional power of Congress to declare war. The Founding Fathers required that such an important issue of war be debated by the elected representatives of the people in the Legislative Branch

SOURCE: Excerpted from Senator Byrd's remarks in the Senate, January 25, 2005.

precisely because no single man could be trusted with such an awe-some power as bringing a nation to war by his decision alone. And yet, that is exactly what the *National Security Strategy* proposes.

Not only does this pernicious doctrine of preemptive war con-tradict the Constitution, it barely acknowledges its existence. The *National Security Strategy* makes only one passing reference to the Constitution: it states that "America's constitution"—that is "consti-tution" with a small *C*—"has served us well." As if the Constitution does not still serve this country well! One might ask if that refer-ence to the Constitution was intended to be a compliment or an obituary?

As National Security Advisor, Dr. Rice was in charge of devel-oping the *National Security Strategy*. She also spoke out forcefully in support of the dangerous doctrine of preemptive war. In one speech, she argues that there need not be an imminent threat be-fore the United States attacks another nation: "So as a matter of common sense," said Dr. Rice on October 1, 2002, "the United States must be prepared to take action, when necessary, before threats have fully materialized."

But that "matter of common sense" is nowhere to be found in the Constitution. For that matter, isn't it possible to disagree with this "matter of common sense"? What is common sense to one might not be shared by another. What's more, matters of common sense can lead people to the wrong conclusions. John Dickinson, the chief author of the Articles of Confederation, said in 1787, "Ex-perience must be our only guide; reason may mislead us." As for me, I will heed the experience of Founding Fathers, as enshrined in the Constitution, over the reason and "common sense" of the Ad-ministration's *National Security Strategy*.

We can all agree that the President, any President, has the in-herent duty and power to repel an attack on the United States. But where in the Constitution can the President claim the right to strike at another nation before it has even threatened our country, as Dr. Rice asserted in that speech? To put it plainly, Dr. Rice has as-serted that the President holds far more of the war power than the Constitution grants him.

And what has been the effect of the first use of the reckless doctrine of preemptive war? In a most ironic and deadly twist, the false situation described by the Administration before the war—namely, that Iraq was a training ground for terrorists poised to attack us—is exactly the situation that our war in Iraq has created.

But it was this unjustified war that created the situation that the President claimed he was trying to prevent. Violent extremists have flooded into Iraq from all corners of the world. Iraqis have taken up arms themselves to fight against the continuing U.S. occupation of their country. According to a CIA report released in December 2004, intelligence analysts now see Iraq, destabilized by the Administration's ill-conceived war, as the training ground for a new generation of terrorists. [*Mapping the Global Future: Report of the National Intelligence Council's 2020 Project*, p. 94.] It should be profoundly disturbing to all Americans if the most dangerous breeding ground for terrorism shifted from Afghanistan to Iraq, simply because of the Administration's ill-advised rush to war in March 2003.

Accountability has become an old-fashioned notion in some circles these days, but accountability is not a negotiable commodity when it comes to the highest circles of our nation's government. The accountability of government officials is an obligation, not a luxury. And yet, accountability is an obligation that this President and his administration appear loath to fulfill.

Instead of being held to account for their actions, the architects of the policies that led our nation into war with Iraq, policies based on faulty intelligence and phantom weapons of mass destruction, have been rewarded by the President with accolades and promotions. Instead of admitting to mistakes in the war on Iraq and its disastrous aftermath, the President and his inner circle of advisers continue to cling to myths and misconceptions. The only notion of accountability that this President is willing to acknowledge is the November elections, which he has described as a moment of accountability and an endorsement of his policies. Unfortunately, after-the-fact validation of victory is hardly the standard of accountability that the American people have the right to expect from their elected officials. It is one thing to accept responsibility for success; it is quite another to accept accountability for failure.

Sadly, failure has tainted far too many aspects of our nation's international policies over the past four years, culminating in the deadly insurgency that has resulted from the invasion of Iraq. I believe that there needs to be accountability for the mistakes and missteps that have led the United States into the dilemma in which it finds itself today, besieged by increasing violence in Iraq, battling an unprecedented decline in world opinion, and increasingly isolated from our allies due to our provocative, belligerent, bellicose, and unilateralist foreign policy.

Institutional Barriers to War Crimes: Failure and Renewal

BRUCE SHAPIRO

Bruce Shapiro traces the "profoundly controversial blueprint for the presidency" that provided the "legal and intellectual scaffolding" for torture and other war crimes. That scaffolding was "firmly, patiently crafted" for nearly thirty years by officials like Donald Rumsfeld and Dick Cheney. After 9/11, the Bush administration gutted the legal and institutional barriers to war crimes—with results that are all too evident. But whistle-blowers, journalists, and even conscientious military officers are challenging this abandonment of legality. Shapiro argues that there is a basis for liberals and true conservatives to unite to reestablish the rule of law.

Bruce Shapiro is the author of *Shaking the Foundations: 200 Years of Investigative Journalism in America* and *Legal Lynching: The Death Penalty and America's Future,* written with Reverend Jesse Jackson and Representative Jesse Jackson Jr. An investigative journalist and political commentator, Shapiro is field director of the Dart Center for Journalism and Trauma. He teaches at Yale University.

SENATORY LEAHY: Does the president have the authority, in your judgment, to exercise a commander-in-chief override and immunize acts of torture?

MR. GONZALES: With all due respect, Senator, the president has said we're not going to engage in torture. That is a hypothetical question that would involve an analysis of a great number of factors.[1]

If Charles Graner and Alberto Gonzales think about each other at all, they probably believe they have little in common. Graner went from high school to work as a corrections officer and joined the Army Reserve. His highest ambition was to be a military police officer. Gonzales rode a power track: the Air Force Academy, Harvard, Rice. Yet in the first weeks of January 2005, these two seemingly dissimilar

SOURCE: Copyright © 2005 by Bruce Shapiro.

[1.] Confirmation hearing of Alberto Gonzales, Senate Judiciary Committee, January 6, 2005.

Americans were called in public hearings to answer for the same thing: their respective roles in war crimes. The Graner and Gonzales hearings were very different proceedings. Graner faced a court-martial for his brutalization of prisoners in Abu Ghraib, a court-martial which concluded with him stripped of rank and pay and imprisoned for ten years. Gonzales—who as White House Counsel wrote and commissioned memos laying the legal groundwork for the handling of prisoners in Afghanistan, Iraq and Guantánamo—testified before a solicitous Senate Judiciary Committee, and despite some opposition the full Senate confirmed his promotion to Attorney General.

The fact that a lowly MP and a U.S. Attorney General are both stained with torture allegations suggests how deeply three years of the war on terror have corrupted public institutions. What shocks is not just the fact of torture, but the failure of every mechanism which is supposed to keep war crimes from happening. When we say Americans aren't supposed to be war criminals, we mean more than some vague assertion of national character. Over many decades, successive presidents and congresses and military leaders embraced specific laws and procedures designed to prevent atrocity in wartime. Some are federal statutes, such as the War Crimes Act of 1996. Some are international treaties: The Geneva Conventions, the Convention Against Torture. Among soldiers, the Uniform Code of Military Justice strictly prohibits abuse of prisoners, and at service academies, aspiring military officers study My Lai and other Vietnam-era massacres in order to understand the kind of leadership needed to prevent such atrocities. Intelligence-oversight laws give Congressional committees authority over secret operations and require intelligence agencies to lay out paper trails of their work.

Yet in Iraq, in Afghanistan, at Guantánamo Bay, military codes, treaty obligations, federal laws, Congressional oversight all failed. A pattern and practice of torture were fostered, backed up, facilitated by White House and Defense Department policy directives. How did it happen? And is there a way back?

It is wrong to think that the road to Abu Ghraib began with the Al-Qaeda attack of September 11. Yes, September 11 set in motion the war in Afghanistan and provided a pretext for the occupation of Iraq; yes, almost immediately, officials at the highest levels of the Bush administration began considering how to position interrogations of prisoners beyond the reach of courts and human-rights laws. But as the White House's own memos make clear, the legal and intellectual scaffolding for these orders to torture was erected according to a fundamental and profoundly controversial blueprint for the presidency [that was] firmly, patiently crafted for nearly thirty years by some of the Bush administration's central figures.[2]

It is possible to point, with only slight oversimplification, to a month and year when this philosophy of presidential power emerged: May of 1970. That month President Richard Nixon, frustrated with the Vietnam War, ordered 54,000 U.S. and South Vietnamese troops to invade neutral Cambodia. He launched his new war—and what would become a three-year campaign of carpet bombing—without consulting Congress. In the White House Office of Legal Counsel, Assistant Attorney General William Rehnquist made a case for the legality of Nixon's new war in a white paper, "The President and the War Power."[3] The proposition that Rehnquist asserted in his memo: Presidential war powers were unreviewable by Congress or courts.

The historical chasm between Cambodia and Iraq abruptly collapsed with the crucial memorandum on torture written for the Bush White House in August 2002 by Rehnquist's latter-day successor at the Office of Legal Counsel, Assistant Attorney General Jay Bybee. In that memo, Bybee famously declared that antitorture laws simply do not apply to "interrogations undertaken pursuant to [Bush's] commander-in-chief authority."[4] As the principal authority for his view of the commander-in-chief's legal impunity,

[2] Relevant memoranda public at this writing and cited in this article include: John Yoo, Memoranda to the White House Counsel, September 25, 2001, and January 2, 2002; Alberto Gonzales, memorandum to the President, January 25, 2002; Jay Bybee, memorandum to the White House Counsel, August 1, 2002; John Goldsmith, memorandum, March 19, 2004; and Donald Rumsfeld, memorandum to the Undersecretary of Defense, January 5, 2003.

[3] William Rehnquist, "The Constitutional Issues: Administration Position," *NYU Law Review* 45 (June 1970).

[4] Jay Bybee, memorandum to the White House Counsel, August 1, 2004.

Bybee invoked Rehnquist's 1970 memo on Cambodia and a subsequent Rehnquist article in the *NYU Law Review*.

Rehnquist had offered the Nixon White House a bold new vision of the commander-in-chief's authority at its most expansive: the president's war power, he wrote acerbically, must amount to "something greater than a seat of honor in the reviewing stand." Cambodia—where the devastation left by American bombs would prepare the way for the Khmer Rouge holocaust[5]—amounted to "the sort of tactical decision traditionally confided to the commander in chief." Those 1970 formulations resonate throughout the Bush administration's 2002 and 2003 policy memoranda. Bybee wants to redefine torture as non-torture; Rehnquist showed how when he argued that the invasion of Cambodia wasn't really an invasion: "By crossing the Cambodian border to attack sanctuaries used by the enemy, the United States has in no sense gone to war with Cambodia."[6] The Bybee memo absolves officials of responsibility through the "necessity defense"; in 1970, Rehnquist argued that pursuing Viet Cong troops into previously neutral territory was "necessary to assure [American troops'] safety in the field."

In ways which go to the heart of post–September 11 policies both foreign and domestic, the invasion of Cambodia in May of 1970 was a watershed. On the one hand, it marked the greatest assertion of expansive presidential warmaking power, crystallized in Rehnquist's white paper cited by Bybee. At the same time, in response to protest against the Cambodian invasion, Nixon centralized the gathering of domestic political intelligence directly in the White House; from his desk in the Justice Department Rehnquist supported this domestic expansion of executive-branch authority, arguing in court for no-knock entry, preventive detention, wiretaps and other recognizable ancestors of today's Patriot Act. Only the Watergate investigation and Nixon's resignation brought that concentration of presidential power to an end.

[5.] The role of U.S. bombing in laying the groundwork for the Cambodian genocide is documented in William Shawcross, *Sideshow: Nixon, Kissinger and the Destruction of Cambodia* (New York: Simon and Schuster, 1979).

[6.] Rehnquist, "The Constitutional Issues."

By the mid-1970s, after investigations and media exposés not only of Watergate but broader abuses, including the CIA's involvement with dictatorships, assassination and torture abroad and the FBI's spying on political dissidents at home, Congress passed a series of reforms designed to halt secret government and human rights abuses: the National Intelligence Reform Act giving Congressional committees oversight of covert operations; the strengthened Freedom of Information Act; the War Powers Act and others. Officials of the Nixon and Ford White House—among them Donald Rumsfeld and Dick Cheney, both top aides to President Ford—bitterly fought these new restrictions, persuading Ford, for instance, to veto the FOIA—a veto overridden by Congress. Post-Watergate reforms in fact had a profound effect, over a generation changing the institutional cultures of the FBI and CIA and establishing the public's sense of entitlement to freedom of information. Ever since, conservative policy-makers have sought repeatedly to regain the expansive executive-branch power lost to post-Watergate reforms.

The attacks of September 11 and the retaliatory invasion of Afghanistan presented a historic opportunity to revive the culture of secrecy and carve out new authority for the president. Within hours of the attacks, old-school conservatives like Admiral James Woolsey were calling for restoration of the CIA's power to assassinate adversaries and engage in sweeping covert operations. As early as September 25, 2001, White House legal advisor John Yoo wrote a memo asserting the president's unilateral power to take military action against any person, organization or state involved in terrorism against the U.S. In October 2001, then-Attorney General John Ashcroft issued a sweeping memorandum undercutting the Freedom of Information Act. Congress passed the Patriot Act and related legislation allowing unprecedented information-gathering on citizens and removing layers of judicial review for national-security wiretaps.

Inside the White House, the attempt to redefine the presidency was explicitly tied to removing legal restrictions on interrogation. It was a three-step process, evident in a string of documents by Yoo, Gonzales, Secretary of Defense Rumsfeld and others. First, define prisoners as stateless pariahs. Second, redefine torture itself, as Bybee did in August of 2002 without any legal precedent, to absolve officials of responsibility. Third, place prisoners physically beyond the reach of American laws which might limit interrogation practices: take them outside the system of American courts by creating Camp X-ray; take them outside military regulations by employing private contractors as interrogators; take them outside U.S. prohibitions on torture by turning them over to the hard men of authoritarian regimes. No American president had ever placed prisoners so far beyond reach of courts and treaties and international law: No Confederate soldier, no Nazi SS officer or Soviet spy, had ever been so thoroughly defined, legally speaking, as a non-person.

In effect, the President defined himself as above the law, and defined detainees as outside the law.[7] The famous photographs of depravity at Abu Ghraib may now be actually impeding public understanding of this radical policy change. While the pornographic violence of Abu Ghraib could be hung on low-level, poorly trained reservists like Charles Graner, the reality is systematic illegal violence by trained interrogators, and even more systematic deceit by their bosses up the chain of command. The new order is exemplified not by Abu Ghraib but by Task Force 6-26, a secret unit of Navy Seals operating in Baghdad—its existence not even acknowledged by the Pentagon, but authorized at the highest levels. A fact-finding mission of Army generals warned in 2004 that Task Force 6-26 was running an off-the-books prison for the purpose of "disappearing" detainees and applying more-than-moderate physical pressure— specifically, beatings which killed at least two individuals. Despite those generals' warnings, Task Force 6-26 with its bland bureaucratic moniker continued operating.[8]

What of meaningful opposition to this culture of torture? Resistance has emerged, principally from three places. A small handful of attorneys and civil rights groups, many working with the Center for Constitutional Rights, refused from the beginning to accept the extralegal and subhuman status of Al-Qaeda prisoners. These lawyers represented the most disdained clients since the abolition of slavery, and systematically began pressing U.S. courts to live up to

[7] I am grateful to Professor Harold Koh, Dean of Yale Law School, for this formulation.
[8] *Washington Post*, December 7, 2004.

their responsibilities: first on behalf of immigrants detained without charge; then on behalf of a handful of U.S. citizens—Yassir Hamdi, Jose Padilla—held incommunicado; and finally, most critically, on behalf of Guantánamo detainees themselves. In a massive setback to the Administration, CCR's lawyers persuaded a U.S. Supreme Court majority (with a notable dissent from Chief Justice Rehnquist) to rule that Guantánamo detainees be covered by the Geneva Conventions' requirements for prisoner-status hearings.

A second important category of resistance came from whistleblowers—individuals within the military, the Justice Department, the CIA—appalled by what was happening. The significance of whistleblowing as a form of conscious civil disobedience cannot be underestimated, particularly within the chain-of-command cultures of the military and law enforcement. To make facts public, individuals have violated military orders, risked rank and position, and defied national-security classification laws. Low-level soldiers shared photos and reports from within Abu Ghraib. FBI and CIA sources went to the press. In some cases, this civil disobedience took organized form: for instance when a group of Judge Advocates General, attorneys within the military justice system, took the unprecedented step of reporting their alarm about Guantánamo to the Association of the Bar of the City of New York. In early 2005, the most eminent opposition to Alberto Gonzales' nomination for attorney general emanated from 12 high-ranking retired military officers—generals and admirals, several of them lifelong Republicans. Though by nature and habit respectful of the presidency and chain of command, and loath to involve themselves in domestic politics, these top-level officers took their oath not to the president but the Constitution. Their principled letter charging Gonzales with collusion in torture changed the dynamic on the Senate Judiciary Committee, persuading Democrats who had cautiously supported Gonzales' nomination to unite against him.

The third center of resistance to war crimes in Afghanistan and Iraq was the American press. This may be a controversial statement. Much has been written—accurately—of how the news media failed in the run-up to the Iraq war, particularly through uncritical reporting of the Administration's claims regarding Sadaam Hussein's weapons of mass destruction. In that sense the press failed as thoroughly as Congress or military leaders or the UN in preventing the Administration heading down the path of war crimes.

Yet after the capture of Sadaam Hussein and the shift from invasion to occupation, the American news media began reporting aggressively on American abuses. It is worth asking why. In part, it was about the dynamic of news: a shift in reporting priorities from frontline combat journalists geared to daily updates to the slow, methodical work of investigative reporters. In part it reflected the efforts of whistleblowers to bring light to the darkest corners of American policy.

The most mainstream press institutions took on war crimes as their beat. The same week Seymour Hersh published photos from Abu Ghraib in *The New Yorker*, *Newsweek*'s investigative team followed the chain of accountability into the White House by revealing the memos on torture and the Geneva Conventions. The *Washington Post* first detailed the practice of "extraordinary rendition," the secret U.S. torture flights ferrying terror suspects into the custody of more brutal allies. Several locally oriented papers—the *Denver Post*, the *Miami Herald*, the *Dayton Daily News* among others—made significant contributions to public knowledge about Guantánamo and other American military prisons. Investigative reporters in essence took on the responsibilities Congress refused to accept: establishing the facts of American occupation, documenting lines of accountability and putting war crimes on the public agenda.

All of these varied interventions share one core principle: the refusal to write off as pariahs prisoners in the War on Terror, whether in Guantánamo, Iraq or elsewhere. A few specific strategies also suggest themselves: the active cultivation of, and support for, whistleblowers; forging new relationships between human-rights groups and non-traditional allies in the military, intelligence agencies and law enforcement; making clear to courts just how contemptuously the Bush administration regards the authority of judges.

It is also time for the antiwar movement to join civil rights lawyers in focusing public attention more sharply and precisely on the mechanisms needed to prevent additional war crimes and further erosion of America's human-rights commitment. It is no longer enough to re-argue the case against the war. Instead it is time to make the case against where the War on Terror has led both abroad and within the United States; pushing to "bring the Constitution home" along with bringing home the troops. Numerous specific measures offer such possibilities—and in particular, the opportunity for mobilizing activists and educating the public. Congress has the power to invoke the sunset provisions of the Patriot Act, reaffirm the FOIA, and strengthen the enforcement provisions of the War Crimes Act and anti-torture laws. Congressional committees investigating torture and military prisons can provide, like the Church Committee which investigated the CIA in the 1970s, opportunities for meaningful reform. This is not some cloudy-eyed liberal dream, but rather, a campaign in which hardnosed military and law-enforcement professionals committed to the balance of powers and rule of law could play a prominent part.

With U.S. laws still failing to restrain clearly illegal policies, it may make sense to turn toward international strategies, including both a general embrace of evolving international standards, and specific laws of universal jurisdiction overseas. In death-penalty and gay-rights cases, the U.S. Supreme Court has shown a new willingness to consider the human rights consensus of other nations. In March of 2005, Supreme Court Justice Anthony Kennedy—a Reagan appointee—invoked "the overwhelming weight of international public opinion," writing for a Court majority banning the execution of juveniles. That "overwhelming weight" extends to torture, a fact surely not lost on justices facing a raft of appeals from the War on Terror.

In the past, campaigns around human rights standards centered on international instruments ranging from the Geneva Conventions to the International Criminal Court. But recent developments suggest that the human-rights laws of individual nations hold promise as an avenue for transnational efforts to raise the human rights floor. In early 2005, the Center for Constitutional Rights appealed to Germany's Federal Prosecutor to initiate an inquiry of Donald Rumsfeld and other U.S. officials under the "universal jurisdiction" doctrines of that country's war-crimes statutes. German law, looking back at historic atrocity, allows for prosecution of killing, torture, cruel and inhumane treatment, forcible transfers and sexual coercion "even when the offence was committed abroad and bears no relation to Germany." The Administration took the threat seriously enough that Rumsfeld personally threatened to boycott an international security conference in Germany if an investigation proceeded. At this writing the suit is still being litigated.

As a legal doctrine, relying upon laws of universal jurisdiction has pitfalls. Such laws could as easily be manipulated into a tool for imposition of U.S. policies. But the abuses of American military prisons are so systematic and severe as to demand a response from citizens and an appeal to any competent authority. And employing Europe's rapidly evolving human rights law as a lever to hold an American administration to evolving standards of decency has healthy recent precedent. When Chilean politicians maintained the immunity of retired dictator General Pinochet, his victims turned to universal jurisdiction elements of Spanish criminal law. The investigation in response to their complaint led to Pinochet's 2001 arrest in London. That arrest, in turn, provoked Chile to finally come to terms under its own constitution with accountability for atrocity, including criminal indictment and house arrest for Pinochet. It would be historically fitting if the United States—whose Declaration of Independence first advanced the argument that human rights transcend national sovereignty—could be similarly shaken by international human-rights standards.

Behind Guantánamo, Abu Ghraib, and torture flights lies a political impulse which ought to alarm true conservatives as deeply as liberals: the determined pursuit of an imperial presidency. In the aftermath of September 11, the Administration's apologists were quick to quote, in distorted fashion, Justice Robert Jackson's World War Two admonition that the Bill of Rights is not a suicide pact. But in 1945, Jackson went on sabbatical from the Supreme Court to initiate the German war-crimes tribunals. On June 7, 1945 he wrote this in his *Report to the President on Atrocities and War Crimes:* "We do not accept the paradox that legal responsibility should be the least where power is greatest."[9]

9. Robert Jackson, *Report to the President on Atrocities and War Crimes* (1945).

Just War—or Just a War?

JIMMY CARTER

Writing on the eve of the invasion of Iraq, Jimmy Carter measured the impending attack against the principles that distinguish just from unjust wars. Jimmy Carter, the thirty-ninth president of the United States, is chairman of the Carter Center in Atlanta and winner of the 2002 Nobel Peace Prize.

As a Christian and as a president who was severely provoked by international crises, I became thoroughly familiar with the principles of a just war, and it is clear that a substantially unilateral attack on Iraq does not meet these standards. This is an almost universal conviction of religious leaders, with the most notable exception of a few spokesmen of the Southern Baptist Convention who are greatly influenced by their commitment to Israel based on eschatological, or final days, theology.

For a war to be just, it must meet several clearly defined criteria.

The war can be waged only as a last resort, with all nonviolent options exhausted. In the case of Iraq, it is obvious that clear alternatives to war exist. These options—previously proposed by our own leaders and approved by the United Nations—were outlined again by the Security Council on Friday. But now, with our own national security not directly threatened and despite the overwhelming opposition of most people and governments in the world, the United States seems determined to carry out military and diplomatic action that is almost unprecedented in the history of civilized nations. The first stage of our widely publicized war plan is to launch 3,000 bombs and missiles on a relatively defenseless Iraqi population within the first few hours of an invasion, with the purpose of so damaging and demoralizing the people that they will change their obnoxious leader, who will most likely be hidden and safe during the bombardment.

The war's weapons must discriminate between combatants and noncombatants. Extensive aerial bombardment, even with precise

SOURCE: Originally appeared in the *New York Times*, March 9, 2003. Copyright © 2003 by the New York Times Company. Reprinted by permission.

accuracy, inevitably results in "collateral damage." Gen. Tommy R. Franks, commander of American forces in the Persian Gulf, has expressed concern about many of the military targets being near hospitals, schools, mosques and private homes.

Its violence must be proportional to the injury we have suffered. Despite Saddam Hussein's other serious crimes, American efforts to tie Iraq to the 9/11 terrorist attacks have been unconvincing.

The attackers must have legitimate authority sanctioned by the society they profess to represent. The unanimous vote of approval in the Security Council to eliminate Iraq's weapons of mass destruction can still be honored, but our announced goals are now to achieve regime change and to establish a Pax Americana in the region, perhaps occupying the ethnically divided country for as long as a decade. For these objectives, we do not have international authority.

The peace it establishes must be a clear improvement over what exists. Although there are visions of peace and democracy in Iraq, it is quite possible that the aftermath of a military invasion will destabilize the region and prompt terrorists to further jeopardize our security at home. Also, by defying overwhelming world opposition, the United States will undermine the United Nations as a viable institution for world peace.

What about America's world standing if we don't go to war after such a great deployment of military forces in the region? The heartfelt sympathy and friendship offered to America after the 9/11 attacks, even from formerly antagonistic regimes, has been largely dissipated; increasingly unilateral and domineering policies have brought international trust in our country to its lowest level in memory. American stature will surely decline further if we launch a war in clear defiance of the United Nations.

What the Rest of the World Watched on Inauguration Day

SISTER JOAN CHITTISTER

Sister Joan Chittister reflects on a photo published on Inauguration Day 2005 that appeared in media worldwide, but not in America. She explores both its meaning and the meaning of the fact that it was seen all over the world, but not in the United States. A Benedictine Sister of Erie, Sister Joan is a bestselling author and regular columnist for the *National Catholic Reporter*.

Dublin, on U.S. Inauguration Day, didn't seem to notice. Oh, they played a few clips that night of the American president saying, "The survival of liberty in our land increasingly depends on the success of liberty in other lands."

But that was not their lead story.

The picture on the front page of *The Irish Times* was a large four-color picture of a small Iraqi girl. Her little body was a coil of steel. She sat knees up, cowering, screaming madly into the dark night. Her white clothes and spread hands and small tight face were blood-spattered. The blood was the blood of her father and mother, shot through the car window in Tal Afar by American soldiers while she sat beside her parents in the car, her four brothers and sisters in the back seat.

A series of pictures of the incident played on the inside page, as well. A 12-year-old brother, wounded in the fray, falls face down out of the car when the car door opens, the pictures show. In another, a soldier decked out in battle gear holds a large automatic weapon on the four children, all potential enemies, all possible suicide bombers, apparently, as they cling traumatized to one another in the back seat and the child on the ground goes on screaming in her parent's blood.

No promise of "freedom" rings in the cutline on this picture. No joy of liberty underlies the terror on these faces here.

SOURCE: Originally appeared in the *National Catholic Reporter*, January 27, 2005. Copyright © 2005 by Sister Joan Chittister, O.S.B.

I found myself closing my eyes over and over again as I stared at the story, maybe to crush the tears forming there, maybe in the hope that the whole scene would simply disappear.

But no, like the photo of a naked little girl bathed in napalm and running down a road in Vietnam served to crystallize the situation there for the rest of the world, I knew that this picture of a screaming, angry, helpless, orphaned child could do the same.

The soldiers standing in the dusk had called "halt," the story said, but no one did. Maybe the soldiers' accents were bad. Maybe the car motor was unduly noisy. Maybe the children were laughing loudly—the way children do on family trips. Whatever the case, the car did not stop, the soldiers shot with deadly accuracy, seven lives changed in an instant: two died in body, five died in soul.

BBC news announced that the picture was spreading across Europe like a brushfire that morning, featured from one major newspaper to another, served with coffee and Danish from kitchen table to kitchen table in one country after another. I watched, while Inauguration Day dawned across the Atlantic, as the Irish up and down the aisle on the train from Killarney to Dublin, narrowed their eyes at the picture, shook their heads silently and slowly over it, and then sat back heavily in their seats, too stunned into reality to go back to business as usual—the real estate section, the sports section, the life-style section of the paper.

Here was the other side of the inauguration story. No military bands played for this one. No bulletproof viewing stands could stop the impact of this insight into the glory of force. Here was an America they could no longer understand. The contrast rang cruelly everywhere.

I sat back and looked out the train window myself. Would anybody in the United States be seeing this picture today? Would the United States ever see it, in fact? And if it is printed in the United States, will it also cross the country like wildfire and would people hear the unwritten story under it?

There are 54 million people in Iraq. Over half of them are under the age of 15. Of the over 100,000 civilians dead in this war, then, over half of them are children. We are killing children. The children are our enemy. And we are defeating them.

"I'll tell you why I voted for George Bush," a friend of mine said. "I voted for George Bush because he had the courage to do what Al Gore and John Kerry would never have done."

I've been thinking about that one.

Osama bin Laden is still alive. Sadam Hussein is still alive. Abu Musab al-Zarqawi is still alive. Baghdad, Mosul and Fallujah are burning. But my government has the courage to kill children or their parents. And I'm supposed to be impressed.

That's an unfair assessment, of course. A lot of young soldiers have died, too. A lot of weekend soldiers are maimed for life. A lot of our kids went into the military only to get a college education and are now shattered in soul by what they had to do to other bodies.

A lot of adult civilians have been blasted out of their homes and their neighborhoods and their cars. More and more every day. According to U.N. Development Fund for Women, 15 percent of wartime casualties in World War I were civilians. In World War II, 65 percent were civilians. By the mid '90s, over 75 percent of wartime casualties were civilians.

In Iraq, for every dead U.S. soldier, there are 14 other deaths, 93 percent of them are civilian. But those things happen in war, the story says. It's all for a greater good, we have to remember. It's all to free them. It's all being done to spread "liberty."

From where I stand, the only question now is who or what will free us from the 21st century's new definition of bravery. Who will free us from the notion that killing children or their civilian parents takes courage?

Part V

The Resisters: "Conscience, Not Cowardice"

INTRODUCTION

Staff Sergeant Jimmy Massey, a twelve-year veteran of the marines, wanted to go to Iraq to fight. "9/11 pissed me off; I was ready to go kill a raghead." Sergeant Kevin Benderman came from a family that had served in the U.S. armed forces since the Revolution; he felt "there was no higher honor than to serve my country and defend the values that established this country."[1] Specialist Joseph Darby had been glad to serve in Bosnia before he was deployed to Iraq.

But as they came to grasp the realities of what was happening in Iraq, all three found themselves in positions that contradicted their most fundamental values and convictions. In the course of manning a checkpoint, Massey's unit had killed thirty civilians in two days. He stopped a car with four people in it, killing three of them. The fourth asked him, "Why did you kill my brother? He wasn't a terrorist. He didn't do anything to you." Benderman saw little children with severe burns who were refused medical treatment by his unit. Darby was handed the now-notorious photographs of prisoners being abused by guards at Abu Ghraib prison.

For those forced to confront the contradiction between what they believed and what they saw and did, the disillusionment when it came was often horrific. "I don't know what I did," says Mike Hoffman, a marine artilleryman. "I came home and read that six children were killed in an artillery strike near where I was . . . I feel responsible for everything that happened while I was there." Specialist Josh Sanders said about his psychiatric intake interview at Walter Reed Hospital, "They asked me if I missed my wife. Well shit yeah, I missed my wife. That is not the fucking problem here. Did you ever put your foot through a five-year-old's skull?"[2]

Each of these soldiers had to find a way to say no. Massey now puts on his marine uniform in his North Carolina hometown a few days a week and carries a sign that says, "I killed innocent civilians

---

[1] Kevin Benderman, "A Matter of Conscience." Originally appeared at http://www .antiwar.com on January 18, 2005.

[2] American Voices Abroad (AVA) and Military Counseling Network (MCN), press release, February 21, 2005. Original quote at Salon.com.

for our government." Benderman refused to return to Iraq for another tour of duty. Darby gave the photos documenting prisoner abuse at Abu Ghraib to his supervisor. A number of enlistees have fled to Canada, where they are awaiting decisions on their applications for refugee status. A growing number of soldiers have simply voted with their feet; the Pentagon reports that since the invasion of Iraq over six thousand soldiers have failed to report for duty.[3] The military has done little to find or punish them so far.

During the era of the Vietnam War, it was not unusual to find resisters in the military. Vietnam was fought by an army of draftees from across the political spectrum, many of whom had been influenced by the political ferment of the 1960s. Since the war continued for ten years, draftees had an opportunity to form opinions about its validity before they were drafted. Currently the military is an enlisted force; it would be natural to assume that more of its members are supportive of government policies. But resistance is there.

Resistance has not been limited to combat soldiers. A group of military lawyers (called Judge Advocates) at the Guantánamo Bay prison objected to and reported abuses and inhumane interrogations at Camp Delta, a secret unit within Guantánamo. By filing memoranda and speaking out to higher officials, these uniformed legal advisers were engaging in their own form of resistance. In 2003, another group of senior military lawyers met in New York with Scott Horton, Chair of the International Law Committee of the Association of the Bar of the City of New York, to express their concerns about "important policy decisions" that had been made in the Office of the Secretary of Defense. For the first time they revealed that top Bush administration officials had made "policy decisions" legitimating torture. Joseph C. Wilson IV, a career diplomat, revealed in 2003 that he had been asked to investigate charges that the government of Niger had sold uranuim to Iraq, to be used in building weapons of mass destruction. In an article in the *New York Times* he revealed that the charges, used to justify the attack on Iraq, were false.

[3.] Monica Davey, "Un-Volunteering: Troops Improvise to Find Way Out," *New York Times*, March 18, 2005.

Beyond individual acts of resistance, returning veterans have formed a number of organizations, such as Iraq Veterans Against the War, which advocates an immediate withdrawal from Iraq, and Operation Truth, which serves as a news forum and a support organization for soldiers in the field. Both organizations seek to tell the American public about what is actually going on in Iraq. Military Families Speak Out supports military resisters, raises questions about the adequacy of government support of soldiers in the field, and speaks forcefully against the waste of human life and resources the war represents. Whistle-blowers have organized the Truth-Telling Project, which encourages civilians and military officials to reveal what they know about government misconduct.

Far from being rewarded for doing the right thing, many of the resisters face serious reprisals. Sergeant Benderman, whose application for conscientious objector (co) status was denied, faces a general court-martial (the most serious) and a jail sentence for remaining in the United States when his unit was redeployed to Iraq. Sergeant Darby was commended for his actions, but his family in western Maryland received death threats.[4] In June of 2003, Sergeant Richard "Greg" Ford, a Coast Guard veteran of thirty years, went to his superior officer to complain that prisoners were being tortured by members of his unit in Samarra, Iraq. He was given thirty seconds to change his mind about making the report. When he refused, he found himself strapped to a gurney and medevaced to Germany as a psychiatric patient.[5] Sergeant Samuel Provance, who spoke out to confirm that there indeed was torture at Abu Ghraib, was disciplined for not having reported it previously. He was transferred to a different unit and stripped of security clearance (a career-ender for a member of a military intelligence unit).[6]

As a CBS reporter said after interviewing some of the resisters, they were motivated by "conscience, not cowardice." These resisters discovered that they had been ordered to participate in illegal actions. They decided that they had to say no. They acted to

4. "Abu Ghraib Whistleblower Targeted," http://www.AlterNet, August 16, 2004.
5. David DeBatto on the radio program *Democracy Now*, December 9, 2004.
6. "U.S. Army 'Flags' Whistleblower," http://www.News24.com, May 26, 2004.

implement their decisions. They rejected the easy course of denial or acquiescence. Like Jimmy Massey, many believe they are responsible for alerting their fellow Americans to the truth: "All you can do is tell people the horrible things you've seen, and let them make up their own minds. It's kind of the pebble in the water: You throw in a pebble, and it makes ripples through the whole pond."

Breaking Ranks

DAVID GOODMAN

This article was the first to detail the responses of ordinary soldiers on the ground to the war crimes they saw around them. David Goodman, a contributing writer for *Mother Jones*, puts together a picture of the anguish soldiers felt in Iraq; the resistance of those who refused deployment; and the campaign of discharged veterans to reach the hearts and minds of the American public.

Mike Hoffman would not be the guy his buddies would expect to see leading a protest movement. The son of a steelworker and a high school janitor from Allentown, Pennsylvania, he enlisted in the Marine Corps in 1999 as an artilleryman to "blow things up." His transformation into an activist came the hard way—on the streets of Baghdad.

When Hoffman arrived in Kuwait in February 2003, his unit's highest-ranking enlisted man laid out the mission in stark terms. "You're not going to make Iraq safe for democracy," the sergeant said. "You are going for one reason alone: oil. But you're still going to go, because you signed a contract. And you're going to go to bring your friends home." Hoffman, who had his own doubts about the war, was relieved—he'd never expected to hear such a candid assessment from a superior. But it was only when he had been in Iraq for several months that the full meaning of the sergeant's words began to sink in.

"The reasons for war were wrong," he says. "They were lies. There were no WMDs. Al Qaeda was not there. And it was evident we couldn't force democracy on people by force of arms."

When he returned home and got his honorable discharge in August 2003, Hoffman says, he knew what he had to do next. "After being in Iraq and seeing what this war is, I realized that the only way to support our troops is to demand the withdrawal of all occupying forces in Iraq." He cofounded a group called Iraq Veterans Against

SOURCE: Originally appeared in *Mother Jones*, October 11, 2004. Copyright © 2004 by the Foundation for National Progress.

the War (IVAW) and soon found himself emerging as one of the most visible members of a small but growing movement of soldiers who openly oppose the war in Iraq.

Dissent on Iraq within the military is not entirely new. Even before the invasion, senior officers were questioning the optimistic projections of the Pentagon's civilian leaders, and several retired generals have strongly criticized the war. But now, nearly two years after the first troops rolled across the desert, rank-and-file soldiers and their families are increasingly speaking up. Hoffman's group was founded in July with 8 members and had grown to 40 by September. Another organization, Military Families Speak Out, began with 2 families two years ago and now represents more than 1,700 families. And soldier-advocacy groups are reporting a rising number of calls from military personnel who are upset about the war and are thinking about refusing to fight; a few soldiers have even fled to Canada rather than go to Iraq.

In a 2003 Gallup Poll, nearly one-fifth of the soldiers surveyed said they felt the situation in Iraq had not been worth going to war over. In another poll, in Pennsylvania last August, 54 percent of households with a member in the military said the war was the "wrong thing to do"; in the population as a whole, only 48 percent felt that way. Doubts about the war have contributed to the decline of troop morale over the past year—and may, some experts say, be a factor in the 40 percent increase in Army suicide rates in Iraq in the past year. "That's the most basic tool a soldier needs on the battlefield—a reason to be there," says Paul Rieckhoff, a platoon leader in the New York National Guard and former JP Morgan banker who served in Iraq. Rieckhoff has founded a group called Operation Truth, which provides a freewheeling forum for soldiers' views on the war. "When you can't articulate that in one sentence, it starts to affect morale. You had an initial rationale for war that was a moving target. [But] it was a shell game from the beginning, and you can only bullshit people for so long."

With his baggy pants, red goatee, and moussed hair, Mike Hoffman looks more like a guy taking some time off after college than a 25-year-old combat veteran. But the urgency in his voice belies his relaxed appearance; he speaks rapidly, consumed with the desire to get his point across. As we talk at a coffee shop in Vermont after one of his many speaking engagements, he concedes, "A lot of what I'm doing is basically survivor's guilt. It's hard: I'm home. I'm fine. I came back in one piece. But there are a lot of people who haven't."

More than a year after his return from Iraq, Hoffman is still battling depression, panic attacks, and nightmares. "I don't know what I did," he says, noting that errors and faulty targeting were common in the artillery. "I came home and read that six children were killed in an artillery strike near where I was. I don't really know if that was my unit or a British unit. But I feel responsible for everything that happened when I was there."

When he first came home, Hoffman says, he tried to talk to friends and family about his experience. It was not a story most wanted to hear. "One of the hardest things when I came back was people who were slapping me on the back saying 'Great job,'" he recalls. "Everyone wants this to be a good war so they can sleep at night. But guys like me know it's not a good war. There's no such thing as a good war."

Hoffman finally found some kindred spirits last fall when he discovered Veterans for Peace, the 19-year-old antiwar group. Older veterans encouraged him to speak at rallies, and steadily, he began to connect with other disillusioned Iraq vets. In July, at the Veterans for Peace annual meeting in Boston, Hoffman announced the creation of Iraq Veterans Against the War. The audience of silver-haired vets from wars in Vietnam, Korea, and World War II exploded into applause. Hoffman smiles wryly. "They tell us we're the rock stars of the antiwar movement."

Several of Hoffman's Marine Corps buddies have now joined Iraq Veterans Against the War, and the stream of phone calls and emails from other soldiers is constant. Not long ago, he says, a soldier home on leave from Iraq told him, "Just keep doing what you're doing, because you've got more support than you can imagine over there."

Members of IVAW led the protest march that greeted the Republican convention in New York, and their ranks swelled that week. But the protest's most poignant moment came after the march, as veterans from wars past and present retreated to Summit Rock in Central Park. Joe Bangert, a founding member of Vietnam Veterans of America, addressed the group. "One of the most painful things when we returned from Vietnam was that the veterans from past wars weren't there for us," he said. "They didn't support us in our questioning and our opposition to war. And I just want to say," he added, peering intently at the younger veterans, "we are here for you. We have your back."

There was no Iraq veterans' group for Brandon Hughey to turn to in December 2003. Alone and terrified, sitting in his barracks at Fort Hood, Texas, the 18-year-old private considered his options. He could remain with his Army unit, which was about to ship out to Iraq to fight a war that Hughey was convinced was pointless and immoral. Or he could end his dilemma—by taking his own life.

Desperate, Hughey trolled the Internet. He emailed a peace activist and Vietnam veteran in Indianapolis, Carl Rising-Moore, who made him an offer: If he was serious about his opposition to the war, Rising-Moore said, he would help him flee to Canada.

The next day, there was a knock on Hughey's door: His deployment date had been moved up, and his unit was leaving within 24 hours. Hughey packed his belongings in a military duffel, jumped in his car, and drove north. As he and Rising-Moore approached the Rainbow Bridge border post at Niagara Falls, Hughey was nervous and somber. "I had the sense that once I crossed that border, I might never be able to go back," he recalls. "It made me sad."

Months after fleeing Fort Hood, the baby-faced 19-year-old still sports a military-style buzz cut. Sitting at the kitchen table of the Quaker family that is sheltering him in St. Catharines, Ontario, Hughey tells me about growing up in San Angelo, Texas, where he was raised by his father. In high school he played trumpet and loved to soup up cars. But when his father lost his job as a computer programmer, he was forced to use up his son's college fund. So at 17, Hughey enlisted in the Army, with a $5,000 signing bonus to sweeten the deal.

Quiet and unassuming, Hughey grows intense when the conversation turns to Iraq. "I would fight in an act of defense, if my home and family were in danger," he says. "But Iraq had no weapons of mass destruction. They barely had an army left, and Kofi Annan actually said [attacking Iraq was] a violation of the U.N. charter. It's nothing more than an act of aggression." As for his duty to his fellow soldiers, he insists, "You can't go along with a criminal activity just because others are doing it."

The GI Rights Hotline, a counseling operation run by a national network of antiwar groups, reports that it now receives between 3,000 and 4,000 calls per month from soldiers seeking a way out of the military. Some of the callers simply never thought they would see combat, says J. E. McNeil, director of the Center on Conscience and War. But others are turning against the war because of what they saw while serving in Iraq, and they don't want to be sent back there. "It's people learning what war really is," she says. "A lot of people are naive—and for a while, the military was portraying itself as being a peace mission."

Unlike Vietnam, when young men facing the draft could convincingly claim that they opposed all war, enlistees in a volunteer military have a tough time qualifying as conscientious objectors. In the Army, 61 soldiers applied for conscientious objector status last year, and 31 of those applications were granted. "The Army does understand people can have a change of heart," notes spokeswoman Martha Rudd. "But you can't ask for a conscientious objector discharge based on moral or religious opposition to a particular war."

Staff Sergeant Jimmy Massey may be the most unlikely of the soldiers who have come out against the war. A Marine since 1992, he has been a recruiter, infantry instructor, and combat platoon leader. He went to Iraq primed to fight. "9/11 pissed me off," he says. "I was ready to go kill a raghead."

Shortly after Massey arrived in Iraq, his unit was ordered to man roadblocks. To stop cars, the Marines would raise their hands. If the drivers kept going, Massey says, "we would just light 'em up. I didn't find out until later on, after talking to an Iraqi, that when you put your hand up in the air, it means 'Hello.'" He estimates that his men killed 30 civilians in one 48-hour period.

One day, he recalls, "there was this red Kia Spectra. We told it to stop, and it didn't. There were four occupants. We fatally wounded three of them. We started pulling out the bodies, but they were dying pretty fast. The guy that was driving was just frickin' bawling, sitting on the highway. He looked at me and asked, 'Why did you kill my brother? He wasn't a terrorist. He didn't do anything to you.'"

Massey searched the car. "It was completely clean. Nothing there. Meanwhile the driver just ran around saying, 'Why? Why?' That's when I started to question."

The doubts led to nightmares, depression, and a talk with his commanding officer. "I feel what we are doing here is wrong. We are committing genocide," Massey told him. He was later diagnosed with post-traumatic stress disorder and given a medical discharge.

Back in his hometown of Waynesville, North Carolina, Massey got a job as a furniture salesman, then lost it after speaking at an antiwar rally. Two or three times a week, he puts on his Marine uniform and takes a long walk around the nearby town of Asheville carrying a sign that reads: "I killed innocent civilians for our government." The local police now keep an eye out for him, he says, because people have tried to run him over.

When asked what he would say to someone who thinks the way he did before the war, Massey falls uncharacteristically silent. "How do you wake them up?" he finally responds. "It's a slow process. All you can do is tell people the horrible things you've seen, and let them make up their own minds. It's kind of the pebble in the water: You throw in a pebble, and it makes ripples through the whole pond."

Jeffry House is reliving his past. An American draft dodger who fled to Canada in 1970 (he was number 16 in that year's draft lottery), he is now fighting to persuade the Canadian government to grant refugee status to American deserters.

"In some ways, this is coming full circle for me," says the slightly disheveled, 57-year-old lawyer. "The themes that I thought about when I was 21 years old now are reborn, particularly your obligation to the state when the state has participated in a fraud, when they've deceived you." A dormant network has been revived, with Vietnam-era draft dodgers and deserters quietly contributing money to support the legal defense of the newest American fugitives.

House's strategy is bold: He is challenging the very legality of the Iraq war, based on the Nuremberg principles. Those principles, adopted by a U.N. commission after World War II in response to the Nazis' crimes, hold that military personnel have a responsibility to resist unlawful orders. They also declare wars of aggression a violation of international law. House hopes that in Canada, which did not support the war in Iraq, courts might sympathize with the deserters' claims and grant them legal refugee status; the first of his cases was to be heard by the Canadian Immigration and Refugee Board this fall.

On an August afternoon, I follow House as he darts through Toronto traffic on his way to see a new client—a young American who had been living in a homeless shelter for 10 months before revealing that he was on the run from the U.S. Navy. He disappears into a run-down brown brick building; moments later, a thin, nervous young man in shorts and a T-shirt emerges onto the sidewalk and introduces himself as Dave Sanders. Over dinner at a nearby Pizza Hut, he tells me his story.

Sanders dropped out of 11th grade in Bullhead City, Arizona, in 2001. He got his GED and was hoping to study computers, but couldn't get financial aid. "The only reason I joined the military was to go to college," he says. That was late 2002, and I ask Sanders whether he then considered he might end up in combat. "I was told," he says, "that everything would be ended by the time I got out of boot camp."

Sanders completed boot camp in March 2003, two days before the United States began bombing Iraq. He started training as a cryptologist; in his spare time he surfed the web, reading news from the BBC and Al Jazeera. He was growing skeptical of the administration's motives in Iraq. "Stuff wasn't adding up," he recalls. "Bush was trying to connect the terrorists with Iraq, and there was no proof for that. I was starting to think that we kind of put the blame on Iraq so we could go over there and make money for companies." He considered what his job might be if he were deployed; as a cryptologist, he could have been handling information leading to raids and arrests. "I didn't want to be a part of putting innocent people in prison," he says. "I felt that what we were doing there was wrong."

In October 2003, Sanders learned that his unit was headed to Iraq. For several weeks he agonized over what to do; then he bought a one-way Greyhound ticket and headed to Toronto. He picked up odd jobs and kept quiet about his predicament, fearing that authorities might send him back to the United States. Finally, he read an article about Jeremy Hinzman, another deserter who had fled to Canada and was being represented by Jeffry House. When I spoke to Sanders, House was helping him file for refugee status.

As we talk, Sanders keeps tapping his feet and twisting his long fingers. "Sorry if I seem nervous," he finally blurts. "I never really talked to the media before. I'm a shy person." I ask if he surprised himself by defying his orders. He nods. "I never really thought I could stand up to a whole institution."

Though Sanders has kept away from the spotlight, other deserters have attracted headlines around the world—and drawn criticism from the war's supporters. Fox's Bill O'Reilly called their actions "insulting to America, and especially to those American soldiers who have lost their lives fighting terrorists."

But Sanders says he doesn't actually consider himself a deserter. "I don't think I did anything wrong by turning down an illegal order," he says. "I don't know what it's called—I think it's Nuremberg?—that's what I followed by leaving." When I ask if he would call himself a pacifist, he says he is not sure what the term means and asks me to explain. Then he shakes his head. "I believe if you're being attacked you have a right to defend yourself. But right now, we are not the ones being attacked. That's a reason I think this is a very unjust war."

Sanders is an only child; his father served in the Marines for 13 years. "My family is pro-war, pro-Bush, pro-everything that's happening," he says. "They would really not support what I'm doing." He has emailed them to tell them that he's alive, but they have not replied. "I miss them," he says, his eyes welling. "I love them. And I hope they can find it in their hearts to forgive me."

Sergeant John Bruhns is sharply critical of soldiers who go AWOL. "I feel that if you are against the war, you should be man enough to stay put and fight for what you believe in," he says. But he also doesn't believe in making a secret of his opinions about the war. "I'm very proud of my military service," he tells me from his post with the Army's 1st Armored Division in Fort Riley, Kansas. "But I am disheartened and personally hurt, after seeing two people lose their limbs and a 19-year-old girl die and three guys lose their vision, to learn that the reason I went to Iraq never existed. And I believe that by being over there for a year, I have earned the right to have an opinion."

Bruhns returned in February from a one-year deployment in Iraq. He is due to complete his Army service next March, but his unit may be "stop-lossed"—their terms extended beyond their discharge dates to meet the Pentagon's desperate need for troops. Critics have called this a backdoor draft, a way to force a volunteer military into involuntarily serving long stints in an unpopular war. A California National Guard member has filed a lawsuit challenging the policy, and Bruhns has considered joining the case.

"I'm really a patriotic soldier," the 27-year-old infantryman tells me; he addresses me as "sir" and stops periodically to answer the squawk of his walkie-talkie. He signed up as a full-time soldier in early 2002, after serving five years in the Marine Corps Reserve. "I was really upset about what happened on 9/11," he recalls, "and I really wanted to serve. I lost a buddy of mine in the World Trade Center. I believe what we did in Afghanistan was right."

But what he saw in Iraq, Bruhns says, left him disappointed. "We were fighting all the time. The only peace is what we kept with guns. A lot of stuff that we heard on the news—that we were fighting leftover loyalists, Ba'ath Party holdovers—wasn't true. When I arrested people on raids, many of them were poor people. They weren't in with the Ba'ath Party. The people of Iraq were attacking us as a reaction to what the majority of them felt—that they were being occupied."

Among his fellow soldiers, Bruhns adds, a majority still support the war. But, he notes, "This is a new generation. We have the Internet, discussion forums, cable news. Soldiers don't just march off into battle blindly anymore. They have a lot more information."

Vietnam figures prominently in soldiers' conversations about Iraq. Nearly every one of the Iraq veterans I spoke with has relatives who served in the military, and nearly every one told me the same story: When they grew cynical about the Iraq war, the Vietnam veterans in their family immediately recognized what was happening—that another generation of soldiers was grappling with the realization that they were being sent to carry out a policy determined by people who cared little for the grunts on the ground.

Resistance in the military "is in its infancy right now," says Hoffman, whose cousins, uncle, and grandfather all did their time in uniform. "It's growing, but it's going to take a little while.

"There was a progression of thought that happened among soldiers in Vietnam. It started with a mission: Contain communism. That mission fell apart, just like it fell apart now—there are no weapons of mass destruction. Then you are left with just a survival instinct. That, unfortunately, turned to racism. That's happening now, too. Guys are writing me saying, 'I don't know why I'm here, but I hate the Iraqis.'

"Now, you realize that the people to blame for this aren't the ones you are fighting," Hoffman continues. "It's the people who put you in this situation in the first place. You realize you wouldn't be in this situation if you hadn't been lied to. Soldiers are slowly coming to that conclusion. Once that becomes widespread, the resentment of the war is going to grow even more."

"I Refuse to Be a Pawn"

JEREMY HINZMAN

Jeremy Hinzman was in the Eighty-second Airborne Division of the U.S. Army and was deployed to Afghanistan in 2002. He had already applied for conscientious objector status by then; while he was in Afghanistan his application was denied. When his unit was redeployed to Iraq, he felt he had no choice but to refuse to go there. He fled to Canada and, like others who took a similar action, he is applying for refugee status and hopes to be allowed to remain in Canada, where he has been joined by his family. One of the factors in Hinzman's decision was his embrace of the moral and spiritual principles of the Society of Friends (Quakers).

I believe that you would have a hard time finding soldiers who, if they spoke honestly and in the absence of fellow soldiers to impress, would tell you that they actually yearn to fight. Granted, there are exceptions to this, but the Army is composed mostly of people who want to make a better life for themselves. The Army is aware of this and is very savvy in marketing it. In exchange for your innocence and morality, the Army provides the most socialistic environment available in the world. Literally everything about a soldier's life is subsidized.

When I enlisted in the Army, I won't deny that I was thinking in a pragmatic manner. However, just because I enlisted, I didn't abdicate my ability to evolve intellectually and morally, which I did as result of the circumstances I found myself involved in.

I object to the Iraqi war because it is an act of aggression with no defensive basis. It has been supported by pretenses that cannot withstand even elementary scrutiny. First, before the U.S. dropped the first bomb, it was quite evident that Iraq had no weapons of mass destruction. Second, the Bush administration had the gall to exploit the American public's fear of terrorists by making the absurd assertion that a secular Baathist government was working with a fundamentalist terrorist group. There was never any intelligence to substantiate this.

SOURCE: Excerpt taken from Jeremy Hinzman's Web site, http://www.jeremyhinzman .net/. Copyright © 2005 by Jeremy Hinzman.

Perhaps I made a mistake by enlisting in the Army, but the U.S. is putting the lives of its soldiers in jeopardy in order to line the pockets of big money. I will not get blood on my hands or put my life in danger for such an endeavor.

Should I apologize for starting to attend Quaker meetings after I enlisted in the Army? It was hard to ignore the Peace testimony that is so integral to the Quaker way of life. Although the timing may have been off, it spoke to me and my situation and made sense. The world is interconnected and violence—for no matter what cause—does nothing but foster more violence while taking away the humanity of its victims and turning them into mere objects. All of creation is infused with the divine, and to act violently against it is to act violently toward God. I wish I would have been privy to this before I enlisted. Just because I wasn't doesn't mean that I should have had to ignore it when it was encountered.

I disagree with [America's] current foreign policy and notion of itself as an empire. I refuse to be a pawn in enforcing this. As a nation, America has certain obligations towards other countries that we now ignore in the quest to serve our own needs. The American public needs to become aware of what a toll its collective lifestyle is inflicting upon the rest of the world. The only way it can be maintained is through the suffering and exploitation of the undeveloped world.

Military Families Speak Out

NANCY LESSIN

Nancy Lessin and her husband, Charley Richardson, founded Military Families Speak Out, an organization of military families opposing the Iraq war, in 2002. Her stepson, Joe, served in the U.S. Marine Corps in Iraq. The following statement is from Nancy Lessin's speech upon receiving the Letelier-Moffit Memorial Human Rights Award from the Institute for Policy Studies. Lessin is the Health and Safety Coordinator for the Massachusetts AFL-CIO.

In August 2002, my stepson—Charley's son Joe—a Marine, deployed for Kosovo. He told us he would be ending up in Iraq, and indeed he did, in spring of 2003.

Fall of 2002 was when the drumbeats for war in this country were getting deafening, and we noticed that all those saying "We gotta go to war!" weren't going anywhere—nor were their loved ones. It was OUR loved ones who would be used as cannon fodder in a war that was about oil markets and dreams of empire—not protecting and defending Country and Constitution, which is what our troops signed up for.

We feared for all who would be in harm's way—our loved ones, all of our troops and the people of Iraq. We had learned a terrible truth, an equation really, from Seymour Hersh. In 1969 Mr. Hersh wrote about My Lai. The equation he exposed was this: racism plus dehumanization equals atrocities. We feared that if Iraq was invaded, we would see it all again.

In fall, 2002 we made our first poster, with Joe's picture on it. It said "Our Son Is A Marine—Don't Send Him To War for Oil."

In October, 2002 we met a father—Jeff McKenzie—at an antiwar demonstration in Washington, D.C. His son, who flew medevac helicopters, would be deploying in January, 2003. In a phone conversation in November, 2002, our two families decided to form an organization—Military Families Speak Out—to use our special need to speak out, and the special voice with which we speak, to try to prevent an invasion of Iraq.

It is now two years later, and the voice of military families opposing this war has grown dramatically.

Our membership today includes well over 1,700 military families with loved ones in every branch of the U.S. military. We have families in every state and in several other countries. We have families who opposed this war from the beginning; and families who supported the invasion, only to find out it was a war based on lies. We are Democrats, Republicans and Independents; we are pacifists, and we are long-time military families who have never spoken out against any military action taken by the U.S. until this invasion of Iraq.

[For example,] Elaine Johnson from South Carolina, whose son Specialist Darius Jennings, age 22, was one of 16 soldiers killed on November 2nd 2003 when a Chinook Helicopter was shot down in Iraq. That helicopter, not properly outfitted with an anti-missile system, was piloted by Sergeant Brian Slavenas of the Illinois National Guard. He too was killed that day; his mother Rosemary Dietz Slavenas is also a member of Military Families Speak Out. Elaine Johnson had the opportunity to meet President Bush a number of months ago. She asked him questions that he could not, or would not, answer. It was not pretty. So much for this administration's concerns for bereaved parents, for "Gold Star" families.

Or Stacy Bannerman from Kent, Washington, whose husband in the National Guard has been "Stop-Lossed" and his tour of duty in Iraq extended . . .

Maritza Castillo's son, Staff Sgt. Camilo Mejia, refused to return to the war after serving in Iraq for 7 months. Camilo wrote a 55 page Conscientious Objector application in which he detailed, among other things, prisoner abuse at a detainee camp in Al Assad. He turned himself in to the military in March, 2004, Conscientious Objector application in hand. In May of this year he was convicted of desertion and received the same one-year prison sentence that Jeremy Sivits, photographer of the Abu Ghraib prison abuse photos, received. Here is just one small piece of what Camilo wrote in his Conscientious Objector application:

"I have held a rifle to a man's face, a man on the ground and in front of his mother, children and wife—and not knowing why I did it. I have walked by the headless body of an innocent man right after our machine guns decapitated him. I have seen a soldier broken down inside because he killed a child. I have seen an old man on his knees, crying, with his arms raised to the sky, perhaps asking God why we were taking the lifeless body of his son. It is the war that has changed me forever . . . By putting my weapon down I choose to reassert myself as a human being."

Larry Syverson of Richmond, Virginia has three sons in the active duty military, two of whom served in Iraq. Larry stands every week in front of the Federal Building in Richmond with a sign that says, "Iraqi Oil is not worth my sons' blood"—and has gotten some grief for this. Larry's son Bryce wrote him from Iraq: "You tell those people to either pick up a gun and come over here and help me out, or pick up a picket sign and join you in getting us the hell home!"

Bill Mitchell from California just returned from Germany where he spent time with Bianca, his would-be daughter-in-law on what was to be her wedding day. Bill's son Michael Mitchell was killed in Sadr City on April 4, 2004—7 days before he was to return home.

And new military families are joining MFSO every single day—24 new families yesterday, and over a dozen so far today. At 8:30 a.m. this morning, this three-sentence, heartfelt email came in to us: "I have a son in the military. This war is a disaster. I want to speak out."

Through our tears, and through our fear—we have joined our voices together with those of Veterans for Peace, Vietnam Veterans Against the War and the new and much-celebrated Iraq Veterans Against the War to become an important part of today's peace and anti-war movement.

Civilians We Killed

MICHAEL HOFFMAN

Michael Hoffman took part in the invasion of Iraq as a U.S. marine. He cofounded Iraq Veterans Against the War (http://www.ivaw.net) in July 2004. Since then he has become a full-time activist. Hoffman believes "the only way to support our troops is to demand the withdrawal of all occupying forces in Iraq."

The chaos of war should never be understated. On the way to Baghdad, I saw bodies by the road, many in civilian clothing. Every time a car got near my Humvee, everyone inside braced themselves, not knowing if gunfire would suddenly erupt out of it. When your enemy is unclear, everyone becomes your enemy.

I will not judge the marine who killed the wounded Iraqi. I do not know what was going on around him or what he experienced in the hours before. But I do know what the stress of combat will do. I remember talking to a friend who told how, after a greatly loved lieutenant was killed in Nassiriya, the unit started shooting anyone that got close. I remember when a pickup truck got too close to my convoy, the armoured vehicle up front shot the passenger to get the message to the driver. Just as these marines should face charges, then those that put us in these situations should have to answer for their actions.

In his book *The Things They Carried*, Tim O'Brien said: "You can tell a true war story by its absolute and uncompromised allegiance to obscenity and evil." This is something people in the U.S. have forgotten after years of watching CNN. War is dirty, always wrong, but sometimes unavoidable. That is why all these horrible things must rest on the shoulders of those leaders who supported a war that did not have to be fought.

I know the commitment it takes to serve your country, but I also know this war has nothing to do with protecting my country.

SOURCE: Originally appeared in the *Guardian*, December 2, 2004. Available at http://www.guardian.co.uk/Iraq/Story/0,2763,1364368,00.html. Copyright © 2004 by Michael Hoffman.

My sergeant put it best a week before we left for the Middle East: "Don't think you're going to be heroes. You're not going for weapons of mass destruction. You're not going to get rid of Saddam, or to make Iraq safe for democracy. You're going for one reason, and that's oil."

War for oil is a term the troops in Iraq know well. That is the only reason left for this war, leaving those on the ground with only one reason to fight—get home alive. When this kind of desperation sinks in, it is easy to make the person across from you less than human, easier to do horrible things to them.

Did the soldiers who committed those acts in Abu Ghraib view Iraqis as equals? Those who committed these acts will have to live with the memories—just as I wonder how many Iraqi children were killed by my artillery battery, or how many Iraqis were trapped in burning vehicles on the road to Baghdad. These are the thoughts that keep me up at night: the bodies of children and the burned remains of Iraqi troops that couldn't get out in time.

But those who put all of us there will never understand this. That is why they need to be judged. But they will never receive the most just punishment: feeling what myself and all the other veterans of this hideous war will deal with for the rest of our lives.

Truths Worth Telling

Daniel Ellsberg

Daniel Ellsberg worked for the Departments of Defense and State during the Vietnam War. In 1969 he gave the study of Vietnam conducted
under the auspices of Defense Secretary Robert McNamara (it became
known as the Pentagon Papers) to the Senate Foreign Relations Committee; in 1971 he released the seven-thousand-page study to the *New
York Times* and seventeen other newspapers. The Pentagon Papers revealed government deception and war crimes—revelations that helped
create a climate of resistance to the war. He is a founder of the Truth-
Telling Project, which encourages whistle-blowing. In the following article Ellsberg makes a compelling case for the necessity of whistle-blowing
activities around the war in Iraq.

On a tape recording made in the Oval Office on June 14, 1971, H. R.
Haldeman, Richard Nixon's chief of staff, can be heard citing Donald Rumsfeld, then a White House aide, on the effect of the Pentagon Papers, news of which had been published on the front page of
that morning's newspaper:

"Rumsfeld was making this point this morning," Haldeman
says. "To the ordinary guy, all this is a bunch of gobbledygook.
But out of the gobbledygook comes a very clear thing: you can't
trust the government; you can't believe what they say, and you
can't rely on their judgment. And the implicit infallibility of
presidents, which has been an accepted thing in America, is badly
hurt by this, because it shows that people do things the president
wants to do even though it's wrong, and the president can be
wrong."

He got it exactly right. But it's a lesson that each generation of
voters and each new set of leaders have to learn for themselves.
Perhaps Mr. Rumsfeld—now secretary of defense, of course—has
reflected on this truth recently as he has contemplated the deteriorating conditions in Iraq. According to the government's own reporting, the situation there is far bleaker than Mr. Rumsfeld has

SOURCE: Originally appeared in the *New York Times*, September 28, 2004. Copyright ©
2004 by Daniel Ellsberg.

recognized or President Bush has acknowledged on the campaign trail.

Understandably, the American people are reluctant to believe that their president has made errors of judgment that have cost American lives. To convince them otherwise, there is no substitute for hard evidence: documents, photographs, transcripts. Often the only way for the public to get such evidence is if a dedicated public servant decides to release it without permission.

Such a leak occurred recently with the National Intelligence Estimate on Iraq, which was prepared in July. Reports of the estimate's existence and overall pessimism—but not its actual conclusions— have prompted a long-overdue debate on the realities and prospects of the war. But its judgments of the relative likelihood and the strength of evidence pointing to the worst possibilities remain undisclosed. Since the White House has refused to release the full report, someone else should do so.

Leakers are often accused of being partisan, and undoubtedly many of them are. But the measure of their patriotism should be the accuracy and the importance of the information they reveal. It would be a great public service to reveal a true picture of the administration's plans for Iraq—especially before this week's debate on foreign policy between Mr. Bush and Senator John Kerry.

The military's real estimates of the projected costs—in manpower, money and casualties—of various long-term plans for Iraq should be made public, in addition to the more immediate costs in American and Iraqi lives of the planned offensive against resistant cities in Iraq that appears scheduled for November. If military or intelligence experts within the government predict disastrous political consequences in Iraq from such urban attacks, these judgments should not remain secret.

Leaks on the timing of this offensive—and on possible call-up of reserves just after the election—take me back to Election Day 1964, which I spent in an interagency working group in the State Department. The purpose of our meeting was to examine plans to expand the war—precisely the policy that voters soundly rejected at the polls that day.

We couldn't wait until the next day to hold our meeting because the plan for the bombing of North Vietnam had to be ready as soon as possible. But we couldn't have held our meeting the day before because news of it might have been leaked—not by me, I'm sorry to say. And President Lyndon Johnson might not have won in a landslide had voters known he was lying when he said that his administration sought "no wider war."

Seven years and almost 50,000 American deaths later, after I had leaked the Pentagon Papers, I had a conversation with Senator Wayne Morse of Oregon, one of the two senators who had voted against the Tonkin Gulf resolution in August 1964. If I had leaked the documents then, he said, the resolution never would have passed.

That was hard to hear. But in 1964 it hadn't occurred to me to break my vow of secrecy. Though I knew that the war was a mistake, my loyalties then were to the secretary of defense and the president. It took five years of war before I recognized the higher loyalty all officials owe to the Constitution, the rule of law, the soldiers in harm's way or their fellow citizens.

Like Robert McNamara, under whom I served, Mr. Rumsfeld appears to inspire great loyalty among his aides. As the scandal at Abu Ghraib shows, however, there are more important principles. Mr. Rumsfeld might not have seen the damning photographs and the report of Maj. Gen. Antonio M. Taguba as soon as he did—just as he would never have seen the Pentagon Papers 33 years ago—if some anonymous people in his own department had not bypassed the chain of command and disclosed them, without authorization, to the news media. And without public awareness of the scandal, reforms would be less likely.

A federal judge has ordered the administration to issue a list of all documents relating to the scandal by Oct. 15. Will Mr. Rumsfeld release the remaining photos, which depict treatment that he has described as even worse? It's highly unlikely, especially before Nov. 2. Meanwhile, the full Taguba report remains classified, and the findings of several other inquiries into military interrogation and detention practices have yet to be released.

All administrations classify far more information than is justifiable in a democracy—and the Bush administration has been especially secretive. Information should never be classified as secret merely because it is embarrassing or incriminating. But in practice, in this as in any administration, no information is guarded more closely.

Surely there are officials in the present administration who recognize that the United States has been misled into a war in Iraq, but who have so far kept their silence—as I long did about the war in Vietnam. To them I have a personal message: don't repeat my mistakes. Don't wait until more troops are sent, and thousands more have died, before telling truths that could end a war and save lives. Do what I wish I had done in 1964: go to the press, to Congress, and document your claims.

Technology may make it easier to tell your story, but the decision to do so will be no less difficult. The personal risks of making disclosures embarrassing to your superiors are real. If you are identified as the source, your career will be over; friendships will be lost; you may even be prosecuted. But some 140,000 Americans are risking their lives every day in Iraq. Our nation is in urgent need of comparable moral courage from its public officials.

What I Didn't Find in Africa

JOSEPH C. WILSON IV

One of the earliest whistle-blowers in the Iraq war, Joseph C.Wilson IV
recounts here the story of the yellowcake uranium that supposedly
went from Niger to Iraq to aid the building of weapons of mass destruction there. After Wilson's report was published in the *New York
Times*, it was revealed by Robert Novak, a reporter, that his wife, Valerie
Plame, was a CIA operative. Plame's undercover career was ended by
this disclosure; her life might well have been in danger, as well as the
lives of those with whom she worked. A special investigator has been
appointed to look into the role of top Bush administration officials in
the disclosure. Wilson served as U.S. ambassador to Gabon from 1992
to 1995 and is now an international business consultant.

Did the Bush administration manipulate intelligence about Saddam Hussein's weapons programs to justify an invasion of Iraq?

Based on my experience with the administration in the months
leading up to the war, I have little choice but to conclude that some
of the intelligence related to Iraq's nuclear weapons program was
twisted to exaggerate the Iraqi threat.

For 23 years, from 1976 to 1998, I was a career foreign service officer and ambassador. In 1990, as chargé d'affaires in Baghdad, I was
the last American diplomat to meet with Saddam Hussein. (I was
also a forceful advocate for his removal from Kuwait.) After Iraq,
I was President George H. W. Bush's ambassador to Gabon and São
Tomé and Príncipe; under President Bill Clinton, I helped direct
Africa policy for the National Security Council.

It was my experience in Africa that led me to play a small role
in the effort to verify information about Africa's suspected link to
Iraq's nonconventional weapons programs. Those news stories about
that unnamed former envoy who went to Niger? That's me.

In February 2002, I was informed by officials at the Central
Intelligence Agency that Vice President Dick Cheney's office had
questions about a particular intelligence report. While I never saw

SOURCE: Originally appeared in *the New York Times*, July 6, 2003. Copyright © 2003 by
the New York Times Company. Reprinted by permission.

the report, I was told that it referred to a memorandum of agreement that documented the sale of uranium yellowcake—a form of lightly processed ore—by Niger to Iraq in the late 1990's. The agency officials asked if I would travel to Niger to check out the story so they could provide a response to the vice president's office.

After consulting with the State Department's African Affairs Bureau (and through it with Barbro Owens-Kirkpatrick, the United States ambassador to Niger), I agreed to make the trip. The mission I undertook was discreet but by no means secret. While the C.I.A. paid my expenses (my time was offered pro bono), I made it abundantly clear to everyone I met that I was acting on behalf of the United States government.

In late February 2002, I arrived in Niger's capital, Niamey, where I had been a diplomat in the mid-70's and visited as a National Security Council official in the late 90's. The city was much as I remembered it. Seasonal winds had clogged the air with dust and sand. Through the haze, I could see camel caravans crossing the Niger River (over the John F. Kennedy bridge), the setting sun behind them. Most people had wrapped scarves around their faces to protect against the grit, leaving only their eyes visible.

The next morning, I met with Ambassador Owens-Kirkpatrick at the embassy. For reasons that are understandable, the embassy staff has always kept a close eye on Niger's uranium business. I was not surprised, then, when the ambassador told me that she knew about the allegations of uranium sales to Iraq—and that she felt she had already debunked them in her reports to Washington. Nevertheless, she and I agreed that my time would be best spent interviewing people who had been in government when the deal supposedly took place, which was before her arrival.

I spent the next eight days drinking sweet mint tea and meeting with dozens of people: current government officials, former government officials, people associated with the country's uranium business. It did not take long to conclude that it was highly doubtful that any such transaction had ever taken place.

Given the structure of the consortiums that operated the mines, it would be exceedingly difficult for Niger to transfer uranium to

Iraq. Niger's uranium business consists of two mines, Somair and Cominak, which are run by French, Spanish, Japanese, German and Nigerian interests. If the government wanted to remove uranium from a mine, it would have to notify the consortium, which in turn is strictly monitored by the International Atomic Energy Agency. Moreover, because the two mines are closely regulated, quasi-governmental entities, selling uranium would require the approval of the minister of mines, the prime minister and probably the president. In short, there's simply too much oversight over too small an industry for a sale to have transpired.

(As for the actual memorandum, I never saw it. But news accounts have pointed out that the documents had glaring errors—they were signed, for example, by officials who were no longer in government—and were probably forged. And then there's the fact that Niger formally denied the charges.)

Before I left Niger, I briefed the ambassador on my findings, which were consistent with her own. I also shared my conclusions with members of her staff. In early March, I arrived in Washington and promptly provided a detailed briefing to the C.I.A. I later shared my conclusions with the State Department African Affairs Bureau. There was nothing secret or earth-shattering in my report, just as there was nothing secret about my trip.

Though I did not file a written report, there should be at least four documents in United States government archives confirming my mission. The documents should include the ambassador's report of my debriefing in Niamey, a separate report written by the embassy staff, a C.I.A. report summing up my trip, and a specific answer from the agency to the office of the vice president (this may have been delivered orally). While I have not seen any of these reports, I have spent enough time in government to know that this is standard operating procedure.

I thought the Niger matter was settled and went back to my life. (I did take part in the Iraq debate, arguing that a strict containment regime backed by the threat of force was preferable to an invasion.) In September 2002, however, Niger re-emerged. The British government published a "white paper" asserting that Saddam Hussein and his unconventional arms posed an immediate danger. As evidence, the report cited Iraq's attempts to purchase uranium from an African country.

Then, in January, President Bush, citing the British dossier, repeated the charges about Iraqi efforts to buy uranium from Africa.

The next day, I reminded a friend at the State Department of my trip and suggested that if the president had been referring to Niger, then his conclusion was not borne out by the facts as I understood them. He replied that perhaps the president was speaking about one of the other three African countries that produce uranium: Gabon, South Africa or Namibia. At the time, I accepted the explanation. I didn't know that in December, a month before the president's address, the State Department had published a fact sheet that mentioned the Niger case.

Those are the facts surrounding my efforts. The vice president's office asked a serious question. I was asked to help formulate the answer. I did so, and I have every confidence that the answer I provided was circulated to the appropriate officials within our government.

The question now is how that answer was or was not used by our political leadership. If my information was deemed inaccurate, I understand (though I would be very interested to know why). If, however, the information was ignored because it did not fit certain preconceptions about Iraq, then a legitimate argument can be made that we went to war under false pretenses. (It's worth remembering that in his March "Meet the Press" appearance, Mr. Cheney said that Saddam Hussein was "trying once again to produce nuclear weapons.") At a minimum, Congress, which authorized the use of military force at the president's behest, should want to know if the assertions about Iraq were warranted.

I was convinced before the war that the threat of weapons of mass destruction in the hands of Saddam Hussein required a vigorous and sustained international response to disarm him. Iraq possessed and had used chemical weapons; it had an active biological weapons program and quite possibly a nuclear research program—all of which were in violation of United Nations resolutions. Having encountered Mr. Hussein and his thugs in the run-up to the Persian Gulf war of 1991, I was only too aware of the dangers he posed.

But were these dangers the same ones the administration told us about? We have to find out. America's foreign policy depends on the sanctity of its information. For this reason, questioning the selective use of intelligence to justify the war in Iraq is neither idle sniping nor "revisionist history," as Mr. Bush has suggested. The act of war is the last option of a democracy, taken when there is a grave threat to our national security. More than 200 American soldiers have lost their lives in Iraq already. We have a duty to ensure that their sacrifice came for the right reasons.

An Open Letter to the Senate Judiciary Committee

BRIGADIER GENERAL DAVID M. BRAHMS (RET. USMC) AND OTHERS

> Before the Senate confirmation hearings for Alberto Gonzales, nominee for Attorney General, a group of very senior retired military officers from many branches of the service detailed their concerns about Gonzales's memo on detention and interrogation. This letter is surprisingly straightforward in expressing the views of regular military officers about the importance of observing the rules of war as detailed in the Geneva Conventions and the *Army Field Manual*.

Dear Chairman Specter and Senator Leahy:

We, the undersigned, are retired professional military leaders of the U.S. Armed Forces. We write to express our deep concern about the nomination of Alberto R. Gonzales to be Attorney General, and to urge you to explore in detail his views concerning the role of the Geneva Conventions in U.S. detention and interrogation policy and practice.

During his tenure as White House Counsel, Mr. Gonzales appears to have played a significant role in shaping U.S. detention and interrogation operations in Afghanistan, Iraq, Guantánamo Bay, and elsewhere. Today, it is clear that these operations have fostered greater animosity toward the United States, undermined our intelligence gathering efforts, and added to the risks facing our troops serving around the world. Before Mr. Gonzales assumes the position of Attorney General, it is critical to understand whether he intends to adhere to the positions he adopted as White House Counsel, or chart a revised course more consistent with fulfilling our nation's complex security interests, and maintaining a military that operates within the rule of law.

Among his past actions that concern us most, Mr. Gonzales wrote to the President on January 25, 2002, advising him that the Geneva Conventions did not apply to the conflict then underway in

SOURCE: The text of this letter and detailed biographical information about the officers can be found at http://www.globalsecurity.org/military/library/report/2005/senate-judiciary-committee-letter_03jan2005.htm.

Afghanistan. More broadly, he wrote that the "war on terrorism" presents a "new paradigm [that] renders obsolete Geneva's" protections.

The reasoning Mr. Gonzales advanced in this memo was rejected by many military leaders at the time, including Secretary of State Colin Powell who argued that abandoning the Geneva Conventions would put our soldiers at greater risk, would "reverse over a century of U.S. policy and practice in supporting the Geneva Conventions," and would "undermine the protections of the rule of law for our troops, both in this specific conflict [Afghanistan] and in general." State Department adviser William H. Taft IV agreed that this decision "deprives our troops [in Afghanistan] of any claim to the protection of the Conventions in the event they are captured and weakens the protections afforded by the Conventions to our troops in future conflicts." Mr. Gonzales' recommendation also ran counter to the wisdom of former U.S. prisoners of war. As Senator John McCain has observed: "I am certain we all would have been a lot worse off if there had not been the Geneva Conventions around which an international consensus formed about some very basic standards of decency that should apply even amid the cruel excesses of war."

Mr. Gonzales' reasoning was also on the wrong side of history. Repeatedly in our past, the United States has confronted foes that, at the time they emerged, posed threats of a scope or nature unlike any we had previously faced. But we have been far more steadfast in the past in keeping faith with our national commitment to the rule of law. During the Second World War, General Dwight D. Eisenhower explained that the Allies adhered to the law of war in their treatment of prisoners because "the Germans had some thousands of American and British prisoners and I did not want to give Hitler the excuse or justification for treating our prisoners more harshly than he already was doing." In Vietnam, U.S. policy required that the Geneva Conventions be observed for all enemy prisoners of war—both North Vietnamese regulars and Viet Cong—even though the Viet Cong denied our own prisoners of war the same protections. And in the 1991 Persian Gulf War, the United States afforded Geneva Convention protections to more than 86,000 Iraqi prisoners of war held in U.S.

custody. The threats we face today—while grave and complex—no more warrant abandoning these basic principles than did the threats of enemies past.

Perhaps most troubling of all, the White House decision to depart from the Geneva Conventions in Afghanistan went hand in hand with the decision to relax the definition of torture and to alter interrogation doctrine accordingly. Mr. Gonzales' January 2002 memo itself warned that the decision not to apply Geneva Convention standards "could undermine U.S. military culture which emphasizes maintaining the highest standards of conduct in combat, and could introduce an element of uncertainty in the status of adversaries." Yet Mr. Gonzales then made that very recommendation with reference to Afghanistan, a policy later extended piece by piece to Iraq. Sadly, the uncertainty Mr. Gonzales warned about came to fruition. As James R. Schlesinger's panel reviewing Defense Department detention operations concluded earlier this year, these changes in doctrine have led to uncertainty and confusion in the field, contributing to the abuses of detainees at Abu Ghraib and elsewhere, and undermining the mission and morale of our troops.

The full extent of Mr. Gonzales' role in endorsing or implementing the interrogation practices the world has now seen remains unclear. A series of memos that were prepared at his direction in 2002 recommended official authorization of harsh interrogation methods, including waterboarding, feigned suffocation, and sleep deprivation. As with the recommendations on the Geneva Conventions, these memos ignored established U.S. military policy, including doctrine prohibiting "threats, insults, or exposure to inhumane treatment as a means of or aid to interrogation." Indeed, the August 1, 2002 Justice Department memo analyzing the law on interrogation references health care administration law more than five times, but never once cites the U.S. Army Field Manual on interrogation. The Army Field Manual was the product of decades of experience— experience that had shown, among other things, that such interrogation methods produce unreliable results and often impede further intelligence collection. Discounting the Manual's wisdom on this central point shows a disturbing disregard for the decades of hard-won knowledge of the professional American military.

The United States' commitment to the Geneva Conventions—the laws of war—flows not only from field experience, but also from the moral principles on which this country was founded, and by which we all continue to be guided. We have learned first hand the value of adhering to the Geneva Conventions and practicing what we preach on the international stage.

Signed,
Brigadier General David M. Brahms (Ret. USMC)
Brigadier General James Cullen (Ret. USA)
Brigadier General Evelyn P. Foote (Ret. USA)
Lieutenant General Robert Gard (Ret. USA)
Vice Admiral Lee F. Gunn (Ret. USN)
Admiral Don Guter (Ret. USN)
General Joseph Hoar (Ret. USMC)
Rear Admiral John D. Hutson (Ret. USN)
Lieutenant General Claudia Kennedy (Ret. USA)
General Merrill McPeak (Ret. USAF)
Major General Melvyn Montano (Ret. USAF Nat. Guard)
General John Shalikashvili (Ret. USA)

Part VI

Halting War Crimes:
A Shared Responsibility

INTRODUCTION

Few would argue that an ordinary citizen bears the same culpability for a war crime as someone who commits or orders one. But all who know about war crimes and fail to take measures to prevent them bear some degree of responsibility.

The Tokyo War Crimes Tribunal found that government officials, whether military or civilian, are responsible for war crimes if "they had knowledge that such crimes were being committed, and having such knowledge they failed to take such steps as were within their power to prevent the commission of such crimes in the future."[1]

Such responsibility is not limited to military personnel and government authorities, however. In the Zyklon B case, for example, the Nuremberg Tribunal found that "the provisions of the laws and customs of war are addressed not only to combatants and to members of state and other public authorities, but to anybody who is in a position to assist their violation." Indeed, as the Nuremberg Tribunal put it in the Flick case, international law "binds every citizen just as does ordinary municipal law."[2] We bear an additional responsibility as citizens of a democracy in which the ultimate authority rests with the people.

Governments have systems for investigating, apprehending, and prosecuting those who violate the law. But history shows many instances in which high government officials use their authority to protect themselves from legal accountability. The Bush administration has deliberately, systematically, and successfully incapacitated the conventional means of law enforcement. How, then, can it be held accountable?

The historian Jeremy Brecher points out that the ability of the Bush administration to pursue its criminal course with impunity depends on "implementation by government officials, support by political constituencies, acquiescence by the indifferent, and inefficacy and division among its opponents." Despite the Bush regime's current

[1] Leon Friedman, ed., *The Law of War: A Documentary History, Volume II* (New York: Random House, 1972), p. 1039.
[2] Quoted in John Carey, William V. Dunlap, and R. John Pritchard, eds., *International Humanitarian Law: Challenges* (Ardsley, N.Y.:Transnational Publishers, 2004), p. 79.

control of the means of law enforcement, its crimes can be brought to a halt if these "pillars of support" are withdrawn. Brecher compares the emerging movement against war crimes to resistance movements against dictatorships that have abolished basic constitutional freedoms. He lays out a strategy that combines revitalizing the institutions of accountability and undermining the Bush administration's pillars of support.

Elizabeth Holtzman, a veteran of the House Judiciary Committee that drew up articles of impeachment against Richard Nixon, explores possible avenues for holding the Bush administration accountable for war crimes through legal and political processes. These avenues might include congressional hearings, an independent commission, a special prosecutor, and other procedures. As she points out, the political process is unlikely to utilize these procedures without significant pressure from civil society, but they indicate targets to which such pressure might be directed.

The resistance to the Vietnam War provides one historical experience that illustrates how the withdrawal of support can undermine the power of governments to pursue unacceptable ends. Michael Ferber, a Vietnam War draft resister, describes how mass refusal to cooperate with the draft intensified public protest against the war and undermined the military's plans to expand the war by increasing the number of draftees. He indicates how similar effects might be achieved in today's very different environment.

Such action is already well under way—and today it is often explicitly tied to the obligation to resist war crimes. Part V already described the resistance of soldiers and government officials. In part VI we present four examples of ordinary people taking on their responsibilities for "citizen law enforcement." "Enforcing International Law Through Civil Disobedience: The Trial of the St. Patrick's Four" describes how a jury in Ithaca, New York, refused to convict protestors who defended their nonviolent disruption of a military recruitment center on the basis of the obligation to resist war crimes. "My Duty as an Able-Bodied American Citizen to Say No" presents the statements of four young women who committed civil disobedience to protest the attack on Iraq. "Reclaiming the Prophetic Voice" describes the strategy of one faith-based organization for mobilizing religious constituencies and the broader community to resist war crimes. In "Counterrecruitment: Cutting Off the Cannon Fodder," a young Latina activist gives an illustration of the growing campaign to help young people resist the blandishments of military recruiters.

These complementary "inside" and "outside" strategies reflect a deeper relation between the actions of governments and those of civil society. As the international law professor Richard Falk points out, the "idea that governments are responsible for adhering to international law" has been carried at two levels. The "governmental level" has "the capacity to impose punishments," but it so far allows "the exemption of leaders of dominant states from accountability." The "civic level" pursues a more consistent application of the law to the leaders of all countries, but lacks "the capacity to enforce" those standards. Civil society must "extend the reach of criminal accountability" to include "those leaders acting on behalf of dominant states." That is just what the emerging movement against American war crimes is trying to do.

Such an approach makes little sense if law is nothing but a means of enforcing the will of the powerful. In "Why War Crimes Matter," the legal scholar Brendan Smith argues that, despite its often-repressive role, both international and national law can also serve as a vehicle for citizens to limit the power of government officials and gain support for their own action. Just as the civil rights and women's movements illustrate how social movements can use the law in their wider strategies for social change, so the movement against war crimes can use the law as part of a strategy to stop the Bush administration's global agenda.

Affirmative Measures to Halt
U.S. War Crimes

JEREMY BRECHER

How can we, as Americans, meet our obligation to halt our country's war crimes? How can we impose law on a vastly powerful government controlled by a determined leadership who control many of the levers of institutional power? Jeremy Brecher, a historian of social movements and a coeditor of this book, points out that even the most autocratic government depends for its power on active supporters and an acquiescent population. He proposes a three-pronged strategy. First, encourage the American people to "repudiate the Bush administration's war crimes" as "contrary to their most cherished values, beliefs, and interests." Second, reinvigorate the "paralyzed institutions" that are supposed to "impose law and democracy on government." Third, undermine the Bush administration's power to commit war crimes by withdrawing popular and institutional cooperation and support.

The worst crimes were dared by a few, willed by more and tolerated by all.

> —Tacitus, *The Histories*

Even the most powerful cannot rule without the cooperation of the ruled.

> —Mohandas K. Gandhi, *Indian Opinion*,
> November 11, 1905

Morality, international law, the U.S. Constitution, and common sense provide many compelling reasons to take affirmative measures to bring the Bush administration's war crimes to a halt. But what might such measures be, and who is in a position to take them?

The Declaration of Independence asserts that "governments derive their just powers from the consent of the governed." Indeed governments derive even their unjust powers from the consent of the governed—or at least from their cooperation and acquiescence. The Bush administration could not last a week if government officials and the press refused to keep its secrets; judges declared its authority illegitimate; soldiers refused to fight its wars; young people refused to enlist in its army; and other countries refused to buy its Treasury bonds.

Like a guerrilla army emerging in response to a military occupation, a large and diverse movement—almost unrecognized even to itself—is arising to halt the Bush regime's war crimes. It is manifested in lawyers who bring war crimes charges against officials in the Bush administration; judges who reject unconstitutional claims to presidential authority; military and government whistle-blowers who reveal to the public what is actually going on in Iraq and in Washington; doctors who expose medical complicity in prisoner abuse; soldiers who refuse to fight in Iraq; people who support their refusal; and myriad ordinary citizens who have protested U.S. military actions in Iraq and beyond.

The halting of U.S. war crimes involves three mutually reinforcing processes. First, encouraging the American people to repudiate the Bush administration's war crimes as contrary to their most cherished values, beliefs, and interests. Second, reinvigorating the currently paralyzed institutions designed to impose law and democracy on government. Third, impeding the means for committing war crimes. These processes provide a broad strategy and concrete affirmative measures that all can take to halt Bush administration war crimes and bring government in line with national and international law.

PUBLIC REPUDIATION OF WAR CRIMES AND WAR CRIMINALS

The first corrective process is the broad public repudiation of U.S. war crimes and the consequent isolation of the Bush administration from public support. This is possible because the Bush project as a whole and in numerous specific actions contradicts the American people's beliefs in international law, constitutional government, and the need for international cooperation, morality, and common sense.

The Bush administration engages in preventive war and maintains that it has the right to do so without UN approval or immediate threat. The American people reject this view.[1] The American public, in contrast, has a strong and continuing belief that all nations, including the United States, are subject to international law. A 2004 poll by the University of Maryland, for example, found that "majorities of the public and leaders do not support states taking unilateral action to prevent other states from acquiring weapons of mass destruction, but do support this action if it has UN Security Council approval. They also both reject preventive unilateral war, but endorse a country's right to go to war on its own if there is strong evidence of an imminent threat." They apply this view to specific U.S. policies. For example, "Strong majorities of the public and leaders also believe the United States would need UN Security Council approval before using military force to destroy North Korea's nuclear capability."[2]

The Bush administration maintains that the President as commander in chief has the authority to attack other countries without congressional approval and torture prisoners without constraint by courts. The American people do not accept this abrogation of the Constitution and the rule of law. Nor do they accept the destruction of basic civil liberties in the name of the war against terror. Three hundred seventy-two local governments have passed resolutions demanding that Congress bring the Patriot Act in line with the Constitution.[3]

The Bush administration's belligerence and unilateralism has isolated the United States from the people and countries of the world. The American people believe that such isolation is dangerous.[4] In one

[1] Americans have tolerated the Bush regime's war crimes less because they don't believe in international law than because those crimes have often been presented as a fulfillment of international law. President Bush portrayed the U.S. attack on Iraq, for example, as the enforcement of UN Security Council resolutions.

[2] Chicago Council on Foreign Relations and University of Maryland Program on International Policy Attitudes (PIPA), "American Public Opinion and Foreign Policy," *Global Views 2004*, http://www.ccfr.org/globalviews2004/.

[3] ACLU release, "ACLU Calls on Gonzales to Engage in Open Dialogue on Patriot Act," March 7, 2005.

[4] See, e.g., University of Maryland Program on International Policy Attitudes release, September 8, 2004.

poll, more than three-quarters of Americans said that the United States should do its share to solve international problems together with other countries. About 70 percent agreed that the primary lesson of September 11 is that the United States needs to cooperate more with other countries to fight terrorism, as opposed to acting more on its own.[5] In contrast to the Bush administration, most Americans support participation in the International Criminal Court, strengthening the United Nations, contributing U.S. troops to UN peacekeeping missions, and signing the Land Mines Treaty.[6] It is doubtful that many Americans would think it wise for a country with 5 percent of the world's people to try to dominate the other 95 percent without their consent.

The forces opposed to U.S. war crimes can use these fundamental disagreements to isolate the Bush administration from public support. By making a public issue of specific violations of U.S. and international law, they can educate the public on what the law is, what the violations are, and why the laws that are being violated embody the interests and beliefs of the people.[7]

This educational process is well under way. In May 2005, for example, a report by Amnesty International set off a firestorm by calling the detention facility at Guantánamo Bay "the gulag of our times."[8] In an orchestrated counterattack, President Bush called the report "absurd"; Dick Cheney said he was "offended"; and Donald Rumsfeld called the comparison "reprehensible." An Amnesty International official characterized their responses as "typical of a government on the

5. PIPA release, January 18, 2005.

6. Ibid.

7. Foreign peoples and governments can contribute to this education by pressing their own governments to disassociate themselves from U.S. criminal activity; supporting the International Criminal Court; utilizing universal jurisdiction to hold U.S. officials accountable in court; and reaching out to Americans of all kinds to explain the significance of what the U.S. government is doing and supporting opposition to it. See Jeremy Brecher and Brendan Smith, "How the World Can Help Americans Halt Bush Administration War Crimes" (Silver City, N.M., and Washington, D.C.: Foreign Policy in Focus, June 8, 2005), available at www.fpif.org/papers/050haltbush .html) and Jeremy Brecher, Terminating the Bush Juggernaut (Silver City, N.M., and Washington, D.C.: Foreign Policy in Focus, May 2003), available at www.fpif.org/ papers/juggernaut/index.html.

8. Amnesty International, Report 2005, Foreword.

defensive."⁹ A *New York Times* editorial observed that "What makes Amnesty's gulag metaphor apt is that Guantánamo is merely one of a chain of shadowy detention camps that also includes Abu Ghraib in Iraq, the military prison at Bagram Air Base in Afghanistan and other, secret locations run by the intelligence agencies. Each has produced its own stories of abuse torture and criminal homicide. These are not isolated incidents, but part of a tightly linked global detention system with no accountability in law.¹⁰

REINVIGORATING THE INSTITUTIONS OF LAW AND DEMOCRACY

The second corrective process is to end the paralysis of the institutions responsible for maintaining accountability of government leaders. That means first of all the legal and political systems. Where they fail, responsibility also falls to institutions of civil society like the media, the academy, the labor movement, and religious communities.

Legal System

A properly functioning legal system investigates, apprehends, and sanctions those who violate the law. Many acts by the Bush regime on their face violate not only international but also U.S. law. But the Bush regime itself controls most of the means of investigation and prosecution and uses its administrative powers to cover up its crimes. Many federal judges have been appointed by President Bush or his Republican predecessors.

Nonetheless, there is a struggle going on within the legal system against the Bush administration's lawlessness and for an assertion of constitutional limits on presidential authority. That struggle involves lawyers, courts, and defendants charged with "crimes" of civil disobedience.

In struggles against autocratic regimes abroad, courts have often

---

9. Lizette Alvarez, "Rights Group Defends Chastising of U.S.," *New York Times*, June 4, 2005.

10. "Un-American by Any Name," *New York Times*, June 5, 2005.

played a critical role in delegitimating the illegal extension of executive powers. In Serbia and Ukraine, for example, courts refused to go along with political leaders' efforts to manipulate the electoral process. Courts are now playing a role in limiting excess claims of executive power in the United States. The Supreme Court's ruling that the Guantánamo prisoners are subject to the jurisdiction of U.S. courts placed the first significant restrictions on the Bush administration's claims that the President as commander in chief can do whatever he chooses without any accountability to anyone. In response to suits brought by the ACLU and others, courts have ordered the release of thousands of pages of documents that have revealed for the first time the extent of torture and prisoner abuse and the crucial role of officials at the highest level.

Defending acts of civil disobedience provides a further opportunity to get the issue of war crimes into U.S. courts. Such actions need not be just individual protests but rather can be the focus of massive and diverse resistance and educational activities. Lawyers not only can provide legal assistance but also can organize to support and publicize the resisters' case.

Actions oriented toward the legal system can weaken the Bush regime's ability to commit war crimes in two ways. When successful in court, they can put limits on the regime's freedom of action and force it to disclose the evidence it has tried to conceal. Whether successful or not, they provide a vehicle for dramatizing the evidence of war crimes and the argument that their perpetrators must be held accountable.

If its power is threatened, the Bush administration may well respond by using its control of the legal system to punish those who would try to hold it accountable for war crimes. But such actions can often be countered by a kind of "political jujitsu" in which the acts of repression themselves become the symbols of the regime's illegitimacy—as Nixon's burglaries, wiretaps, and other "dirty tricks" against opponents became the source of his downfall. Such abuse of power can be utilized to show the public that the regime's purpose is not to protect the American people or bring democracy to the world, but rather to protect war criminals from accountability.

Political System

The American political system has been deeply complicit in the Bush administration's war crimes. While many congressional Democrats voted against authorizing war on Iraq, many others and almost all Republicans supported it. Presidential candidate John Kerry called for more troops for the Iraq occupation and barely mentioned such scandals as Abu Ghraib and Guantánamo. Initial congressional hearings on Abu Ghraib and other obvious war crimes were so desultory as to comprise part of the cover up.

The confirmation hearings on Alberto Gonzales constituted an early attempt to begin holding the Bush administration accountable to Congress for its crimes. Democratic opposition far exceeded expectations because, as Senator Russ Feingold put it, "He simply refused to say without equivocation that the president is not above the law." Thirty-five Democratic senators voted against Gonzales's confirmation.

The Gonzales hearings revealed the emergence of a new national coalition opposed to the Bush violations of international law and the Constitution. It included major law and human rights organizations; religious leaders; and retired generals, admirals, and diplomats. This coalition is likely to be the spearhead of future efforts to hold the Bush administration accountable for war crimes in the political arena. It is calling for further congressional hearings and an independent investigation of prisoner abuse by a special prosecutor or independent commission.

Under pressure from civil society, the political system has begun to respond. Congressman Edward Markey successfully attached a House amendment to the 2005 Iraq emergency supplemental appropriation bill prohibiting the U.S. government from continuing the practice of extraordinary rendition.[11] Congresswoman Barbara Lee has

[11.] Further information about the Markey amendment is available at http://www.house.gov/markey/Issues/iss_human_rights_2pr050316.pdf. On June 16, 2004, the Senate unanimously adopted an anti-torture amendment to the Defense Department Authorization bill. Senator Dick Durbin offered the amendment; cosponsors were Senators McCain, Specter, Levin, Feinstein, Leahy, and Kennedy. The House took no action, however. Later in the year, the Senate approved an amendment to its Intelligence Reform bill, S. 2845, which would have extended the ban to the CIA, by introduced a resolution calling for Congress to disavow "the doctrine of preemption because it poses a threat to international law and to the national security interests of the United States."[12] Congresswoman Lynn Woolsey, along with twenty-seven of her colleagues, has introduced a resolution calling for the immediate withdrawal of U.S. troops from Iraq.[13]

Such efforts accelerated after Amnesty International called Guantánamo "the Gulag of our time." Two days after the Amnesty International report, top Democratic representatives led by Rep. Henry Waxman announced plans to introduce legislation to create a bipartisan House select committee to investigate the evidence of detainee abuse and torture in Iraq, Afghanistan, and Guantánamo Bay. Supporters included Democratic Leader Nancy Pelosi, Democratic Whip Steny Hoyer, House Democratic Caucus Chairman Robert Menendez, and many other leading House Democrats. "The failure of Congress to conduct responsible oversight, which is our constitutional duty, is shameful," Waxman observed.[14] A few days later, Democratic Senator Joseph Biden introduced a bill to create a commission to study allegations of detainee abuse and called for Guantánamo to be shut down.[15]

When political leaders become too isolated from the values and interests of those they represent, they become vulnerable. "The internal stability of a regime can be measured by the ratio between the number and strength of the social forces that it controls or conciliates, in a word, represents, and the number and strength of the social

---

a vote of 96 to 2. The amendment was dropped from the conference committee's final bill at the urging of then–National Security Director Condoleezza Rice. See http://www.bordc.org/legislation.htm.

[12] H. Con. Res 141 is available at http://www.fcnl.org/issues/int/sup/iraq_resolution-lee 318-03.htm.

[13] H. Con Res. 35 text available at http://www.woolsey.house.gov/newsarticle.asp?RecordID=401.

[14] "Democrats to Introduce Legislation to Create Select Committee to Investigate Prisoner Abuse," press release, May 27, 2005, and "Dems Introduce Bill Aiming to Create Committee to Investigate Abuse," *Raw Story*, May 27, 2005.

[15] E. J. Dionne, Jr., "Hyperbole and Human Rights," *Washington Post*, June 3, 2005.

forces that it fails to represent and has against it."[16] Lyndon Johnson, after the greatest presidential election victory in history, withdrew from the campaign for reelection. The reason? He had led the United States into a catastrophic war that had been repudiated by the American people. Richard Nixon triumphed over the peace candidate George McGovern. Within a few months he had resigned from office in disgrace. The reason? He engaged in multiple criminal activities that violated the basic norms and values of the American people, especially undermining the law and the Constitution. If the Bush administration comes to be widely perceived as pursuing an illegal and unpopular war by criminal means, all the bombs in the Pentagon's arsenal will be inadequate to protect its power.

Civil Society

Where legal and political institutions fail to control governmental crime, civil society organizations often provide the next line of defense for democracy and the rule of law. The media, the academy, the labor movement, and religious communities can be important arenas for action.

From 9/11 through the invasion of Iraq, the U.S. media largely abandoned their responsibility to ask critical questions and investigate official lies and malfeasance. Since the Iraq occupation, however, the media have played a key, though still far from adequate, role in exposing U.S. war crimes.

Universities have been a primary recruiting ground for the cadres of the Bush administration and for the arguments justifying their crimes. But scholars have also provided some of the challenges to those arguments. Law professors like Harold Koh, Dean of the Yale Law School, have demolished the legal views put forward by Alberto Gonzales and others. Archaeologists like MacGuire Gibson of the University of Chicago warned against and then decried the destruction of the treasures of early civilization in Iraq. Medical pro-

---

[16.] Quoted in Gene Sharp, *The Politics of Nonviolent Action*, vol. 1, *Power and Struggle* (Boston: Porter Sargent, 1973), pp. 15–16.

fessionals have exposed the death and disease propagated by the U.S. occupation of Iraq.

The AFL-CIO has refused to support the Iraq war the way it did the Vietnam War, but it has also failed to oppose it. However, a very active U.S. Labor Against the War organization has mobilized many unions and many rank-and-file trade unionists against the Iraq war.

Many denominations and parishes actively opposed the U.S. attack on Iraq. After the attack their activity diminished. The beginning of 2005 saw the emergence of new forms of religious opposition, such as the founding of the group Clergy and Laity Concerned About Iraq.

All of these spheres provide arenas for education about the Bush administration's war crimes and for organizing resistance to them.

IMPEDING WAR CRIMES

The third corrective process is resistance to war criminals' illegitimate authority. The Bush administration's capacity to commit war crimes depends on having soldiers, mercenaries, intelligence agents, government officials, and others who will obey orders. And it depends on having an acquiescent population who will not impede their actions.

As we saw in part V, resistance in the military and refusal to reenlist is growing. So is refusal to enlist—aided by counterrecruitment efforts. And so is the revelation of war crimes and cover-ups by military and civilian whistle-blowers. These are all encouraged by growing public disaffection with the Iraq war and other Bush policies.

While refusal to fight directly weakens the capacity of the Bush regime to engage in war crimes, it also has powerful secondary effects. Such refusals pose stark moral questions to other people and call them to examine their own responsibilities.

Soldiers and their families have a special place in the mythology used to silence opposition to war. War supporters often portray questioning of government policy as a desecration of their service and sacrifice. But when the soldiers and their families begin to question the morality and legality of a war, this pillar of support is threatened.[17]

Refusal to fight also makes the top military brass and other policy makers worry that the military may become a "broken force" filled with demoralized troops, losing prestige, confronting negative public opinion, and held in contempt in foreign countries.

If the Bush regime is unable to raise the troops it needs for its global ventures, it will be forced either to give up those ventures or to turn to conscription—an alternative whose political impact the administration must shudder to even consider.

Not everyone is in a position to refuse to fight. But U.S. laws make it a crime to "aid, counsel, or abet" draft resistance, desertion, or refusal of military orders. A growing number of people are taking a stand against a criminal war and its associated war crimes by publicly violating those laws.

If broad public opposition, the reinvigoration of the institutions of democratic accountability, and the growth of military and civilian resistance are not sufficient to bring the Bush administration's war crimes to a halt, they may lay the groundwork for the use of mass action for that purpose. During the late 1960s, opponents of the Vietnam War organized a recurrent event called the Moratorium. Once a month people around the country protested in whatever way they considered suitable—from shutting down schools and workplaces to holding seminars, religious services, rallies, and marches. By October 1969, an estimated two million Americans were participating.

Democratization movements in other countries have often staged similar periodic mass protests—even if in a repressive envi-

---

[17.] Abuse of those in the military has accelerated this process. Short on troops, in 2004 the military began a "stop-loss" policy of involuntarily extending enlistments—in reality conscription of those already in the military. Bogged down in a war it hadn't planned for, the Pentagon was often unable to provide armor and supplies for its troops. In an act of supreme contempt for those who had served their country, the army's Walter Reed Medical Center in Washington, D.C., started making some wounded soldiers pay for the food they eat at the hospital. People in the military and their families began to question these conditions—leading to lawsuits against the Pentagon and highly publicized confrontations between angry GIs and the Secretary of Defense.

ronment people could do no more than beat pots out of their windows. More recently, mass mobilizations have defended democracy and constitutional rule in Serbia, Ukraine, and many other countries.[18] Ultimately there will have to be, in Gandhi's phrase, a "matching of forces" between the people of the United States and those who claim the right to nullify both the U.S. Constitution and international law.

It is not possible to project an exact scenario for terminating the Bush regime's war crimes and bringing those responsible to justice. A chain will break at its weakest link, but it is often impossible to know which link is weakest until the pressure is applied. Affirmative measures are needed to increase the pressure until these war crimes are brought to a halt. Such action can provide a starting point for bringing the officials of all states, whether weak or strong, under the rule of law.

[18.] For accounts of a wide range of democratization movements, see Gene Sharp, *Waging Nonviolent Struggle* (Boston: Porter Sargent, 2005). The approach proposed in this article draws heavily on Sharp's three-volume *Politics of Nonviolent Action* (Boston: Porter Sargent, 1980).

Watergate and Abu Ghraib: Holding War Criminals Accountable in the U.S. Courts and Congress

ELIZABETH HOLTZMAN

The attorney Elizabeth Holtzman served four terms in the U.S. Congress, where she played a key role in the Watergate investigations as a member of the House Judiciary Committee that drew up the articles of impeachment against President Richard Nixon. In 1973 she won a court order halting the bombing of Cambodia, which went all the way to the Supreme Court before it was ultimately overturned. She has served as Brooklyn district attorney and New York City comptroller. She recently forced the CIA to agree to release all information on cooperation of U.S. intelligence agencies with former Nazis.

In the following article Holtzman lays out possible ways to hold the Bush administration accountable for criminal acts. The War Crimes Act, the Torture Act, and other legislation by Congress have incorporated important aspects of international law in the U.S. criminal code— and thereby made top government officials subject to investigation and prosecution for war crimes. But only public pressure is likely to bring such law enforcement into effect.

Although the terrible revelations of torture at Abu Ghraib surfaced in April 2004, no higher-ups have yet been held accountable. The fact of the torture has shamed and outraged many Americans, in addition to creating a greater threat of terrorism against the United States. But it has prompted no investigative commissions with a mandate to find the whole truth or full-scale congressional hearings on who was responsible.

Nonetheless, higher-ups can be held to account. Difficult as it may be, our institutions of government can be pressured to do the right thing, and public and media insistence on thorough investigations and appropriate punishments for those responsible, no matter how high up the chain of command, could bring about those results.

There are several examples of how public opposition changed even the most entrenched government policy. Neither President

Johnson nor President Nixon wanted to end the Vietnam War, but growing public anger—characterized by growing demonstrations, among other things—forced Congress, finally, to end the war. Similarly, in Watergate, Congress did not commence impeachment proceedings to hold President Nixon accountable for the obstruction of justice and other abuses that had become increasingly apparent, until the American people demanded action after the Saturday night massacre. (That was when Nixon fired Special Prosecutor Archibald Cox to keep him from getting incriminating personal tape recordings.) And, of course, the most important example of the last fifty years is the civil rights movement, which changed the system of segregation in the South through sustained and peaceful public protest.

THE WAR CRIMES ACT OF 1996

No less a person than Alberto Gonzales, then White House Counsel to President George W. Bush, expressed deep concern about possible prosecutions under the War Crimes Act of 1996 for U.S. mistreatment of Afghanistan war detainees.

This relatively obscure statute makes it a federal crime to violate certain provisions of the Geneva Conventions. The Act punishes any U.S. national, military or civilian, who commits a "grave breach" of the Geneva Conventions. A grave breach includes the "willful killing, torture or inhuman treatment" of detainees. Violations of the statute that result in death carry the death penalty.

In a memo to President Bush, dated January 25, 2002, Gonzales urged that the U.S. opt out of the Geneva Conventions for the Afghanistan war—despite Secretary of State Colin Powell's objections. One of the two reasons he gave the President was that opting out *"substantially reduces the likelihood of prosecution under the War Crimes Act."* [Emphasis added.]

Attorney General John Ashcroft also sent a memo to President Bush making a similar argument. Opting out of the Geneva Conventions, Ashcroft said, would give the "highest assurance" that there would be no prosecutions under the War Crimes Act of "military officers, intelligence officials or law enforcement officials" for their misconduct during interrogations or detention.

Plainly, both Gonzales and Ashcroft were so concerned about preventing War Crimes Act prosecutions that they were willing to risk having the United States come under serious international criticism, and even possibly exposing our own captured troops to mistreatment, which opting out of Geneva could cause.

The specter of prosecution was particularly troublesome because the Conventions used broad terminology. Noting that violations may consist of "outrages upon personal dignity" and "inhuman treatment," Gonzales advised the President in his memo that it would be "difficult to predict with confidence" which actions would constitute violations of the War Crimes Act and which would not.

Moreover, Gonzales opined, it was "difficult to predict the motives of prosecutors and independent counsels" acting in the future. (The "future" could be a very long time indeed, because there would be no statute of limitations on War Crimes Act prosecutions where the victim died.)

Although Gonzales did not spell out which government officials he was worried about, his reference to "independent counsels" suggests that he was focusing on prosecutions of highest-level individuals. In the past, "independent counsels" had been appointed to investigate both President Nixon and President Clinton. (During Watergate and for a time afterward, the independent counsel was called a special prosecutor.) The independent counsel statute, which had recently expired, applied to presidents and other highest-level government officials.

President Bush followed the advice given by his White House Counsel and his Attorney General with some slight modifications. It remains to be seen whether the gimmick of "opting out" of the Geneva Conventions for the war in Afghanistan will provide the promised "solid defense" to prosecution.

PROSECUTIONS UNDER THE WAR CRIMES ACT FOR U.S. MISCONDUCT IN IRAQ

Whatever its applicability to Afghanistan, the applicability of the War Crimes Act to Iraq is an entirely different matter. Under Gonzales's logic, the War Crimes Act applies whenever the Geneva

Conventions apply. Since President Bush has repeatedly stated that the Geneva Conventions apply to Iraq, the War Crimes Act applies to Iraq and imposes criminal penalties for serious mistreatment of detainees by U.S. personnel in Iraq.

Prosecutions under the War Crimes Act for violations in Iraq do not need to challenge the legality of "opting out of the Geneva Conventions." Nor do they need to deal with the issues involving the Administration's convoluted definition of torture; violations of the War Crimes Act can consist of inhuman treatment alone—whether torture took place or not.

Although the term *inhuman treatment* is not defined in the War Crimes Act or in the Geneva Conventions, there is little doubt, using the normal meaning of the phrase, that U.S. personnel subjected Iraqi detainees to inhuman treatment by, for example, forcing hooded prisoners into stressful positions for lengthy periods of time, using dogs to bite and intimidate naked prisoners, compelling prisoners to engage in or simulate sexual acts, dragging naked prisoners on the ground with a leash around the neck, beating prisoners, and on and on.

A huge body of evidence documents the inhuman treatment, aside from the notorious Abu Ghraib photos. Major General Antonio Taguba's inquiry found "sadistic, blatant and wanton criminal abuses." The report issued by a panel headed by former Secretary of Defense James Schlesinger found "widespread" abuses. And the International Red Cross repeatedly protested the treatment of Iraqi prisoners.

The key question, however, is not just whether inhuman treatment occurred in violation of the War Crimes Act, but how high up the responsibility goes for those abhorrent acts. Under well-established principles of international law, officials in the chain of command who order the inhuman treatment or who, knowing about it, fail to stop it are responsible. Although not completely free from doubt, even if the "chain of command" doctrine were not incorporated into the War Crimes Act, higher-ups would likely be responsible for ordering inhuman treatment under normal federal criminal law principles of conspiracy or aiding or abetting the crime. This was undoubtedly the reason that Gonzales wanted to block possible future prosecutions of higher-ups by "independent counsels."

President Bush likes to blame a few "bad apples" for the serious mistreatment of Iraqi prisoners. But the problem is not limited to a few bad apples at the bottom of the barrel. For example, Lieutenant General Ricardo Sanchez, the top military officer in Iraq, ordered inhuman treatment at least for a brief period of time, before he revised the interrogation protocols. Secretary of Defense Donald Rumsfeld issued orders for interrogation that were later withdrawn after protest by military lawyers. Did Secretary Rumsfeld and Lieutenant General Sanchez violate the War Crimes Act?

And what about President Bush himself? At a congressional hearing shortly after the Abu Ghraib story broke, Attorney General Ashcroft testified that President Bush never ordered the torture of the Afghanistan war and Iraqi detainees. But the Attorney General did not describe what the President did order, and all presidential directives on interrogations have not been made public.

In making his claim, the Attorney General may have been using the now discarded Orwellian definition of *torture* that the Justice Department devised specifically to avoid prosecutions under the U.S. statute making it a crime to engage in torture (Section 2340–2340A of the U.S. Code, Title 18).

Under Justice's notoriously narrow definition, torture was not torture if the torturer was simply seeking information from the victim. Only gratuitous or purely sadistic torture qualified as torture. Moreover, to meet the definition, the pain caused had to be the equivalent of losing an organ or bodily function, or dying. It is very unlikely that the President or any high-level U.S. official ordered torture for torture's sake, so Ashcroft's testimony to that extent may have been perfectly truthful. (That definition of *torture* was formally abandoned just before Gonzales's confirmation hearings, undoubtedly to avoid extensively publicizing the fact that extremely cruel and vicious treatment of prisoners had been authorized at the highest levels of our government.)

On the other hand, there are tantalizing suggestions that Ashcroft, even though truthful, may have been incorrect. For example, in a May 22, 2004, memo about interrogations in Iraq, made public by court order, an FBI agent repeatedly cites an Executive Order issued by President Bush that authorized "e.g., sleep deprivation, stress positions, loud music, etc." (The FBI claims that its agent was mistaken.)

In addition, President Bush's oft-quoted Executive Order of February 7, 2002, requiring that detainees be treated humanely, by its very terms does not apply to the CIA. That leaves open the question of what standards of interrogation the President laid out for the CIA and whether his failure to impose the requirement of humane treatment on the CIA signaled permission for that agency to engage in torture or inhuman treatment of detainees. The possibility that the CIA engaged in torture or inhuman treatment of detainees was given greater substance when Porter Goss, Director of the CIA, testified in March 2005 that the CIA was not at that time using torture against detainees, but refused to testify about past practices except behind closed doors. (It was also given further substance by reports that some CIA personnel were dismayed at the change in the definition of *torture*, which could expose them to liability under the antitorture act.)

To resolve the question, then, of the responsibility of higher-ups for torture and inhuman treatment in Iraq, there needs to be full disclosure of directives issued by the President and other top officials on the treatment of detainees and a full inquiry into what the President and other top government officials knew about the serious mistreatment of detainees and what steps they took to stop the mistreatment once it came to their attention.

If the President did authorize inhuman treatment, or if he knew it was ongoing and failed to stop it, is he punishable under the War Crimes Act? White House Counsel Gonzales did not put limits on who might be liable in his January 2002 memo. But the Attorney General in his congressional testimony specifically denied that President Bush committed any crime. In so doing, the Attorney General may have been relying on a doctrine (advanced by the Justice Department in its memorandum on the definition of *torture*) that a president, as commander in chief and acting in the interest of national security, can override U.S. laws. During his confirmation hearings to replace Ashcroft, Alberto Gonzales was repeatedly asked to repudiate the position that a president has the right as commander in chief to break U.S. laws, but refused to do so.

The claim that a president, whether President Bush or any other president, is above the law strikes at the very heart of our democracy. It was the centerpiece of President Richard Nixon's defense in Watergate — one that was rejected by the courts and lay at the foundation of the articles of impeachment voted against him by the House Judiciary Committee.

Of course, the national security argument in Watergate was a red herring. President Nixon's men's break-in at a psychiatrist's office and the wiretapping of journalists and White House staff phones, among other things, had nothing to do with national security but instead were blatantly political efforts to get damaging information on political opponents.

Courts have not directly ruled on a president's powers to violate the U.S. antitorture statute or the War Crimes Act. But they have found limits on a president's claims of unchecked power as commander in chief. The U.S. Supreme Court rejected President Harry Truman's claim that as commander in chief he could seize steel mills during the Korean War to keep them running. Similarly, the Supreme Court repudiated President George W. Bush's claim that as commander in chief he had unlimited powers to incarcerate prisoners at Guantánamo. As Justice Sandra Day O'Connor stated, "A state of war is not a blank check for the President." Indeed, Congress itself during the Vietnam War used its power of the purse to impose restrictions on the conduct of the war, including, for example, prohibiting incursions into Cambodia after the fatal Kent State shootings.

Although untested as a check on presidential power, the War Crimes Act of 1996 may yet fulfill Gonzales's darkest fear and become a crucial tool for holding presidents and other top officials accountable for inhuman treatment and torture — and, thus, of preserving the rule of law in America.

HOLDING HIGH ADMINISTRATION OFFICIALS ACCOUNTABLE

It is never easy to hold powerful officials accountable for their misdeeds, but it is still important to try to do so. Even if, after a full investigation, no higher-ups turn out to be responsible under U.S. civil or criminal laws for the terrible misdeeds at Abu Ghraib and elsewhere, the mere fact of a thorough and serious inquiry could go far in preventing similar abuses in the future.

If Watergate is any example, accountability at the highest level requires a number of factors: public exposure of the misdeeds; public awareness that the misdeeds violate the law; independent and fearless public officials and prosecutors—and of course a crusading press.

EDUCATING THE PUBLIC AND THE PRESS

The press plays a key role in educating both public officials and the American people about a problem and focusing attention on it. In Watergate, it was the work of the press, and in particular the persistence of two enterprising young *Washington Post* reporters, Bob Woodward and Carl Bernstein, that laid the groundwork for the resignation of President Nixon and the conviction of his top aides, two Attorneys General, and several Cabinet Secretaries for an assortment of crimes against our democracy.

While the press did a generally excellent job in breaking the Abu Ghraib story and in educating the American public about the facts of the brutal mistreatment of prisoners that took place there and elsewhere, it has not focused as much on the question of high-level accountability for those acts.

The consequences are predictable. Take the example of Gonzales's January 2002 memo to President Bush. The media gave substantial coverage to his recommendation that the United States opt out of the Geneva Conventions. The media also focused on his first reason for the recommendation: that the Conventions were "quaint" and inapplicable to the "new" paradigm of twenty-first-century terrorism. The public outcry was predictable.

But the press did not pay similar attention to Gonzales's second reason: that opting out would reduce the possibility of prosecutions under the War Crimes Act. As a result, the American people remained largely in the dark about the War Crimes Act. They generally did not know that the Act made it a federal crime to engage in inhuman treatment of detainees, or that the Act applied to Iraq.

They did not know that, by recommending that the United States opt out of Geneva, the White House counsel—and the President apparently through his approval—were trying to create a legal loophole that would permit U.S. government personnel to engage in possible criminal behavior with impunity. It was entirely predictable, under these circumstances, that there would be no public outcry about violations of the War Crimes Act or a broad demand for accountability of higher-ups under it.

It is also not surprising that little attention was paid to the War Crimes Act during the hearings on Gonzales's confirmation as Attorney General. It would have been easy to ask Gonzales what actions by U.S. officials gave rise to his concern about possible prosecution under the War Crimes Act. It would also have been easy to ask what U.S. officials he was worried about. But for some reason, the press never did, and the Senate showed a lack of curiosity about the subject.

Questions about the War Crimes Act would have been particularly apt because as Attorney General, Mr. Gonzales might have to prosecute violations of the Act—and his role in trying to shield government officials from prosecution under the Act could raise possible issues of conflict of interest.

How can the press be encouraged to report about this issue? Perhaps the best way to get the press to take this subject seriously is to make it clear that the potential liability of higher-ups is not a frivolous matter. No less a personage than a White House Counsel, later Attorney General, believed that the U.S. criminal law (including the War Crimes Act) imposed possible criminal liability on those who seriously mistreated detainees. International, if not U.S., law might then impose criminal liability on those who ordered or condoned the serious mistreatment.

There is no certain way to educate the press. One method is to get experts in the subject matter, such as respected legal scholars, to write about it—in books, articles, and op-eds. (A White Paper would be a very useful beginning.) These writings could then be circulated to editorial writers, managing editors of papers, columnists, and reporters. Letters to the editor of newspapers and magazines could refer to those writings and question why higher-ups have not been held accountable—as well as demand more coverage of the subject.

These writings could be circulated in ways designed to reach a larger public—through Web sites, blogs, and the like. Peaceful protests and the use of celebrities are other ways to attract attention to the problem.

Once this issue is seriously covered by the press and the public begins to express serious concern about it, there is much greater likelihood that Congress might initiate efforts to investigate and hold higher-ups accountable.

OPTIONS FOR CONGRESSIONAL ACTION

What actions could Congress take? Given that the President's party controls both the House and the Senate, it is unlikely that any serious action will be taken by either congressional body to uncover wrongdoing by higher-ups in the mistreatment of U.S. detainees. Nonetheless, it is important to understand what needs to be done.

The best outcome would be to have full congressional hearings or a fully independent inquiry conducted by a commission such as the so-called 9/11 panel. That inquiry should have the power to seek all documents (including presidential documents) respecting the treatment of detainees, and to question higher-ups, including Secretary Rumsfeld and the President himself. The objective of the inquiry would be to see who, including those at the highest level of our government, directed the inhuman treatment (or torture) of detainees, and what those officials did, if anything, when they learned of the mistreatment. If the inquiry found that the President or Secretary of Defense (or other high-level government officials) directed or knowingly condoned the inhuman treatment or torture of U.S. detainees, a special prosecutor should be appointed, with guarantees of full independence, to determine whether there is any criminal liability under the War Crimes Act (and the U.S. antitorture statute) or any other applicable criminal statute. Unlike Whitewater investigator Kenneth Starr, the special prosecutor should have no political ties to the administration or its political opponents.

Short of that result, there is still much that public officials can do.

Members of Congress and the Senate could write and ask Gonzales to identify which persons he was trying to protect from prosecution—and what acts they engaged in or were expected to engage in—as referred to in his January 2002 memo to President Bush. They could ask the White House for all orders and directives issued or signed by the President with respect to the treatment of detainees, whether at Abu Ghraib or elsewhere. They could request all documents that would have alerted the President and other top officials to the conditions of interrogation and documents that would have reflected oral briefings of top officials about these conditions. Legislation could be introduced requiring the disclosure of this information, if it is not otherwise forthcoming.

Even if the President's party blocks hearings, refuses to issue subpoenas for documents showing the involvement of higher-ups in the inhuman treatment of U.S. detainees, or stymies other legislative approaches to get at the full truth, congresspersons and senators can still act on the problem. They can still raise public awareness of the need for full disclosure and increase public pressure for action by introducing bills, holding press conferences, writing letters to appropriate officials, asking questions at hearings, and so forth.

In addition, there may be other legislative steps that cannot be blocked by a partisan majority. Take, for example, an obscure parliamentary device that allows members of the House of Representatives to pose factual questions to the President or members of his cabinet. The resolution is privileged, which means that any congressperson introducing it may call it up for a vote on the House floor at any time—something that is not normally the case for other resolutions and bills—and control half of the one hour of debate permitted. (A resolution of inquiry was used to force the House inquiry into President Ford's pardon of Richard Nixon.) While the resolution seeking the information may be defeated or referred to a committee (and thus consigned to oblivion), the debate on the floor of the House could generate substantial publicity and could create additional momentum for investigation or disclosure.

If Attorney General Alberto Gonzales appears at any future hearings, such as hearings involving the Justice Department, or if he is nominated for any other position in government, questions about criminal liability under the War Crimes Act could be raised at that time. Similarly, if there is a vacancy in the position of Attorney

General and someone else is appointed, that person, as a condition of confirmation, could be asked to conduct a full investigation into criminal liability under the War Crimes Act.

In this respect, Watergate provides some guidance. Special Prosecutor Archibald Cox was appointed only because of a series of happenstances. Prior to his appointment, the possibility had surfaced that higher-ups might be involved in the Watergate break-in and cover-up. As luck would have it, there was a vacancy in the position of Attorney General. Both Attorneys General John Mitchell and Richard Kleindienst had resigned because of their connection to the Watergate scandal. When President Nixon nominated Elliot Richardson to fill the vacancy, the Senate refused to confirm him unless he agreed to appoint a special prosecutor with full independence. Richardson complied. In that case, senators knew there had to be a thorough criminal investigation into Watergate and used the leverage of the Senate confirmation hearings to get their way. That is a far cry from what occurred during the process of confirming Gonzales for Attorney General—even making allowances for the fact that the President's party controlled the Senate.

Still, calls for the appointment of a special prosecutor by the Attorney General to investigate possible criminal liability under the War Crimes (and antitorture) laws can be issued, and members of Congress and the Senate can press for it.

In the final analysis, there is no sure way to compel the government to investigate itself or to hold high-level government officials accountable under applicable criminal statutes. But if the public does not seek to have it happen, it will not happen. Those in the public who care deeply about the rule of law and government accountability must keep this issue alive. Failure to investigate wrongdoing in high places and tolerating misconduct or criminality can have only the most corroding impact on our democracy and the rule of law that sustains us.

Blue-Ribbon Panel Calls for Independent Commission on Prisoner Abuse

THE CONSTITUTION PROJECT'S LIBERTY AND
SECURITY INITIATIVE

In the summer of 2005, pressure began to build for a full investigation of prisoner abuse in Afghanistan, Iraq, and Guantánamo. A distinguished bipartisan group called for an independent commission, modeled on the 9/11 Commission, to investigate allegations of abuse of terrorist suspects. Signers included former UN Ambassador Thomas Pickering, former FBI Director William Sessions, and former news anchor Walter Cronkite. Notably, the group included such conservative figures as David Keene, Chairman of the American Conservative Union, Bob Barr, former Republican member of Congress, and Dr. Roger Pilon, Vice President for Legal Affairs, Cato Institute. The statement was subsequently endorsed by Marine Corps Brigadier General (Ret.) David Brahms, Navy Rear Admiral (Ret.) John Hutson, and the National Institute of Military Justice. The statement was prepared by the Constitution Project, an initiative based at the Georgetown University Public Policy Institute, which "seeks consensus solutions to difficult legal and constitutional issues" through "constructive dialogue across ideological and partisan lines."

We [the undersigned members of the Constitution Project's Liberty and Security Initiative] request that the Congress and the President establish a bipartisan commission, modeled after the 9/11 Commission, to investigate the issue of prisoner abuse. Specifically, we recommend that such a bipartisan commission investigate the various allegations of abuse of terrorist suspects by the United States, and make recommendations to guide U.S. officials in the future.

We recognize that several government investigations are already underway or have recently been completed. However, these investigations, including the recently completed Pentagon report, are not government-wide, and are not structured to provide recommendations to the President and the Congress on specific measures that might be taken to prevent any such abuse in the future. One of

SOURCE: Statement of the Constitution Project's Liberty and Security Initiative, released May 25, 2005, by the Constitution Project, available at www.constitutionproject.org.

the principal accomplishments of the 9/11 Commission was the comprehensive and detailed list of recommendations it provided. We believe a similar approach is warranted in the context of prisoner abuse allegations.

We also recognize the complexity of the tasks faced by those charged with defending our nation's security in an age of global terror. In our view, however, that very complexity creates a need for a high-level, broad-gauged panel to assess the national security, foreign policy and human rights implications of the issue. The experience of the 9/11 Commission demonstrates that such a panel can engage in credible, effective fact-finding and can propose reforms that garner support from both the executive and legislative branches, as well as the public.

Members of the Liberty and Security Initiative Who Have Endorsed the Statement Above:*

CO-CHAIRS
David Cole, Professor of Law, Georgetown University Law Center.
David Keene, Chairman, American Conservative Union.

MEMBERS
Floyd Abrams, Esq., Partner, Cahill Gordon & Reindel LLP.
Dr. Azizah Y. al-Hibri, Professor, The T. C. Williams School of Law, University of Richmond; President, Karamah: Muslim Women Lawyers for Human Rights.
Bob Barr, Member of Congress (1995–2003); CEO, Liberty Strategies, LLC; the 21st Century Liberties Chair for Freedom and Privacy at the American Conservative Union; Chairman of Patriots to Restore Checks and Balances; practicing attorney; Consultant on Privacy Matters for the ACLU.
Walter Cronkite, former Managing Editor, CBS Evening News; Special Correspondent, CBS News.
John J. Curtin, Esq., Partner, Bingham McCutchen, LLP.
Mickey Edwards, Director, Aspen Institute-Rodel Fellowships in Public Leadership; Lecturer, Woodrow Wilson School of Public and International Affairs, Princeton; former Member

*Organizational information is listed for identification purposes only.

of Congress (R-OK); former Chairman, House of Representatives Republican Policy Committee.

Reverend Dr. C. Welton Gaddy, Executive Director, The Interfaith Alliance.

Dr. Morton H. Halperin, Director of U.S. Advocacy, Open Society Institute; Senior Vice President, Center for American
Progress.

David Lawrence, Jr., President, Early Childhood Initiative Foundation; former publisher, *Miami Herald* and *Detroit Free Press*.

Robert A. Levy, Senior Fellow in Constitutional Studies, Cato
Institute.

Thomas R. Pickering, former Undersecretary of State for Political
Affairs; former United States Ambassador and Representative
to the United Nations.

Dr. Roger Pilon, Vice President for Legal Affairs, Cato Institute.

John Podesta, President and Chief Executive Officer, Center for
American Progress; White House Chief of Staff, Clinton
administration.

John Seigenthaler, Founder, The Freedom Forum First Amendment Center at Vanderbilt University; former President,
American Society of Newspaper Editors; former Administrative Assistant to Attorney General Robert F. Kennedy.

William S. Sessions, former Director, Federal Bureau of Investigation; former Chief Judge, U.S. District Court for the Western
District of Texas.

John Shore, Founder and President, noborg LLC; former Senior
Advisor for Science and Technology to Senator Patrick Leahy.

Geoffrey R. Stone, the Harry Kalven, Jr., Distinguished Service
Professor of Law, The University of Chicago.

John F. Terzano, Vice President, Vietnam Veterans of America
Foundation.

John Whitehead, President, Rutherford Institute.

Roger Wilkins, Clarence J. Robinson Professor of History and
American Culture, George Mason University.

Resisting War Crimes:
Vietnam and Iraq

MICHAEL FERBER

Like opponents of the Iraq war today, activists opposing the Vietnam War had few conventional vehicles for political efficacy. Echoing the civil disobedience techniques of the civil rights movement, young draft resisters turned in their draft cards and refused induction. Michael Ferber describes how a similar strategy of resistance might be effective today.

Ferber was a founder of the Vietnam-era draft resistance movement and stood trial for conspiracy with Dr. Benjamín Spock. Ferber has worked as a peace movement lobbyist in Washington and has been head of New Hampshire Peace Action. He teaches literature at the University of New Hampshire. His books include *The Resistance,* a history of draft resistance in the 1960s, two books on William Blake, one on Percy Shelley, and *A Dictionary of Literary Symbols.*

The scope and depth of the American antiwar movement, which had marched and lobbied and blocked traffic throughout the country in 2003, was most strikingly revealed, I think, by its enormous effort in 2004 to elect a candidate who supported the war. Had Howard Dean been the Democratic nominee, instead of the tedious and finger-to-the-wind "centrist" John Kerry, who had voted for the invasion of Iraq and argued we needed more troops there, the frenzied outpouring of Deaniac doorbell-ringers can easily be imagined. That is not to say Dean would have beaten George W. Bush, as he had some liabilities, but he grew from an unknown former governor of a tiny state to the hero of millions almost entirely because he had spoken out from the beginning against the Iraq invasion. When Kerry got the nomination, so angry were these millions over the invasion that they held their noses and worked like dogs for Senator Anybody-but-Bush, even though he sounded a lot like Bush.

Bush won anyway. Now what do we do, we millions, whose candidate lost but who now are joined, according to the polls, by a majority of the American people, who say they believe the invasion was a mistake? Small demonstrations continue, letters are written to

Congress, ads taken out, but many of us have run out of steam or cannot decide where to direct what steam we can still summon. Lobbying the new Congress, more Republican than the last one, looks hopeless. What do we do?

During the first four years of the Vietnam War, from 1964 to 1968, lobbying also seemed hopeless. I had a sharp lesson in its futility myself, when, as a college student home for the summer in 1965, I took advantage of an excellent lobbying opportunity on my next-door-neighbor's front porch. He was the chairman of the county Democratic party, and sitting with him one evening was our congressman, also a neighbor and friend of my parents, a liberal who, a few years later, was to lead a congressional campaign against chemical and biological weapons. Over lemonade I made my best speech against the war, citing every fact I had researched earlier that summer. I sensed the congressman was sympathetic, and uncomfortable. When they had both politely heard me out, the county chairman turned to the congressman: "Well, Max, this is all very interesting, but as your chairman I must direct you to support our President in the war." It was jocular enough, but chilling. Our President was Lyndon Johnson, a Democrat, who was surprisingly liberal on civil rights and poverty and other issues dear to those politicians who were most unhappy (privately) over the war. Few of them would dare oppose him over Vietnam. Only when a Republican President inherited the war did they find their voices and switch their votes.

So lobbying seemed a waste of time, at least until 1969. But those days were a time when creative new ideas about resistance and social transformation were bubbling up, notably from the black civil rights movement, which in turn had learned from the nonviolent campaigns of Gandhi in India. Boycotts, sit-ins, hunger strikes, and "filling the jails" had widened our imagination of what was possible without turning to violence. For the young, male, civilian portion of us, and those in their families and circles of friends, a new strategy quickly arose: organized mass draft resistance. The draft had been in place since 1948, and it was cranking out thousands of draftees for Vietnam every month. Individuals here and there were refusing induction, hundreds were fleeing to Canada, small bands had set fire to their draft cards (a federal felony), others had signed "We Won't Go" statements, but it was only with a group called "The Resistance" in 1967 that the strategy gelled: young men would return their draft cards to the government (also a felony) with a pledge to refuse induction, and they would not leave the country but fill the federal prisons, generating as much publicity as possible as they did so.

Within a year several thousand had relinquished their cards and hundreds had refused induction. Churches offered "symbolic sanctuary" to resisters awaiting arrest. Trouble brewed for the government at induction centers and federal courts, not to mention the print and broadcast media, which were often quite sympathetic to the young men who could have avoided the draft altogether. In March 1968, when General William Westmoreland returned from Vietnam and asked for another two hundred thousand troops (on top of the half million already deployed), Johnson's staff took out their calculators and said no. To get that many more men would mean raising the draft quotas so high they would multiply the number of resisters many times. Turmoil would follow; the political costs were too high.[1]

The rejection of the General's request was a turning point in the war, for it could only be won on the ground, though of course America did not end its savage attacks, now mainly from the air, until five years later. Draft resistance was not the only factor, of course, but it was decisive in preventing the United States from destroying Vietnam completely, and in drastically limiting its military options. Other factors were the astounding tenacity of the Communist forces, and along with it the demoralization of the U.S. Army, which by about 1970 had ceased to be an effective fighting force.

What can we learn from that draft resistance almost forty years later? First, you never know what will work. Draft resistance as a mass strategy was risky, and many antiwar groups opposed it as meaningless middle-class moralism. But nobody had a better idea,

---

[1] Michael S. Foley, *Confronting the War Machine: Draft Resistance During the Vietnam War* (Chapel Hill: University of North Carolina Press, 2003), pp. 257–60.

so it went forward; the resisters cast their bread upon the waters. Second, it is not usually by governments that wars are stopped. It is by resistance from below, from ten here and twenty there causing trouble, and keeping it up until governments finally respond to them. Senators will not save us. All that energy on behalf of Kerry might have gotten rid of George Bush, but Kerry might have done even worse things in Iraq, just as Hubert Humphrey, the Kerry of 1968, might have ordered just as many horrors in Vietnam as Richard Nixon did—until resistance forced his hand.

Of course we do not yet have conscription again, so we lack the tool it gave us in 1967. But will it come back? The draft was suspended in 1973, but draft registration was reinstated in 1980 by Jimmy Carter in response to the Soviet invasion of Afghanistan. Draft board members retired, though many stayed on call until their twenty-year terms were up, and no one has been drafted since 1973. But in late 2003, for the first time in thirty years, the Selective Service System issued a call for volunteers to serve on draft boards, and Congress appropriated an extra $28 million for the purpose. Is it an accident that it was also in late 2003 that it first became obvious that the Iraq invasion had not succeeded? In late 2004 representatives of the Selective Service System were alerting peace churches such as the Brethren that they should prepare to place conscientious objectors as they used to do.

Presidents do not like to face military defeat, so Bush may well feel he must bolster American troop strength just to protect the oil, never mind bringing about "democracy." And to do that, having drained the Reserves and National Guard dry, he may have to resort to a draft. And that will give us our opportunity.

Yet we needn't wait. Now is the time for young men—and women—to begin to declare themselves: if we are drafted while U.S. troops are in Iraq, we will refuse to serve. The presence of "We Won't Go" statements in advance of an actual draft will act as a shot across the bow of the war planners. Now too we should be signing a new "Call to Resist Illegitimate Authority," like the one that supported resisters in 1967. Bush, moreover, has already imposed a kind of draft, a "back-door draft," on the National Guard and Reserves by extending tours by several months and by recalling regular troops for a full second tour. And, as we have seen earlier in this book, court challenges, desertions, and no-shows by guardsmen and reservists and regular soldiers are mounting. Here is where we civilians must enter in and help: by serving as their megaphone—multiplying their effectiveness by spreading news of their refusals as widely as we can—and by offering moral, legal, and financial help to the refusers and their families. And here again churches must come forward and offer "sanctuary" to those who wish to claim it.

Perhaps the largest problem we faced in the resistance of the 1960s was the fact that, though you may turn in your draft cards together, or even desert the army together, in the end you must stand trial and go to prison alone, months or even years after the initial impulse of solidarity led you to your act of resistance. We faced this fact, and tried to create communities of support for those in prison and their families, but it was hard to sustain and our success was mixed. We must prepare to do better. Already with this new war we have resisters before courts-martial; we need to make them feel appreciated and honored for their courage. We have some advantages over the movement of forty years ago, not least the speed of communicating with each other, a speed that might help us intervene or at least boost the morale of the growing number of those refusing to fight. The disappearance of communism from the world, too, means that the little sects of Leninists and Maoists that so bedeviled our meetings and made fresh thinking so much harder have disappeared as well; the FBI liked these groups, because they were easy to infiltrate and manipulate and could be used to wreck the larger, more serious, more democratic, organizations.

And we have the advantage of that much more history to learn from, not only the experiments of the resistance to the Vietnam War but the tremendous movements of nonviolent reform and revolution that have swept across the world since then, from Polish "Solidarity" to the Philippine resistance to Ferdinand Marcos, from the banging of pots against pans in Augusto Pinochet's Chile to the orange scarves of the Ukraine. These are a treasury of lore and experience that ordinary citizens came up with; they are a gift to us, if we will take it.

Enforcing International Law Through Civil Disobedience: The Trial of the St. Patrick's Four

BILL QUIGLEY

Nonviolent civil disobedience in protest of war has a long tradition in the United States, dating back at least to Henry David Thoreau's going to jail to protest the U.S. war against Mexico. Today many war opponents ground their action specifically in international law. As one of the "St. Patrick's Day Four" protestors described in this article told the jury trying him, it was his duty under international law and the Nuremberg principles to take nonviolent action to stop an illegal and immoral war. Unexpectedly, most of the jury seemed to accept his argument.

Bill Quigley is a law professor at Loyola University School of Law in New Orleans and one of the advisory counsel in the trial of the St. Patrick's Four.

On March 17, 2003, two days before the invasion of Iraq, four members of the Catholic Worker community in Ithaca, New York, walked into the waiting room of the local army-marine recruiting center in Lansing, New York. They then carefully poured their own blood on the walls, the windows, the posters, cardboard mannequins of soldiers, the door, and the American flag. They read a statement, then knelt in prayer and awaited the authorities.

The four, Daniel Burns, forty-three, Clare Grady, forty-five, Teresa Grady, thirty-eight, and Peter DeMott, fifty-seven, were each arrested and charged with felony criminal damage to property, criminal mischief in the third degree.

Because of the date of their actions, they became known as the "St. Patrick's Four." The four decided to represent themselves at their upcoming jury trial with assistance of advisory counsel.

They always admitted that they poured their blood to try to stop the invasion of Iraq. They chose to pursue trial strategies together and to try, as best they could, to put the legality of the war in Iraq on trial.

Their first defense was that their actions were absolutely legal under international law because they were trying to stop an illegal war. Because the United Nations had not approved the invasion of Iraq, the invasion was a series of serious illegal acts that constitute war crimes. Therefore, they had a right under the Nuremberg principles to try to stop war crimes.

Their second defense was that even if their actions were technical violations of law, they were authorized by the law of necessity, which allows the breaking of minor laws in order to prevent more serious harm (for example, breaking into a stranger's home in an emergency like a fire if you are trying to rescue a child). With this element they planned to present evidence of the widespread devastation caused by the invasion of Iraq in order to compare it to the damage to the recruiting center.

Early on, they refused an offer of the District Attorney's Office to plead guilty to a misdemeanor. They refused because they did not feel they were guilty.

A pretrial ruling stopped the defendants from calling witnesses on international law, the Nuremberg defense, and the doctrine of necessity. The judge did allow them to testify about their own state of mind and what they thought about these issues.

As the morning of trial dawned, reporters on the local paper created a pool on how long it would take the jury to convict—the longest bet was a couple of hours.

The St. Patrick's Four conducted their own jury selection from a table on which supporters had placed three daffodils in a small glass vase. They started out by telling the jury exactly what they had done. Clare Grady told how the defendants had gone to the recruiting center and poured their blood on the walls, the recruiting posters, the windows, and the flag. She admitted that she and the others took their actions to try to stop the war in Iraq. Then she started questioning the pool of potential jurors: Did anyone believe it was wrong to protest the war in Iraq? Did people think the President could make a mistake? Did anyone object to nonviolent disobedience? Did anyone feel the war in Iraq was wrong? Did people know how many people died in Iraq? Did anyone know how many Iraqi people died in the invasion? Were people familiar with the Boston Tea Party? Can you accept that pouring blood on the flag is no different legally than pouring blood on any other piece of cloth, or does the damage to the flag make it impossible for you to follow the presumption of innocence?

Dozens of people were questioned about the war in Iraq. Many were against; many were for; most felt strongly. People who had been sitting in court all day volunteered to the judge that they could not be fair, even before the prosecution or defense questioned them. Many were openly angry. It was like popcorn finally reaching full heat. Juror after juror said they could not be fair and left, and the judge immediately replaced them in the panel.

It took until 6:00 p.m. to seat a full jury and alternates.

Over sixty people had been questioned about the war in Iraq and their ability to sit on a jury to determine the legality of a nonviolent protest. For dozens of citizens of Tompkins County, New York, the civic obligation of jury duty had also been transformed into a focus group on the war in Iraq. What became absolutely clear is that there are very few people who do not have very strong feelings about the war in Iraq. Some jurors said the war was a horrible mistake and they could never convict anyone of doing anything to oppose it. Other jurors declared that even though they thought the invasion may have been a mistake, this was no time to criticize the war while troops were on the ground—prompting other potential jurors to break out in applause. Stereotypes were shattered as VFW members scoffed at the judgment of the President and business lobbyists said they were passionately against the war. Supporters and opponents of the war did not fall into neat categories.

The next day the prosecutor started her case. She showed the jury big pictures of bloody walls and windows and the bloody American flag. The only contested prosecution witness was the person who submitted a bill for cleaning. He was cross-examined about the different bills submitted at different times and the fact that though he paid the two people who cleaned up just $7 to $10 an hour for a total of fourteen hours of work, he charged the government $45 an hour and a couple of hundred extra for his time and for supplies, thus calling into question whether the damage was over $250 or not—a key element for the felony charge. The prosecution rested.

Now it was time for the defense. It was up to the St. Patrick's

Four, and them alone, to tell the jury and the larger community why they poured their blood and why they thought this act was moral and legal.

Peter DeMott testified as a father, a husband, the oldest of nine children, and as a marine and army veteran who served in the war against Vietnam. He stated it was his duty as a Christian and under international law and the Nuremberg principles to take nonviolent action to stop an illegal and immoral war undertaken by his country. He also spoke of great concern about the U.S. service people who are suffering in Iraq and elsewhere from the ravages of war, and especially about the toxic effects of depleted uranium (DU) on the troops in Iraq and the Iraqi people.

Teresa Grady testified about being raised to embrace all of God's children and to greatly appreciate the diversity of people while growing up in New York City. She spoke as the mother of a teenage boy and stressed the importance of educating young people about the real impact of signing up for the military, the reality that the recruiters gloss over. She cited the number of people killed in Iraq during the time of the trial alone, which pointed to the desperate need for the prevention of this war.

Daniel Burns testified that as a father of a small child, he felt that the loss of a single child would be too great for anyone to bear, and that he was thinking very much of that when he took his action. Burns said he felt there had been an emergency about to occur in Iraq and that our country is essentially "on fire," with the emergency continuing in Iraq and the tragedy continuing here as well in the form of U.S. military people still coming home dead, wounded, and scarred.

Clare Grady told of her eyewitness knowledge of the suffering in Iraq at the hands of the U.S. sanctions when she visited there with a Voices in the Wilderness delegation in 1999. She described how she visited with Iraqi mothers and, despite the language barrier, shared with them the joy of their children, kissing each other's photographs of their children.

In the fourth day of the trial, all the defendants rose and said together, "The defense rests." The jury was dismissed for the Easter weekend.

Teresa Grady closed with a reading of "We Are Catholic Workers and We Are Still Pacifists," repeating that no matter what, they and others were committed to love as a solution rather than violence. Clare Grady thanked the jury for their time and reminded them that while everyone in the trial had the weekend to catch up and take a breath, the people of Iraq were dying by the dozens as were many U.S. soldiers. Daniel Burns gave a brief summation of the case and asked the jury to look at their action not in the narrow legalistic context that the prosecutor wanted, but in the context of the war in Iraq, in the context of history of nonviolent civil resistance, and in the context of justice. Burns said Iraq is the building and the building is on fire, and that although they were not able to stop the fire of war, they should not be penalized for trying. He reminded the jurors of their promise to dispense justice and asked them to send the world a message of justice and peace by deciding justly.

The jury started deliberations at 11:30 A.M. One of the court personnel was overheard saying in disgust, "These people are making a mockery of this whole process!"

As the afternoon inched forward, supporters were heard saying, "Every hour is a victory." Finally, the judge sent the jury home for the night.

The next day the jury was out all morning, and the judge ordered them lunch. The TV reporter said her managers wanted to know what was going on. Hadn't the defendants admitted that they did it? What was taking so long?

At 8:50 P.M., after twenty hours of deliberation, the jury said it was deadlocked and the judge declared a mistrial. The packed courtroom gave the jurors a tremendous ovation and repeated it as they filed out.

The DA was stunned; the media were stunned; the community was elated. But the greatest news of all? Within twenty-four hours, it was reported that the jury was deadlocked 9–3 in favor of acquittal of the defendants.

The district attorney later agreed to dismiss the charges, telling the court that he did not think a retrial would have a different outcome. But he also said that the local U.S. attorney had agreed to bring federal charges against the St. Patrick's Four. In February 2005, nearly a year after the jury's refusal to convict, a federal court indicted them for "conspiracy to impede an officer of the United States."

Because the war in Iraq is both illegal and a continuing war crime, and because international law and international treaties are explicitly a part of U.S. law by reason of two provisions of the U.S. Constitution and many decisions of the U.S. Supreme Court, people who are trying to stop it are in fact trying to uphold a higher law.

This is not a new position. In the 1940s, U.S. Supreme Court Justice Robert Jackson, who not only served as the chief American prosecutor at the Nuremberg trial but was also appointed to help formulate the international legal principles for the trial, stated, "The very essence of the Nuremberg Charter is that individuals have international duties which transcend national obligations of obedience imposed by the individual state." This articulation of the principles of international law developing from the postwar trials was echoed by Judge Bernard Victor A. Röling of the Tokyo War Crimes Tribunal, who said, "The most important principle of Nuremberg was that individuals have international duties which transcend national obligations of obedience imposed by the nation state . . . This means that in some cases individuals are required to substitute their own interpretation [of international obligations] for the interpretation given by the state." As Judge Röling said, the world "has to rely on individuals to oppose the criminal commands of the government."

The case of the St. Patrick's Four started as a trial of brave and conscientious protestors. But it was clear that somewhere along the way the nature of the trial changed; the war in Iraq itself had gone on trial. The defendants' acquittal provided an opportunity to lift up the concerns of the people of Iraq and a victory for those who try to stop the violence there.

This is a story of a jury who answered the plea to not be bound by the narrowness of the law. Some would say it is jury nullification. I say it is justice.

The jury did their part. What is our part?

"My Duty as an Able-Bodied American Citizen to Say No"

OONA CLARE DEFLAUN, ANA FLORES, ANNA RITTER, AND MARIE GRADY

> On December 21, 2002, four sixteen- to seventeen-year-old girls from upstate New York were arrested for walking into a military recruiting office and refusing to leave. One of them, Oona Clare DeFlaun, when asked what if anything had influenced her, answered: "A couple of years ago I found a quote from the Nuremberg War Crimes Tribunal . . . It says, 'Individuals have international duties which transcend the national obligations of obedience. Therefore [individual citizens] have the duty to violate domestic laws to prevent crimes against peace and humanity from occurring.' This quote made an impact on me and has resonated with me ever since. And I think it applies to this action. My purpose in being there was not to violate a local law but to uphold well-recognized international law."[1]

OONA CLARE DEFLAUN

In protest of the impending war on Iraq, I, as well as twelve other people, "died in" at the local army recruiter's office . . . our small group broke off, and we crossed the road to the other mall where the recruiter's office is. We went into the lobby and took down army and marine posters and put up pictures and signs of our own. Two of our group, our "spokespeople," went back into the recruiter's office and introduced us. The recruiter, a young man, was shaken and upset by our presence and wanted us to leave, but we made it clear that we were there, not to protest him personally, but to protest the work he was doing. We wanted to educate him and all the recruitees about the horrors of war, not to mention "Gulf War Syndrome," most likely caused by depleted uranium and/or anthrax vaccines.

As we were lying on the floor, with red paint smeared on our faces, we read a fact sheet about depleted uranium and Martin Luther King Jr.'s Christmas sermon from 1967, given just months before he was killed. In it he tells us that we don't have to like

SOURCE: Copyright © 2004 by Oona Clare DeFlaun.

[1.] *Nonviolent Activist*, March–April 2004, http://www.warresisters.org/nva0304-4.htm.

everybody, that would be very difficult, but we do have to love even our worst enemies. "Love is understanding, creative, redemptive good will toward all people."

After numerous warnings, we were arrested. We were taken to the state police office and processed, which took a couple of hours, and eventually we were released with court dates.

ANA FLORES

I am sixteen years old, and I am the youngest of four. I have three older brothers, two who registered for selective service and one who has not yet fallen into the trap of the military institution. I did this action for my brothers.

I am currently a junior at Ithaca's Alternative Community School and have many friends that are my age and older. I know that they could also be lured into the military, only because they are told that the military will pay for all their education, and instead be forced to fight in a war that is full of lies and deception. I did this action for them.

I took the liberty to speak for the voiceless people of Iraq, for all the innocent men, women, children, and babies that have been killed by U.S. bombs since the Gulf War and will continue to be killed in this next war. I did this action for them. I lay there in the recruitment office for the men and women who are currently in the military, so they don't have to be sent off to war to kill and be killed in this war. [As] my uncle Peter DeMott said, "We're here to recruit you into the peace movement!"

SOURCE: Copyright © 2004 by Ana Flores.

ANNA RITTER

Although I risked arrest and was prepared for it, I did not do the action to get arrested; I did it because I feel that it is my duty as an able-bodied American citizen to say no to the atrocities that my government is going to commit. Therefore I feel that by taking direct action my voice will be better heard.

If there is a war it will affect the young people the most, because we would be among those sent to kill our brothers and sisters on foreign soil.

MARIE GRADY

As I was feeding my baby sister her dinner, I was thinking about what I should say about why I was a part of the action on Saturday. What it all boils down to is this: I know that there are big sisters in Iraq right now who are helping to feed their baby sisters, and I wonder what they are thinking. The U.S. government is hot to trot. They want to bomb Iraq as soon as possible. I hope that what I did will help to stop this war. I think of the big sisters here, whose little brothers are going to be sent to kill the babies of Iraq, and the sisters and brothers, and fathers and mothers too for that matter. And the Iraqi sisters and brothers who'll be sent to fight the American sisters and brothers . . .

We went to the recruitment office on Saturday with pictures of children, some of whom are probably dead. We went and lay down on the floor as if we were dead. We went to bring that ugly, disgusting face of needless and premature death to the place where it all starts. You don't see the kind of pictures we brought in the shiny brochures that they hand out there. So I went for all the Iraqi kids, especially the older sisters who must be worrying about what will happen if we bomb them even more than we already have. Will they get to watch their baby siblings grow up? Or will they all be dead in a couple of months? If I were in their position I would want somebody to try to stop the war, and so I have to do everything I can to stop it. For them, and for me.

Reclaiming the Prophetic Voice

JOHN HUMPHRIES

Reclaiming the Prophetic Voice, a faith-based group in Connecticut, has begun its own grassroots campaign of resistance to American war crimes. It includes such traditional activities as outreach to religious leaders and parishioners, public witness, and lobbying. But it also features the *Call to Resist the War in Iraq,* which openly endorses resistance in the military. And it provides counseling and support both for those in the military who are questioning their role and for young people who are considering whether to enlist. By focusing on U.S. war crimes, it hopes to challenge people of faith and the broader community to take on their moral responsibilities.

John Humphries, a member of the RTPV steering committee, is a longtime peace activist, community organizer, and nonviolence trainer. He is a member of the Hartford Friends Meeting and the founder of the Quaker Peacebuilder Camp.

As the United States plunged into war against Afghanistan in the months following 9/11, the Reverends Allie Perry and Kathleen Mc-Tigue wondered why there was so little visible response from religious leaders. Where was the moral outcry? After several weeks of perplexed discussion, they decided to stop waiting for the "leaders" to lead and to begin organizing to take action. Beginning with a small steering committee of like-minded friends, they formally launched Reclaiming the Prophetic Voice (RTPV) in April 2002 as a Connecticut-based interfaith network of clergy and laypeople willing to stand together against a militaristic response to terrorism. They believed that if they began to speak and act boldly and prophetically, other people of faith would find their voices. The informal, streamlined structure of RTPV allowed the group to act quickly. The participation of Christian denominational leaders and Jewish and Muslim clergy, along with RTPV's ability to mobilize fairly large numbers of people, gave it credibility. RTPV lobbied legislators, helped galvanize a statewide peace coalition, and participated in civil disobedience before and immediately following the invasion of Iraq.

RESPONDING TO WAR CRIMES

As the graphic details of abuses at Abu Ghraib prison and other military detention facilities surfaced last year, RTPV once again observed a lack of an organized, vocal response from the religious community. "Where's the moral outrage? Where are the voices of our national religious leaders?" the group wondered.

Although torture is merely the most blatant aspect of the ongoing crime of an illegal war that has caused the deaths of more than 100,000 civilians, the general revulsion against torture offers an opportunity to reach out to people not active in the peace movement—the people in the pews. Clearly, these war crimes cross the boundary of what is morally acceptable. By framing torture as a moral issue, RTPV encourages people of faith to question the underlying assumptions of the war on terror.

To counter the tendency to blame the soldiers on the ground, RTPV has chosen to focus on the responsibility of the high government officials who gave the orders, sending men and women, physically and morally, into harm's way. RTPV has sought ways to be allies for the soldiers and their families, who are themselves victims of our government's immoral military adventures.

THE 1967 CALL TO RESIST

In pondering how to respond in a way that might challenge others to find their voices and take action, RTPV has drawn inspiration from the 1967 *Call to Resist Illegitimate Authority*. This was a statement that was initially signed by well-known cultural, religious, and intellectual figures, who were then joined by thousands of others.

The 1967 *Call* challenged the legality of the Vietnam War and the legitimacy of the government that was pursuing it. It argued that the war was unconstitutional and illegal because it was not declared by Congress as required by the U.S. Constitution; violated the obligation under the UN Charter to settle disputes peacefully; and violated the Geneva Conventions of 1949, which outlawed as war crimes many of the activities the U.S. military was conducting in Vietnam (all of these arguments can clearly be made about the current war in Iraq).

The 1967 *Call* described various forms of resistance, including refusal by those in the armed forces to obey specific illegal and immoral orders, application for conscientious objector status, refusal of induction, organizing further resistance in the military, and seeking sanctuary outside the United States.

Because the statement included a pledge of moral and financial support to draft resisters, merely signing the 1967 *Call* could be construed as a violation of the Military Selective Service Act of 1967. That act made it a crime to "counsel, aid and abet" those subject to the draft to "neglect, fail, refuse and evade service in the armed forces."

The U.S. Justice Department brought charges against Dr. Benjamin Spock, the Reverend William Sloane Coffin, Marcus Raskin, Mitchell Goodman, and the draft resister Michael Ferber. It accused them of conspiracy in "counseling, aiding, and abetting" young men to avoid and resist the Selective Service System. After a highly publicized trial, most were convicted. When a federal appeals court overturned the conviction due to prejudiced rulings by the judge, the Justice Department unexpectedly dropped the charges.

The *Call to Resist Illegitimate Authority* had a significant impact on the growth and development of the antiwar movement. The *Call* put the authority of highly respected intellectual and religious leaders behind the young draft resisters. The risk that thousands took by signing the statement led many others to consider their own responsibilities to take action to end the war. It challenged the legality of a war that had been legitimated by the fact that it was conducted by a popularly elected President and acquiesced in by Congress. What became known as the trial of the "Boston Five" was front-page news, helping move the moral, legal, and political issues raised by the antiwar movement from the margin to the mainstream.

RTPV'S *CALL TO RESIST*

In December 2004, the RTPV steering committee decided to draft its own statement: *Call to Resist the War in Iraq.*[1] The objective was not to produce the definitive statement that all groups across the country would sign and support, but rather to craft a powerful statement that could inspire others to develop their own—generating discussion, outreach, and signature campaigns in dozens of local communities.

The statement begins by presenting the case against the war, identifying the interlocking and mutually reinforcing moral, legal, and social reasons for opposing it. The text goes on to highlight individual and shared responsibility for active resistance: "We believe it is our duty as both Americans and members of the international community to insist that our government immediately adhere to the international agreements binding us."

Seeking to establish the statement as a form of civil disobedience, the members of RTPV applaud military personnel who are seeking ways to avoid service and pledge "to do all that we can to encourage others to follow their example." The text includes specific commitments to "support and . . . spread the word about the GI Rights Hotline and other efforts to support soldiers in withdrawing from the military"; to "counsel young men turning eighteen on the moral obligations as well as risks inherent in a refusal to register with the Selective Service"; and to provide financial assistance for their legal defense. Finally, the signers pledge to "encourage young men and women not to comply" with any reinstated draft.

RTPV concludes its statement by grounding its actions in the international law principle of individual responsibility: Anyone with knowledge of illegal activity and an opportunity to do something is a potential criminal under international law unless the person takes affirmative measures to prevent the commission of the crimes. The declaration's signers commit themselves "to undertake all affirma-

[1] www.ReclaimingthePropheticVoice.org.

tive measures available to us to fulfill our obligations under these treaties, which have guided our world for half a century."

At the core of this statement is the understanding that the authority and powers of the U.S. government have been usurped for illegitimate and immoral purposes, making it necessary for U.S. citizens, both individually and collectively, to take action to halt the war crimes being perpetrated in their names. By publicly committing to such action, RTPV seeks to challenge others to meet their own responsibilities under international law.

In March 2005, the venerable Fellowship of Reconciliation endorsed RTPV's *Call to Resist*.[2] This national endorsement will likely lead other groups to adopt the statement.

PUBLIC ACTION ATTRACTS NATIONAL ATTENTION

In January 2005, RTPV organized a public witness on the New Haven Green to mark Martin Luther King, Jr.'s birthday. The program included reading from King's April 1967 sermon at Riverside Church, altering the text by inserting *Iraq* for most of the references to *Vietnam*. Participants honored the U.S. soldiers and Iraqi civilians who had been killed in the war by reading the names of all the dead soldiers and an equal number of Iraqis. RTPV highlighted its *Call to Resist* with a choral reading and public signing.

In addition to the local media coverage, RTPV's action received national attention. During the week prior to the event, the group's media release was posted on the CommonDreams Newswire.[3] As a result, RTPV received e-mail and phone inquiries from activists throughout the country wanting more information about the *Call to Resist*, about the lists of names, and about the action campaign being launched. Some groups that contacted us incorporated the *Call to Resist* and/or the reading of the names into their own events marking Martin Luther King Day.

[2.] http://www.forusa.org/media/IraqCalltoResist.html.
[3.] http://www.commondreams.org/news2005/0112-09.htm.

A STRATEGY FOR COORDINATED RESISTANCE

Following its public action, RTPV has continued reaching out to clergy and denominational leaders, speaking with them about the *Call to Resist* and the action campaign. In these discussions, the group presents the challenge: "This is how we are responding to the atrocities of war crimes and our responsibility to take affirmative measures. How are you going to respond? How will your congregation or denomination respond?"

RTPV's action campaign implements aspects of the *Call to Resist*. Specifically, the group is organizing to provide support for military personnel considering a refusal to serve in Iraq and to support counterrecruitment efforts that seek to dissuade young people from entering the military or National Guard.

RTPV is organizing workshops on GI rights counseling and advocacy with the intention of establishing a network of clergy and laypeople who can provide a source of support and information for soldiers and their families in communities throughout the state. The group plans to make the network a visible witness against the war by securing media coverage and advertising that will list the names and contact information of those who have been trained. At the same time, RTPV will publicize the GI Rights Hotline[+] through leafleting and advertising that targets communities surrounding military bases and National Guard facilities.

Supporting counterrecruitment activities is the other pincer in a strategy designed to squeeze the military by exacerbating the growing shortage of active-duty personnel. RTPV is soliciting volunteers to receive training and go into the public schools, and group members are organizing public actions at recruiting stations with the active participation of young people.

The group has also begun meetings with members of Congress, issuing them the same challenge being given to clergy and faith communities: "What affirmative measures are you going to take?" RTPV is presenting them with a concrete proposal to investigate the Bush administration's war crimes by demanding the appointment of

+ http://girights.objector.org/.

an independent commission with the power to subpoena testimony and evidence.

RTPV's leaders believe that a focus on war crimes has greater potential than calls to cut the funding for the war, which can too easily be construed as denying soldiers the support they need. Furthermore, military spending is a local bread-and-butter issue. One of Connecticut's Democratic members of Congress publicly stated her intention to support the supplemental appropriation for the Iraq war because it provides defense contracts in her district.

Calling for a war crimes commission has the potential to tap into the public revulsion over the graphic photos of abuse. A broad-based push to appoint such a commission can overcome stiff resistance, just as the families of 9/11 victims successfully lobbied for the creation of the 9/11 commission.

As RTPV moves forward with these strategies, it encourages other groups to develop their own creative actions. Some may pursue a different set of affirmative measures, but everyone has a responsibility to act. Drawing upon contacts with groups around the country, RTPV is seeking ways to increase the coordination of local and regional efforts. Although RTPV's leaders do not yet have a clear vision of how such coordination will unfold, they have been sharing strategies and action ideas with other activists across the country. The group feels that the peace movement can be strengthened by evaluating successes and failures and by having the movement's leaders challenge each other to be more strategic and less reactionary. In order to succeed in bringing the troops home and halting Washington's war crimes, activists must move beyond banners and protests and begin to take greater risks. Religious leaders and communities of faith must reclaim their prophetic voice and translate words of resistance into meaningful action.

Counterrecruitment:
Cutting Off the Cannon Fodder

MARELA ZACARIAS

The reluctance of Americans to serve in a war that most consider un-
wise at best, if not immoral and illegal, has led the military to desperate
efforts to recruit American youth. Minority groups with limited economic opportunities, already overrepresented in the "volunteer" military, are prime targets for recruitment. A counterrecruitment campaign
has rapidly emerged around the country to challenge the recruitment
drive and offset the misinformation often used to lure youth into the
military. Marela Zacarias describes such efforts in the Hartford, Connecticut, region. Born in Mexico City, Zacarias is a political activist and
muralist who serves as artist-in-residence at Central Connecticut State
University in New Britain and teaches art in a variety of community
settings.

One afternoon in February 2004, a reporter watched as two "sharp-
dressed" Marines talked with students waiting for the bus on the
steps of Bulkeley High School in Hartford, Connecticut. "They
winked at the girls as they walked by. They compared military service to video games as they bantered with the young boys who clus-
tered around them. One student asked one of the Marines if he was
scared to die. 'A Marine doesn't get scared,' the older man said. 'You
know why? "Say hello to my little friend." That's why.' As he quotes
Al Pacino from *Scarface*, the Marine pretends to shoot an imaginary
machine gun and laughs."[1]

Military recruiting in high schools, particularly inner-city high
schools, is aggressive and consistent. In Connecticut cities like Hartford and New Haven, most of the student population comes from a
low-income background and is for the most part African-American
and Latino. Military recruiters concentrate their efforts on recruiting young men and women who find "no better choice" than joining a branch of the military. Cuts in social services, lack of jobs, and
the drive of some of these young men and women to succeed lead

[1] Penelope Overton, "Resistance Campaign," *Hartford Courant*, March 13, 2005.

them to choose the only "good job" that is being offered to them: to become a soldier. Call it the poverty draft.

As part of an organization called Latinos Contra la Guerra (Latinos Against the War), I work in alliance with other peace activists to organize counterrecruitment in Connecticut high schools. Part of an emerging national effort, we have operated counter-recruitment tables in ten schools in Hartford, West Hartford, East Hartford, Bloomfield, Norwich, and New London. A 1986 federal appeals court ruling requires any school that opens its doors to recruiters to also open its doors to opposing views.

We go into the schools with attractive information booths. We stock them with cookies, candy, and antiwar buttons and stickers. We play antiwar music videos by the rapper Eminem and others. We hand out pamphlets in English and Spanish with statistics that we've culled from reports and news articles. A yellow pamphlet describes alternative ways for students to pay for college or travel abroad. A green one addresses students who are already planning to enlist. A white one exposes some of the misinformation given out by recruiters.

Army recruiters do everything they can to paint an attractive picture of a soldier's life. They promise seventy-five thousand dollars for college education along with cash bonuses (up to twenty thousand dollars) for those who "enlist on active duty for four years, with special monetary incentives for candidates who have college degrees, sign up for high-priority jobs or agree to move quickly into training."[2] They promise travel opportunities, and they say that the probability of being sent to Iraq is very slim.

The beautiful picture recruiters paint for the young men and women is, in most cases, an illusion. Recruitment is simply part of a soldier's duty, part of his or her job. We have talked to many veterans from various wars who have told us that there is a quota they have to fulfill every month, and that it really doesn't matter if they lie because in the contract the new recruit signs there is a clause that protects the U.S. military from being held accountable for

---

[2] "Army Having Difficulty Meeting Goals in Recruiting; Fewer Enlistees Are in Pipeline; Many Being Rushed into Service," *Washington Post*, February 21, 2005.

any remark made by the recruiter. Only the rules stated in the contract are valid.

When we ask the students in a high school why they are thinking of joining the military, the most common reasons we hear are: to pay for college; to get a decent job/job skills; to escape their communities (poverty, abusive relationships, etc.); to travel; a sense of patriotic duty; for the benefits; to gain discipline/structure in their lives; and because it's "cool" and "sexy" to be a soldier.

Our role as counterrecruiters in the high school is to give the students all the information they need to have a balanced view of what it entails to join the military. For example, the army promises seventy-five thousand dollars for college. But in reality only a small proportion of enlisted personnel who complete four years in the army actually receive these benefits. Many of the soldiers who come back to civilian life cannot find a job, either because the skills that they learned (to wire a submarine, to kill the enemy effectively) are not applicable to civilian life or because they are disabled. Indeed, a high proportion of the homeless are military veterans.

We also inform students about discrimination in the military. People of color make up one-third of the armed forces, but only 18 percent of all officers.[3] Fifty-five percent of the women in the military reported sexual harassment.[4] Between August 2002 and February 2005, 307 cases of sexual assault against female military personnel were reported in Iraq, Kuwait, and Afghanistan.[5] The military is an employer that openly discriminates against homosexuals. According to the Department of Defense, there were 1,231 gay discharges in 2000, and 1,075 incidents of antigay harassment were documented in 2001.[6]

After we present some of these facts to the students, many of them stay around to talk to us and ask many questions. Some bring their friends to listen to what we have to say; some just take the lit-

---

[3] U.S. Department of Defense, *The 2000 Defense Almanac.*

[4] U.S. Department of Defense, *Defense Equal Opportunity Council Task Force Report* (1996).

[5] "Military Women Say They Face Sex Harassment," Scripps Howard News Service, March 9, 2005.

[6] http://www.sldn.org/templates/law/record.html?section=22&record=473.

erature. Many of the inner-city high school students with whom we have contact are heavily influenced by the mass media, so a lot of the things we say are completely new to them.

A reporter recently described the way one of our members, Milly Guzman-Young, approached Latino students in a crowded high school cafeteria that included dozens of Junior ROTC cadets:

> She didn't hesitate to grab an arm and make her pitch to Latino students in rapid-fire Spanish. She told them that military recruiters "target our schools and our neighborhoods to get us to fight in their war."
>
> Instead of staying away from the cadets, Guzman-Young walked up to their table and sat right down. At first, the group of young black and Latina women rolled their eyes, but within minutes they were nodding.
>
> "She said a lot of things that I didn't know," said Shyla Bennet, a 17-year-old junior in her third year of JROTC. "I don't know if I'm going to join or not, but I'm going to check this stuff out."
>
> Guzman-Young talked Lisa Clarke, an 18-year-old senior enrolled in JROTC, into pinning a "Peace is Patriotic" button on her dress uniform. They talked about how Clarke might finance her plan to go to culinary school.
>
> "I'd always thought I'd join the Air Force, because my family is big into it, but lately all that I've been seeing about dead soldiers has me thinking I won't," Clarke said. "She said I can find other ways to pay for school."[7]

The No Child Left Behind Act requires all schools that get federal funding to give all students' personal information to the military, including information about hobbies and skills. But students may demand to be removed from military recruiters' lists by submitting a form for a "section 9528 exemption." We pass out the forms in the schools; at least 225 Hartford students that we know of have already submitted them.

---

[7] Overton, "Resistance Campaign."

For the first time since September 11, military recruiters are consistently falling short of their quotas for new enlistments. The *Washington Post* recently reported that "for the first time since 2001, the Army began the fiscal year in October with only 18.4 percent of the year's target of 80,000 active-duty recruits already in the pipeline. That amounts to less than a half of last year's figure and falls well below the Army's goal of 25 percent." The active-duty army is "in danger of failing to meet its recruiting goals." The Marine Corps, which has "historically had the luxury of turning away willing recruits," missed its recruiting goal for the first time in ten years when it fell 3 percent short in January.[8] The Army National Guard announced in December that it had fallen 30 percent below its recruiting goals in the previous two months. (National Guard members and army reservists now make up nearly 40 percent of the 148,000 troops in Iraq.)[9] Five of the six military reserve components have failed to meet their recruiting goals for the first four months of the current fiscal year.[10]

By going into the high schools to talk to students, we hope to educate them about the realities of war, to diminish the recruiters' efforts to take more low-income youth to war, and to inspire others to join our struggle. We find that most people want us there. They want the information. And they want to make up their own minds. As a fifteen-year-old Latina student in Hartford said to us, "You mean the recruiters can tell me one thing, like they're going to let me go to Germany, and then send me to Iraq once I sign on the dotted line? That ain't right!"[11]

---

8. "Marines Miss January Goal for Recruits," *New York Times*, December 3, 2004.
9. "Guard Reports Serious Drop in Enlistment," *New York Times*, December 4, 2004.
10. "5 Units of Military Reserve Miss Recruiting Goals," *New York Times*, February 17, 2005.
11. Overton, "Resistance Campaign."

The Accountability of Leaders: A Challenge to Governments and Civil Society

RICHARD FALK

The Nuremberg Tribunals made government officials accountable for obeying international law but did not create effective means of enforcement. A civic movement continued to demand accountability and eventually helped establish international courts and other intergovernmental means of holding government officials accountable to international law. Richard Falk traces the ups and downs of the intergovernmental and civil society movements to impose accountability on leaders. As the United States pursues a clearly illegal course with impunity, Falk advocates a "struggle waged by global civil society" to "extend the reach of criminal accountability to include those leaders acting on behalf of dominant states."

Falk is the Albert G. Milbank Professor Emeritus of International Law and Practice at Princeton University and Visiting Distinguished Professor of Global Studies at the University of California, Santa Barbara. He is the author, coauthor, or editor of more than forty books on international law and the law of war, including *The Great Terror War* (2003) and *The Declining World Order: America's Imperial Foreign Policy* (2004).

CRIMINAL ACCOUNTABILITY: STATES AND CITIZENS

At the Nuremberg Tribunals that followed World War II, America insisted that the surviving leaders of Nazi Germany and imperial Japan be neither shot when captured nor set free, but rather prosecuted as war criminals in a court of law that gave those accused a full opportunity to present a defense. Nuremberg has often been criticized as "victors' justice," and so it was, but the victorious powers that managed the process insisted that in the future the legal accountability of leaders would apply to the behavior of all sovereign states. And not just the losers. Justice Robert Jackson, the chief American prosecutor at Nuremberg, expressed this intention in his opening statement: "The ultimate step in avoiding periodic wars, which are inevitable in a system of international lawlessness, is to make statesmen responsible to law. And let me make clear that while this law is first applied against German aggressors, the law includes, and if it is to serve a useful purpose it must condemn, aggression by any other nation, including those which sit here now in judgment."[1]

However, there was a disturbing unwillingness by the victors of World War II to fulfill the expectations created by Jackson's statement. The Nuremberg approach continues to lack credibility whenever it collides with the stubborn realities of geopolitics. The state system is still beholden to dominant states that insist upon their prerogative to wage illegal "wars of choice," thereby dangerously and often imprudently subordinating legality to political expediency.

Even in the cold-war era, the Nuremberg flame was kept burning by a series of initiatives rooted in civil society. These initiatives, based on individual conscience, expressed the view that leaders are legally obliged to uphold international law in the area of war and peace. If they fail to do so, citizens have a right, even a duty, to refuse to participate in official policies even if ordered to do so.

This civic movement on behalf of official accountability climaxed in the latter stages of the Vietnam War and in relation to the nuclear arms race during the 1970s and 1980s. It produced antiwar heroes such as the Berrigan brothers and many young men who chose prison rather than obey orders to fight in Vietnam, orders which they considered illegal under international law. Religious leaders, including Martin Luther King, Jr. and William Sloane Coffin, condemned the criminality of American policies in a widely influential book, *In the Name of America*.[2] Daniel Ellsberg explained his release of the Pentagon Papers (which included many classified documents) as driven in large part by his reading of the Nuremberg judgment. Telford Taylor, a respected and scholarly former military

---

[1] Text in R. Falk, G. Kolko, and R. J. Lifton, eds., *Crimes of War* (New York: Random House, 1971), p. 85; see also Karl Jaspers, *The Question of German Guilt* (New York: Capricorn, 1961).

[2] *In the Name of America* (New York: Clergy and Laymen Concerned About Vietnam, 1968).

officer who was an important member of the prosecution team at Nuremberg, wrote a widely read indictment of American policy, *Nuremberg and Vietnam*.[3] The renowned British philosopher Bertrand Russell convened a tribunal to examine charges of war crimes in Vietnam that included among its members leading intellectual figures such as Jean-Paul Sartre.

These and many other developments confirmed the role of an emergent global civil society in keeping alive the central idea that governments are responsible for adhering to international law even in times of war and with respect to national security. There is no doubt that this civic trend was controversial, especially in the United States, but it kept alive a public consciousness that helped make possible a revival of Nuremberg principles.

After decades of forgetfulness induced by the consuming rivalry of the cold-war era, there occurred in the 1990s a dramatic revival of the idea that neither states nor their leaders were above the law with respect to war making and crimes against humanity. Milestones of the recent rebirth of the Nuremberg approach to war crimes have included the establishment by the UN Security Council of special international criminal tribunals to address allegations of official crimes in the course of the breakup of the former Yugoslavia and arising from the mass killings in Rwanda; the indictment in a Spanish court and the subsequent British detention for extradition of the former Chilean dictator Augusto Pinochet; the indictment of Slobodan Milošević while he was still head of state in Yugoslavia, and his subsequent prosecution in The Hague; a worldwide movement that led to the establishment in 2002 of a permanent International Criminal Court (ICC). This momentum, although resisted and weakened by opposing trends, seemed to point to the gradual emergence of a law-governed world system.

Thus there have been two interacting traditions of support for international law, each with its own strengths and weaknesses. The intergovernmental tradition shows a pattern of alternating assertiveness and neglect. The transnational civic tradition often intensifies

---

[3.] Telford Taylor, *Nuremberg and Vietnam: An American Tragedy* (Chicago: Quadrangle Books, 1970).

in response to intergovernmental irresponsibility. The intergovernmental level can gain public and media attention and impose punishments; its main weakness is inconsistent and highly selective
implementation and the exemption of leaders of dominant states
from accountability. The civic level is more consistent than the intergovernmental, thereby filling a moral vacuum; but it lacks the
authority or capacity to enforce, and has difficulty gaining public
and media attention. Such developments as the establishment of
the International Criminal Court and the Belgian national judicial
experiment with "universal jurisdiction" in the 1990s were largely
the work of collaborative efforts between a transnational coalition of
NGOs and moderate governments working to strengthen the role of
international law in the political governance of the planet.[4]

THE BUSH ERA

As soon as George W. Bush arrived at the White House, it became
clear that issues of international accountability for war crimes would
be handled in a highly partisan spirit that cast doubt on what had
seemed so promising in the years immediately preceding. Bush took
the unprecedented step of withdrawing the American signature
from the treaty setting up the ICC and then had the State Department negotiate a series of bilateral treaties ensuring that no American citizens would ever be handed over to the ICC for prosecution.[5]

But at the same time, the U.S. government pushed harder
than ever for the prosecution of Serbian political and military
leaders thought to be responsible for war crimes in Bosnia and
Kosovo. And in the context of Iraq, the U.S. government crafted a

---

[4] See John Borneman, ed., *The Case of Ariel Sharon and the Fate of Universal Jurisdiction* (Princeton, N.J.: Princeton Institute for International and Regional Studies
Monograph Series, no. 2, 2004). See also Stephen Macedo, ed., *Universal Jurisdiction: National Courts and the Prosecution of Serious Crimes Under International Law*
(Philadelphia: University of Pennsylvania Press, 2003).

[5] The signature of a treaty does not bind the party; ratification does, and there was
never a prospect that the U.S. Congress would ratify the treaty establishing the ICC.
Bush's withdrawal of signature was a domestic and international signal of the American repudiation of the whole process of establishing an international institution addressing issues of accountability.

dubious Iraqi war crimes procedure that would bring Saddam Hussein and his subordinates to trial in a setting that would virtually guarantee convictions, and with a mandate to impose the death sentence (which would not have been allowable if the trials had been in an international venue). Such a self-serving approach to criminal accountability has caused widespread public criticism of the United States, especially when its behavior seems to challenge most flagrantly the restraints on war making that are part of international law.

The attacks of September 11th have greatly complicated the situation. Even before 9/11 American leaders were exhibiting a rather scary geopolitical hubris. For example, back in 1988 the first George Bush said, "I will never apologize for the United States. I don't care what the facts are." This generalized ethos of unconditional nonaccountability was reiterated by his son in the course of the 2004 State of the Union address: "America will never seek a permission slip to defend the security of our country." The clear implication of this assertion was that the United States would never regard itself as constrained in its decisions to wage wars on other countries either by the United Nations Charter or by international law. More dramatically, the casting off of legal and ethical limits on American behavior, while insisting on such limits for enemies, conveyed to the world an image of a belligerent and cynical imperial power aiming at world domination.

Although it has been hard to pin down the precise parameters of aggressive war, the clear instances are easily discerned on the basis of the directives of the United Nations Charter. Articles 2(4) and 51 establish that it is impermissible to use force against another state except in circumstances of self-defense or in the furtherance of a mandate issued by a decision of the UN Security Council.[6] The essential idea in the charter is that war making by a state against another state is aggression unless it can qualify as self-defense, which is deliberately defined narrowly in article 51 of the charter.

So understood, there is no substantial doubt that the war against Iraq launched by the United States in March 2003 was a

[6.] It was such a mandate that gave a color of legality to the First Gulf War in 1991.

flagrant instance of aggressive war.[7] Despite strenuous American efforts to obtain a mandate from the Security Council, none was given.[8] Granted, the Afghanistan war was undertaken without Security Council authorization, but at least there was a plausible case for American claims of a defensive necessity such that the 9/11 attacks provided a legal basis for a self-defense claim.[9] And unlike the Kosovo War, which also lacked a legal foundation, in Iraq as of 2003, there did not exist the mitigating circumstance of a humanitarian emergency.[10]

A NECESSARY STRUGGLE

There is little doubt that the Iraq War qualifies as an aggressive war that constitutes a crime against peace. As such, those who planned and executed this war should be subject to indictment and prosecution. Other crimes associated with the conduct of the war and the subsequent occupation should also give rise to accountability by reference to the laws of war and international humanitarian law.

With U.S. backing, the crimes of Saddam Hussein and his chief lieutenants are to be the object of prosecution by Iraqi judicial procedure closely tied to the American occupation. This prospect will accentuate the double standard at play when it comes to

---

[7] This assessment of the illegality with respect to the Iraq War has been overwhelmingly confirmed by mainstream international law specialists. A representative panel at the 2004 annual meeting of the American Society of International Law composed of Anne-Marie Slaughter, Thomas M. Franck, James Crawford, Mary Ellen O'Connell, and myself unanimously reached such a conclusion of illegality. See "Iraq, One Year Later," *Proceeding of the 98th Annual Meeting of the American Society of International Law* (Washington, D.C., 2004), pp. 261–74.

[8] For a discussion of the feeble efforts by American officials to invoke earlier Security Council resolutions to support the legality of the Iraqi invasion, see ibid., note 8, pp. 263–69.

[9] Discussed in Richard Falk, *The Great Terror War* (Northampton, Mass.: Olive Branch Press, 2003), pp. 61–72. Even though the war had a legal basis, it was undertaken in a manner that makes its legality questionable and quite possibly imprudent as well. The main legal doubts concerned the absence of a clear Security Council authorization and the failure by the U.S. government to treat war as a last resort.

[10] See the analysis to this effect in the report of the Kosovo Commission: *Kosovo Report* (Oxford: Oxford University Press, 2000), pp. 163–98.

accountability for international crimes. It will also demonstrate that the U.S. government is not opposed to procedures of accountability so long as it can exempt its own officials and personnel, and those of its friends. Such a partisan posture invites the impression of hypocrisy and has the effect of reinforcing cynical views that holding individuals responsible for crimes of state is one more instance of the strong imposing their will on the weak. This is most unfortunate as the acts being punished are crimes that need to be deterred and punished if the peoples of the world are to be better protected against the abuses of governments.

U.S. policies have sparked a counterreaction of civic initiatives expressing a transnational consciousness in support of universal standards of accountability. More than fifteen distinct tribunals have examined the criminality of various aspects of the Iraq War, with sessions in Japan, Britain, Belgium, the United States, Turkey, Germany, Sweden, and others.

Global civil society must wage a struggle to extend the reach of criminal accountability to include those leaders acting on behalf of dominant states. Especially in democratically organized states, it is a matter of extending the rule of law to foreign as well as domestic policy. As the disasters of Vietnam and Iraq show, it might enhance the effectiveness of America's role as global leader if its own policies and conduct were constrained by the self-imposed discipline of international law.

Why War Crimes Matter

Brendan Smith

Can law be an effective means for halting war crimes? Brendan Smith argues that, despite their evident limitations, both international and domestic law provide opportunities to resist Bush administration lawlessness. According to Smith, a scholar of international law and social movements as well as a coeditor of this book, these opportunities include utilizing legal and constitutional restraints on arbitrary state power; taking advantage of the law's unintended developments; and using law to legitimate and encourage the claims of social movements. He shows how each of these can contribute to a movement to bring Bush administration war crimes to an end.

Our strength as a nation state will continue to be challenged by those who employ a strategy of the weak using international fora, judicial processes and terrorism.

> —*President George W. Bush's 2005 National Defense Strategy Report*

I don't care what the international lawyers say, we are going to kick some ass.

> —*President George W. Bush*, as quoted by Richard Clarke, *Against All Enemies*

Surely there is little expectation that members of the Bush administration will soon be subject to war crimes prosecution in U.S. courts. At the same time, however, we see fear among these officials—evidenced in the declassified Alberto Gonzales memo to President Bush expressing concern about criminal prosecution—over the danger of war crimes enforcement. What explains the simultaneous cynicism of citizens and fear of U.S officials? This article considers this contradiction and argues that the law, in particular war crimes law, can be incorporated into the strategy for halting the Bush administration's global agenda.[1]

[1.] See part III of this book for a discussion of the Administration's global agenda.

LIMITATIONS OF THE LAW

Traditional legal theorists claim that law functions "above" the political realm, meaning legal legitimacy rests on a quasi-scientific process that operates separate and independent from politics.[2] The result is a body of rules and an enforcement system that treat all citizens equally in terms of access and outcome.

As citizens, we often instinctively reject this doctrine because our everyday experience indicates otherwise. We may have read reports that while the U.S. Supreme Court reviewed a case with Vice President Cheney as defendant, Justice Antonin Scalia went duck hunting with the Vice President. Or we may have sought a lawyer's advice about a complaint against a corporation and were advised there was little chance of success against such a wealthy defendant. Our experiences indicate the law fails to fulfill many of its promises.[3]

Moreover, if national law remains ineffective, human rights and humanitarian law such as the Geneva Conventions are of no use whatsoever. Without an enforcement mechanism, international law allows states to act with impunity. Legal scholars respond by pointing to the shaming, normative, and reciprocal powers of human rights law, but as one scholar points out, "Can you have a system of law if you don't have a cop on the beat to enforce it?"[4]

This experience of the limitations of the law injects healthy cynicism into people's thinking about war crimes. Without hope of bringing those culpable to justice, many of those who want to halt the Bush administration's agenda reject legal frameworks and instead concentrate their efforts on electing public officials or organizing protests in Washington.

[2] The reasons include: the technical expertise of practitioners; judicial subservience to the Constitution, statutes, and precedent; and the objective nature of legal reasoning.
[3] This commonsense view of the law parallels several schools of legal thought including Legal Realism and Critical Legal Studies, as well as the Marxist legal tradition. The Realist formulation is that laws are "rules of the game of economic struggle," which asymmetrically empower groups bargaining over the benefits of production.
[4] Harry Kreisler, "Transnational Legal Process and World Order: Conversation with Harold Hongju Koh," October 3, 2003, http://www.globetrotter.berkeley.edu/people3/Koh/koh-cono.html.

THE NEOCONSERVATIVE ANTILAW MOVEMENT

While many people turn away from the law, neoconservatives are engaged in a systematic elimination of whole swaths of international human rights and humanitarian legal rules and structures.[5] With startling speed and effectiveness, this antilaw movement has rewritten, rejected, or ignored the Geneva Conventions, the UN Charter, and other key international treaties and conventions.

An early indication of this strategy came with President Bush's refusal to apply the Geneva Conventions to prisoners of war captured during the Afghanistan War. (See "Crimes of War and Occupation" in part I of this book for the illegality and results of this decision.) Soon the United States refused to adhere to UN Charter requirements for the use of force (see "An Illegal War" in part I). The Administration's Under Secretary of State and 2005 nominee for UN ambassador, John Bolton, has so little respect for institutions of international law that he argued: "If I were doing the Security Council today, I'd have one permanent member because that's the real reflection of the distribution of power in the world . . . [and that member would be] the United States."[6]

Legal prohibitions on state-sanctioned murder are also under attack. When sued by several Guantánamo detainees, the Justice Department argued that courts would not have jurisdiction over these detainees even if they were being summarily executed. According to the Ninth Circuit Court, "the U.S. government has never before asserted such a grave and startling proposition . . . a position so extreme that it raises the gravest concerns under both American and international law."[7] President Bush also bragged of extrajudicial killing, illegal under both U.S. and international treaty

---

[5] There is also an important domestic element to this antilaw strategy. It includes packing the courts with Federalist Society judges to roll back seventy years of legal precedent that permitted social legislation; tort and medical malpractice reform; and increasing privatization of civil suits through mandatory private adjudication requirements.

[6] "The World According to Bolton," *New York Times*, March 9, 2005.

[7] See *Gherebi v. Bush*, Ninth Circuit, December 18, 2003. The United States asserts the power "to do with [the detainees] as it will, when it pleases, without any compliance with any rule of law of any kind, without permitting [them] to consult counsel, and without acknowledging any judicial forum in which its actions may

law, in his 2003 State of the Union speech, claiming that more than three thousand suspected terrorists "have been arrested in many countries. And many others have met a different fate. Let's put it this way: They are no longer a problem for the United States."

The antilaw movement extends to the neoconservatives' successful attack on universal jurisdiction for war crimes and their opposition to the International Criminal Court.[8] According to Samantha Power, writing in the *New York Times*, the Bush administration has done all it can to undermine the ICC: "In Bush's first term, the United States suspended military aid to more than 20 countries that refused to shield Americans from potential prosecution, including Mali (a fledging democracy), Ecuador (a partner in drug interdiction efforts), and Croatia (a fragile government trying to stem a nationalist tide)."[9] The most shocking example is the Administration's refusal to refer a genocide complaint against the Sudanese province of Darfur to the ICC. The reason? "We don't want to be party to legitimizing the ICC," explained Pierre-Richard Prosper, the U.S. Ambassador-at-large for War Crimes Issues.[10]

Domestic manifestations of the rejection of the rule of law include the Patriot Act and the U.S. Justice Department's practice of filing legal briefs against U.S. citizens "under seal," meaning neither defendants nor their attorneys are permitted to view copies of the government's legal claims.[11] Some local effects have been the illegal arrest of hundreds of Muslim Americans in the days after September

---

be challenged . . . Indeed, at oral argument, the government advised us that its position would be the same even if the claims were that it was engaging in acts of torture or that it was summarily executing the detainees. To our knowledge, prior to the current detention of prisoners at Guantánamo, the U.S. government has never before asserted such a grave and startling proposition . . . a position so extreme that it raises the gravest concerns under both American and international law."

[8.] In March 2005, the Bush administration also withdrew from an international protocol that allowed foreigners on death row in U.S. prisons to take their cases to the International Court of Justice in The Hague. Adam Liptak, "U.S. Says It Has Withdrawn from World Judicial Body," *New York Times*, March 10, 2005.

[9.] Samantha Power, "The Court of First Resort," *New York Times*, February 12, 2005.

[10.] Ibid.

[11.] This represents a profound violation of due process, whereby litigation is conducted behind closed doors, available only to the government and the court. See David Cole, "Accounting for Torture," *Nation*, March 21, 2005.

11th and the illegal detention of Jose Padilla, a U.S. citizen, for more than two years without access to a lawyer or court hearing. Ignoring these basic constitutional requirements indicates that officials in the Administration will simply break the law when they think they can get away with it.[12]

OPPORTUNITIES PROVIDED BY THE LAW

While laws like the Patriot Act certainly function in support of the Bush administration's larger goals, if law exclusively served the interests of the powerful, the neoconservative agenda would simply require applying the legal apparatus to implement the war on terror. Instead, neoconservatives fear of the rule of law. Why?

They are afraid because elements of the law can function as obstacles impeding neoconservative projects. This understanding provides an opportunity for people coming together into social movements challenging the Bush administration's agenda to identify, fortify, and utilize these legal obstacles.[13]

The law represents neither the liberal ideal of a neutral system dispensing equal justice nor simply a tool for the powerful to dominate the powerless. Instead the law is an arena in which social forces with fluctuating degrees of power contest their interests. Within this arena there are three elements that are useful to social movements: (1) protections from arbitrary state power, (2) capitalizing on unintended developments, and (3) popular constitutionalism.

[12.] The antilaw agenda is not restricted to the fields of humanitarian or human rights law. It extends to the Bush administration's decisions to withdraw from the Kyoto global-warming treaty, the Comprehensive Test Ban Treaty, and the Anti-Ballistic Missile Treaty. It also includes shifting from rule-based trade institutions to bilateral trade agreements where U.S. negotiators are able to directly strong-arm individual governments into trade deals.

[13.] This article addresses only the law's relevance to social movements and, as a result, does not consider the law's ability to resolve disputes among citizens; its offerings of consistency, continuity, universal application, and predictability; its power to describe, organize, and record principles, rules, and prior interpretations and results; and its capacity to maintain social order both through its coercive power and citizens' belief in its moral authority.

Fortifying Protections from Arbitrary State Power

Legal structures can shield citizens from the exercise of arbitrary state power. Basic legal instruments—such as the U.S. Constitution and the English Magna Carta—primarily establish a state's authority over its citizens. But in return for this grant of authority, the state agrees to minimal rules under which it is permitted to exercise its control over its citizenry—in the words of Justice Robert Jackson, we, as citizens, would "submit ourselves to rules only if under rules." These constraints on the state are the basis for rights such as due process and equal protection under the law; and this skeletal structure is far better than the unmediated force of naked state power.[14]

Examples of protection from arbitrary state power include the Fifth Amendment, which prohibits the state from depriving citizens of "life, liberty, or property, without due process of law." As a result, state officials are barred from stealing people from their homes and detaining them indefinitely. If government officials wish to exercise their power to detain an individual for any extended period, they must convince a judge that the detention is warranted according to established rules, as well as provide the accused basic rights such as legal representation and humane treatment.

The Geneva Conventions and United Nations Charter provide similar minimal legal structures barring arbitrary and lawless state behavior.[15] Indeed, at their root, these provisions limit the very worst expressions of excessive state authority by establishing rules of war to which all states adhere to ensure humane treatment of their own soldiers and civilians. According to the legal expert Richard Falk, the importance of the war crimes concept is "to

---

[14] According to the historian Edward P. Thompson, "The form and rhetoric of law acquire a distinct identity which may, on occasion, inhibit power and afford some protection to the powerless." Edward P. Thompson, *Whigs and Hunters* (New York: Pantheon, 1975), p. 266.

[15] Article VI of the U.S. Constitution explicitly incorporates international instruments such as the Geneva Conventions into federal American law, making them the "supreme law of the land." Such incorporation is reinforced by U.S. laws like the War Crimes Act, which makes grave violations of the Geneva Conventions a crime punishable by imprisonment or even death.

reinforce a boundary—to paint the limiting condition of state behavior in bold colors."[16]

At minimum, therefore, the U.S. Constitution and the Geneva
Conventions require that leaders vested with constitutional authority
not engage in war crimes activity. But the Bush administration is systematically removing these national and international obstacles. Citizens of all stripes and persuasions—even those in the elite spheres of
society—are prone to view such actions as a threat to basic constitutional requirements. Indeed, Americans almost unanimously believe
that some law is an absolute necessity, whether on the highway or
between nations. They also believe that the law should be enforced
regardless of the social position of the lawbreaker.

The violation of these principles opens the opportunity to build
a broad coalition across civil society. Fighting war crimes allows
those with specific objections to the Bush administration's policies to
join with those holding deeper concerns about containing lawless
government behavior. Activists fighting to end the Iraq War, retain
civil liberties, or even protect Social Security can join with members of the legal community, military leaders and soldiers, moderate
nations, and ordinary Americans to fortify the legal restraints on the
Bush administration.

Many groups are already using war crimes law to demand that
Bush administration officials be restrained. Lawyers and judges, often at the tail end of progressive changes in society, have actually
been leading the fight to hold the Bush administration accountable.
Driven mainly by their deep concern with the violation of fundamental constitutional and international law, more than a thousand
law professors and U.S. legal institutions organized in opposition to
the U.S. war crime of launching an "aggressive war in violation of
the U.N. Charter" against Iraq.[17] The American Civil Liberties
Union sued U.S. Defense Secretary Donald Rumsfeld on behalf of

[16.] Richard Falk, "The Question of War Crimes: A Statement of Perspective," in *Crimes
of War*, ed. R. Falk, G. Kolko, and R. J. Lifton (New York: Random House, 1971), p. 9.
[17.] A sign of the legal establishment's deep resistance to the Bush administration's antilaw focus is the fact that fifteen corporate law firms are now providing free representation to about seventy Guantánamo detainees. See Gail Appleson, "Republican
Judge Takes Aim at Bush Terror Policies," Reuters, December 30, 2004.

eight Afghan and Iraqi detainees for breaching the U.S. Constitution and Geneva Conventions. The claim alleges Rumsfeld ordered "the abandonment of our nation's inviolable and deep-rooted prohibition against torture and other cruel, inhuman and degrading treatment."[18]

Some in the coalition may not consider themselves part of the peace movement and in fact may support portions of the neoconservative agenda; nevertheless, they stand opposed to the Bush administration based on a desire to live in a world that constrains state power. Framing issues in terms of war crimes that violate established legal principles will help build alliances and common strategies between the peace movement and these groups.

Capitalizing on Unintended Developments in the Law

Legislators and jurists often draft laws or establish precedents that are later applied to unanticipated situations. Almost every constitutional article and amendment has undergone this process, ranging from the application of the due process clause to freedoms of speech and religion. While there is no "natural" or necessary development of legal doctrines, they sometimes contain a germ that social movements can identify and nurture to help embrace wider human and social needs.

An example of this process is the "invention" of women's right to the use of contraceptives. Neither the Constitution nor the Bill of Rights mentions anything about privacy, marriage, or procreation. Nevertheless, in *Griswold v. Connecticut* the Supreme Court extended the Fourteenth Amendment's due process clause to infer a right to marital privacy and therefore also the right to contraception.[19] Conservatives like Judge Robert Bork detested this development, arguing that *Griswold* represented "not legal reasoning, but fiat."[20] Despite the fact that the due process clause was established at the end of the Civil War to protect the "life, liberty, or property" of

---

[18.] *Ali et al. v. Rumsfeld*, ACLU complaint for declaratory relief and damages, available at http://www.aclu.org/SafeandFree/SafeandFree.cfm?ID=17574&c=280.

[19.] *Griswold v. Connecticut*, 381 U.S. 479 (1965).

[20.] Robert H. Bork, *The Tempting of America: The Political Seduction of the Law* (New York: Free Press, 1990).

former slaves, the women's movement successfully expanded the interpretation of due process concepts to contraceptive freedom and eventually other gender-based rights.

The same process is occurring with respect to precedents established by the Nuremberg Tribunals. The primary debate leading up to Nuremberg centered not on whether war criminals were worthy of punishment, but rather whether or not to establish standards for their prosecution. Winston Churchill, Britain's wartime prime minister, considered the Nazis "outlaws" and therefore subject only to summary execution.[21] However, President Truman, a former small-town judge, insisted on formal trials with "notification to the accused of the charge, the right to be heard, and to call witnesses in his defense."[22]

While Truman argued for the specific right to a trial only in the context of holding Nazi war criminals accountable, the success of his arguments and the precedent set by the subsequent Nuremberg Tribunals evolved into the creation of complex war crime tribunals in Rwanda and the former Yugoslavia.[23] Moreover, despite the fact that Nuremberg trials embodied the worst form of "victor's justice"—in that American crimes of bombing Japanese and German civilians were ignored—Truman's notion of legitimate democratic justice established a framework to be applied to future dictators and tyrants.[24]

This process might be considered a "positive externality" of Truman's imposition of the Nuremberg Tribunals that we now apply to the Bush administration's crimes. In the words of one commentator,

[21] Summary execution became the official practice of the British government from 1943 to the end of the war. See "The Nuremberg Trials: International Law in the Making," in *From Nuremberg to The Hague: The Future of the International Criminal Court*," ed. Philippe Sands (Cambridge, England: Cambridge University Press, 2003).

[22] Ibid., p. 5.

[23] As Richard Falk writes in his contribution to this book, "Nuremberg has often been criticized as 'victors' justice,' and so it was, but the victorious powers that managed the process insisted that in the future the legal accountability of leaders would apply to the behavior of all sovereign states."

[24] Although the American practice of purposefully targeting Germans and Japanese civilians was excluded from the Nuremberg Tribunals, these very acts later became illegal under article 33 of the Fourth Geneva Convention and the First Additional Protocol of 1977. This process represents another unintended development of the law.

"Like a sheriff with a posse of deputies, international law is slowly catching up with the Bush administration."[25]

Social movements need to join this "posse" and capitalize on the unintended development of war crimes law. One possibility is to support former congresswoman Elizabeth Holtzman's suggestion for a campaign to apply the War Crimes Act to Bush administration officials. (See Elizabeth Holtzman's contribution to this volume for a full discussion.) This federal statute was passed in 1996 for the purpose of prosecuting people who committed war crimes against Americans. In March 2003 Congress passed a resolution to remind "Iraqis who are holding United States and British troops as prisoners [that they] could potentially be eligible for prosecution under the War Crimes Act of 1996."[26] While this legislation was intended for Saddam Hussein, social movements can encourage its use to develop the "unintended consequence" of holding administration officials accountable for their crimes.[27]

Using Popular Constitutionalism to Halt War Crimes

Since the founding of the Republic, citizens have engaged in struggles about the meaning and relevance of rights and obligations found in constitutions, human rights documents, and other instruments. This process has allowed social movements to use the legal arena to legitimate their claims, as well as draw on the law for inspiration.

Once laws, such as the U.S. Constitution, UN Charter, and Geneva Conventions, have been published and circulated, citizens

25. Simon Tisdall, "International Law Starts to Bring Washington Back into the Fold," *Guardian*, March 11, 2005.
26. Congressman Walter Jones, "Jones Calls for P.O.W. Captors to Be Treated as War Criminals," press release, March 27, 2003. Available at http://www.jones.house.gov/html/release.cfm?id=191.
27. Other possibilities include encouraging modern developments of universal jurisdiction whereby severe human rights violations, including war crimes, are subject to prosecution in any court in the world, regardless of their origin; joining lawsuits filed in Germany by the Center for Constitutional Rights against Secretary Rumsfeld; blocking efforts by the Bush administration to delegitimate the ICC, including in the Sudan; and passing universal jurisdiction resolutions in towns and cities throughout America.

read them as a promise by the state to respect such assigned rights and obligations as equality, freedom, justice, and due process. And even though these abstract principles are often broken, the promise endures. The result, according to the famed civil rights lawyer Victor Rabinowitz, "is that very large numbers of the people accept, believe in, and rely on these abstract principles. Often they demand that the promise be kept; they even may be willing to march and riot in the streets, and sit down in the factories and churches to enforce the promises."[28]

Regardless of the original intent of the law or judicial claims of popular misinterpretation, individuals and groups up and down the social stratosphere—workers, the middle class, even members of Congress—often believe that the state's promise must be honored.

This process is sometimes termed *popular constitutionalism* or a *constitutional insurgency* whereby a social movement "rather than repudiating the Constitution altogether, draws on it for inspiration and justification."[29] According to the constitutional law professor James Pope, "From the American revolution through the Virginia and Kentucky resolutions, the nullification movement, constitutional abolitionism, populism, the civil rights movement, and down to the recent rise of right-wing 'militias,' constitutional insurgencies have exerted a pervasive influence" on American society.[30]

The civil rights movement used popular constitutional notions of equal treatment under the law to articulate and legitimate their claims. They were able to justify allegedly illegal acts, such as civil disobedience, strikes, and boycotts, by arguing they were engaged in "citizen's enforcement" of the American principle of equality.[31] At the same time, the Constitution itself served as an inspiration for

[28] Victor Rabinowitz, "The Radical Tradition in the Law," in *The Politics of Law*, ed. David Kairys (New York: Basic Books, 1982), p. 683.

[29] James Gray Pope, "Labor's Constitution of Freedom," *Yale Law Journal* 941 (1997): 943.

[30] Ibid., pp. 944–45.

[31] As early as 1947, civil rights leaders were using the UN Charter in the same manner by filing human rights petitions at the United Nations challenging the status of African-Americans in the United States. Rhonda Copelon, "The Individual Framework of International Human Rights," in *The Politics of Law*, p. 223.

their struggle. In 1963, on the steps of the Lincoln Memorial, Dr. Martin Lincoln King, Jr. proclaimed, "When the architects of our republic wrote the magnificent words of the Constitution and the Declaration of Independence, they were signing a promissory note . . . that all men, yes, black men as well as white men, would be guaranteed the unalienable rights of life, liberty, and the pursuit of happiness."[32]

The development of international war crimes law offers social movements the same opportunity to express their needs and expectations in terms of established legal structures. Demanding that the Bush administration adhere to constitutional and international law will likely resonate with the majority of Americans. At the same time, evoking the UN Charter or Geneva Conventions does not mean citizens cannot "enforce" these principles through civil disobedience and other methods.

We see this process in the summoning of international law to frame nonviolent civil disobedience against the Iraq War. Religious leaders, for example, have applied the abstract principles set down in the Geneva Conventions and the court decisions convicting Japanese war criminals to assert their obligation under international law to take "affirmative measures" against the war crimes of the Bush administration. Their statement, A Call to Resist, reads: "We believe it is our duty as both Americans and members of the international community to insist that our government immediately adhere to the international agreements binding us." (See John Humphries's contribution to this book for a full account of this statement.)[33]

These international documents allow social movements to operate "inside the law," thereby offering a blanket of authority and

---

[32] Martin Luther King Jr., "'I Have A Dream' Speech," August 28, 1963. Available at http://www.stanford.edu/group/King/.

[33] Part VI of this book provides other current examples, including the statements by high-school-age resisters and the St. Patrick's Four's civil disobedience, which show groups using the Nuremberg principles and the U.S. Constitution to frame their resistance efforts against the war in Iraq. In his piece, Richard Falk discusses how actors in civil society have used constitutional and international law for inspiration and justification for more than fifteen civic war crimes tribunals held around the world.

inspiration to legitimize their actions within the framework of accepted American discourse. At the same time, this popular international constitutionalism allows Americans to join the rest of the world in support of the global expansion of human rights and the rule of law.

CONCLUSION

The Administration's framing of war crimes in terms of punishing a few low-level soldiers at Abu Ghraib is not simply about avoiding its own accountability. Rather, it is part of a systematic and sophisticated antilaw strategy employed by neoconservatives. Their approach rests on an old and simple premise: for a powerful governing party and country, legal structures impede efficient application of power. Based on this premise, they are eliminating all legal restraints. This new paradigm cannot be permitted to evolve.

Rather than an embodiment of liberal equality or a transmission belt for the powerful to exert control over the powerless, the law functions as an arena in which different social forces with varying degrees of power come together to contest their interests. As a result, depending on the strength and number of social forces struggling in this arena at any given point, the law will support different outcomes.

Law does not develop automatically, and if ignored it often functions against citizen's interests. Law is also not just about what happens inside the courtroom. Indeed, the majority of court victories have come about thanks to the pressure brought to bear by widespread social movements. Courts upheld labor laws only under threat of the 1937 strike wave; the right of African-Americans to vote in the South arrived only after decades of civil rights struggle. Meaningful institutional change requires a process whereby civil society interacts with legal institutions. It cannot be realized through one channel or the other; it requires both.

Social movements must not cede the legal arena to conservative forces; they need to force the law to meet their new social goals. Addressing war crimes is not only about accumulating evidence to hold high officials accountable. Thinking and framing issues in terms of international legal norms opens numerous opportunities, such as supporting efforts to retain the legal restraints on arbitrary state power, leveraging progressive developments of the law, and empowering social movements through popular constitutionalism.

The neoconservatives are already aware of these risks. According to Under Secretary of State Bolton, "It is a big mistake for us to grant any validity to international law even when it may seem in our short-term interest to do so—because, over the long term . . . those who think that international law really means anything are those who want to constrict the United States."[34] Bolton's opposition to international law in any form indicates his concern that despite their control of the White House, neoconservatives know they are threatened by the posse of forces amassing in the international law arena.

[34] James P. Lucier, "Just What Is a War Criminal?" *Insight on the News*, August 2, 1999, Daily Insight. Available at http://www.insightmag.com/news/1999/08/02/SpecialReport/Just-What.Is.A.War.Criminal-215455.shtml.

CONCLUSION

Most Americans hold these truths to be self-evident: torture is wrong; attacking another country that hasn't attacked you is wrong; occupying another country with your army and imposing your will on its people is wrong. These acts are not only immoral. They are illegal.

Most Americans believe that even the highest government officials are bound by law. They reject the Bush administration's view that as commander in chief the President can exercise the unlimited powers of a king or dictator. They do not believe that the law is whatever the President says it is—that if the President says something isn't torture, then it's OK to order it.

Most Americans don't agree that their president can unilaterally annul treaties like the Geneva Conventions. They don't accept, as Alberto Gonzales put it in a 2002 legal memo, that if the president simply declares there's a "new paradigm," he can thereby "render obsolete Geneva's strict limitations on questioning of enemy prisoners."

Aggression, military occupation, and torture were the war crimes, crimes against peace, and crimes against humanity for which the Axis leaders were prosecuted at the Nuremberg and Tokyo trials after World War II. The United States supported similar charges against Slobodan Milošević and Saddam Hussein.

But what about the U.S. attack on Iraq, justified by false charges that Iraq had weapons of mass destruction? What about the leveling of Fallujah and the targeting of hospitals and urban neighborhoods? What about torture at Abu Ghraib and Guantánamo? If a single standard is applied, these too are war crimes.

The U.S. attack on Iraq was a violation of the UN Charter, which states, "All members shall refrain in their international relations from the threat or use of force against the territorial integrity or political independence of any state." As United Nations Secretary-General Kofi Annan bluntly stated, the invasion of Iraq was "illegal."[1]

[1] "Iraq War Illegal, Says Annan," BBC News, September 16, 2004.

The U.S. occupation of Iraq constitutes an illegal continuation of the illegal U.S. attack on Iraq, conducted under the cover of an imposed regime. So does the plan to create permanent U.S. military bases in Iraq. Current U.S. policy is to continue this illegal occupation.

The United States and its supporters in Iraq have killed tens of thousands of Iraqi civilians. The Bush administration currently plans to continue the policies that have led to this slaughter of the innocent.

Authorized agents of the U.S. government have tortured prisoners at Abu Ghraib, Guantánamo, and elsewhere around the globe. The top officials in the Bush administration whose policies legitimated this torture remain in power, and the policies and doctrines that justified it remain in place.

The U.S. government is defying the Geneva Conventions as a matter of policy. It holds captives in secrecy without disclosing their existence to the International Committee of the Red Cross; spirits them across borders; denies them due process of law; and engages in cruel, brutal, and humiliating treatment of prisoners.

In support of their illegal international polices, U.S. officials are engaged in violations of human rights against both citizens and noncitizens abroad and at home. They seize and lock up those they deem a threat without due process of law, hold them incommunicado, and treat them inhumanly, in violation both of international law and of the U.S. Constitution.

These acts are sometimes attributed to a few "rogue" individuals acting on their own. But extensive evidence indicates that they actually result from policies enacted at the highest levels of the military and governmental chain of command.

These acts are sometimes justified in terms of protecting Americans, fighting terrorism, and bringing democracy to oppressed nations. Regardless of whether such claims are sincere or self-serving, they cannot justify war crimes. Nor can the undoubted fact that crimes are also being committed by insurgents and others in Iraq.

The Bush administration justifies these crimes under the doctrine that the U.S. government may do whatever it chooses in pursuit of its own national interests, regardless of its responsibilities under international law. But that justification cannot legitimate a pattern of lawlessness that violates both U.S. and international law.

WAR CRIMES AND CONSTITUTIONAL DEMOCRACY

U.S. war crimes present a profound challenge to the principles of national as well as international law. Indeed, the actions of the Bush administration have disturbed many who may not consider themselves part of the peace movement but who do care profoundly about the U.S. Constitution.

For many centuries there has been a struggle to put limits on the authority of governments and their officials.[2] Under the principles of constitutional government, government officials are themselves required to obey the law. The authority of government officials was made conditional on their own obedience to law.[3] Every schoolchild used to be taught that the U.S. Constitution provided "government under law"—that the United States was "a government of laws not men."

The U.S. Constitution made the President the commander in chief of the armed forces but provided many legal constraints on the President's authority. Only Congress had the authority to declare war, to conscript, to tax, or to appropriate funds. The President was subject to laws passed by Congress and interpreted by the courts.

The United Nations Charter, the Geneva Conventions, and other treaties ratified under the authority of the United States are the supreme law of the land under article 6 of the U.S. Constitution. Some are further reinforced by U.S. laws like the War Crimes Act, which makes grave violations of the Geneva Conventions a crime punishable by imprisonment or even death.

The United States has a law enforcement system responsible for investigating, apprehending, and sanctioning criminals. Unfortunately, those who control the government have many opportunities to extend their authority beyond the limits provided in laws and

---

[2] In Anglo-American tradition, these limits are often traced to the Magna Carta.

[3] Under the principles of democracy, the laws were in turn made subject to the will of the people.

constitutions—even to the point of committing crimes. Such "extended authority" has an old and ugly name: usurpation.[4]

Modern America has not been immune to such extended authority. In the 1960s, Lyndon Johnson launched the Vietnam War without a congressional declaration of war; used a false account of an attack in the Gulf of Tonkin to panic Congress into granting him unlimited authority to make war; and ultimately sent half a million troops to Vietnam. Public antagonism eventually led Johnson not to run for reelection.

In the 1970s, Richard Nixon engaged in the massive abuse of presidential powers that came to be known as the Watergate scandals. On the heels of a landslide electoral victory, the Nixon administration was subjected to investigation by a special prosecutor and by Congress; Nixon resigned rather than undergo impeachment.

Today, the Bush administration has subverted constitutional government from within. It has paralyzed the constraints that would limit Executive authority. A memo written by Assistant Attorney General Jay Bybee stated that prosecution of the U.S. law prohibiting torture could be barred "because enforcement of the statute would represent an unconstitutional infringement of the President's authority to conduct war." When asked at his Senate confirmation hearings whether he agreed that the President could simply refuse to obey a law he considered unconstitutional, President Bush's Attorney General nominee Alberto Gonzales assented. As Dean Harold Koh of the Yale Law School commented, "If the President has the sole constitutional authority to sanction torture, and Congress has no power to interfere, it is unclear why the President should not also have unfettered authority to license genocide."

The "new paradigm" the Bush administration has used to legitimate its war crimes is in truth not so new. It embodies practices well-known to autocratic regimes throughout history. Seize on an emergency when people are panicked. Issue decrees that override established laws. Authorize your own henchmen to act outside the law. Restrict the courts. Appoint prejudiced judges. Threaten

[4] For the concept of *extended authority*, see Charles Lindblom, *Politics and Markets* (New York: Basic Books, 1977).

326 ■ In the Name of Democracy

opponents. Conceal information. Construct phony plots and threats. Manufacture trumped-up law cases and phony evidence of wrongdoing. Criminalize the normal operations of dissent. The objective of such actions—to instill fear, confusion, acquiescence, submission, and withdrawal into private life—is often achieved, at least for a time.

The movement against autocracy and for democratic government is centuries old and worldwide. The movement against American war crimes is very much part of that struggle.

A MOVEMENT FOR LAW ENFORCEMENT

The legal system is designed to enforce the law. But the Bush administration has managed to paralyze the legal processes that might bring it to the bar of justice. Halting Bush administration war crimes requires a revitalization of the checks and balances that limit executive power. This requires blocking the illegitimate activities of the Bush administration and activating the individuals and institutions that are derelict in their duty to enforce the law on high government officials.

There are four obvious objectives for a movement against U.S. war crimes:

- ◆*Halt the crimes.* This requires policy changes such as withdrawing U.S. forces from Iraq, closing the U.S. prison in Guantánamo Bay, releasing or immediately putting on trial all captives, and shutting down U.S.-controlled death squads all over the world.
- ◆*Bring war criminals to justice.* Impunity breeds crime. The mechanisms for investigation, prosecution, and trial of criminals must be applied to anyone, from the President on down, who is responsible for war crimes. This is first of all a responsibility for the U.S. legal system, including its courts, and ultimately all court officials, including all members of the bar. If the American legal system is derelict in its duty, the responsibility passes to courts in the rest of the world.
- ◆*Draw the lessons.* Unchecked presidential authority and flouting of international law led the United States to a national catastrophe

in Vietnam, but the obvious lessons were deliberately obscured or denied. We are paying the price today. Only an extensive and extended public confrontation with the implications of U.S. war crimes can lay the basis for saving us from still further catastrophes in the future.

◆ *Establish barriers to future war crimes.* The Bush administration's war crimes were made possible by the dismantling of legal and constitutional barriers to government secrecy, deceit, manipulation, and lawlessness. Their perpetuation has been made possible by the dismantling of legal restrictions on presidential authority and the seduction or intimidation of those whose duty it is to enforce such restrictions. Our democratic heritage and the recent experiences of many countries in eliminating dictatorships point to specific institutional arrangements—from independent prosecutors to battlefield legal supervision and from freedom-of-information laws to international courts empowered to hear war crimes charges—that can be effective in preventing war crimes in the future.

THE RESPONSIBILITY OF AMERICANS

International law prohibits war crimes, but there are few effective institutional means of implementing that prohibition. Therefore the first responsibility for opposing such crimes lies with the people of the countries that commit them.

As citizens of the United States, it is we who have the duty to make our country stop committing war crimes. Indeed, anyone with knowledge of illegal activity and an opportunity to do something is a potential criminal under international law unless the person takes affirmative measures to prevent the commission of the crimes.

How many Americans can honestly claim to know nothing about this "illegal activity"? It's reported in detail in the daily newspapers and shown in full color on the nightly news, from the phony reports of Iraq's yellowcake uranium to the shooting of ambulances to the horrors of Abu Ghraib.

People in many countries have found themselves to be citizens of states that conduct wars of aggression, kill civilians, tyrannize occupied territories, and torture prisoners. The actions of France in Algeria; the Soviet Union in Afghanistan; Russia in Chechnya; India in Kashmir; Israel in Palestine; Syria in Lebanon; and Iraq in Kuwait all put their citizens at risk for complicity in war crimes. U.S. actions in Vietnam, Nicaragua, Afghanistan, and Iraq, among other places, have put American citizens at similar risk.

Such criminal acts have often been conducted by legally recognized states and governments. The governments conducting such crimes—from the French brutalities in Algeria to Milošević's outrages in Kosovo—have often been legally elected. Neither established legitimacy nor popular election obviates the responsibility of governments to obey international law or of their citizens to halt their government's criminal acts.

Where national and international institutions fail to halt such crimes, it is the responsibility of the people to do so. "Affirmative measures" to halt war crimes are now a moral and even a legal obligation for all Americans.

AFFIRMATIVE MEASURES

As Richard Falk points out, the movement to make governments obey international law has both a governmental and a civil society level. The current need is for "global civil society" to "extend the reach of criminal accountability to include those leaders acting on behalf of dominant states."

Many Americans are already taking "affirmative measures" to halt U.S. war crimes and bring their perpetrators to justice. As the occupation of Iraq has continued, more and more members of the armed forces have begun to resist. Military and civilian whistle-blowers have leaked accounts and photos of prisoner abuse. Thousands of people have been arrested for antiwar civil disobedience. Others have risked prosecution by pledging their support to military resisters. Journalists and independent tribunals have exposed U.S. war crimes. Generals, admirals, diplomats, and others have spoken out internally and publicly against abusive U.S. policies. Lawyers and human rights organizations have brought a wide range of cases challenging U.S. war crimes. The American Bar Association, the

ACLU, and other legal organizations have demanded independent investigations of criminal activity by government officials.

Like movements against dictatorships that have abolished basic constitutional freedoms, this is a movement to reassert the basic constitutional principle that the rule of law applies to the highest officials of the government. Such a "civic movement on behalf of official accountability" asserts, in Falk's words, that citizens have "a right, even a duty, to refuse to participate in official policies even if officially ordered to do so."

Gandhi pointed out that "even the most powerful cannot rule without the cooperation of the ruled." Such a resistance movement advances not so much by amassing power to itself as by withdrawing the elements of cooperation and acquiescence that give usurpers their power. When soldiers refuse to fight; youth refuse to enlist; activists interfere with induction centers; officials refuse to hide the truth; lawyers, judges, and elected officials refuse to accept abuse of governmental authority; and more and more ordinary citizens support such efforts—the days of those who usurp legitimate authority are numbered.

Such affirmative measures are as necessary to ensuring democratic, constitutional rule in the United States as they are to promoting peace around the world. Making "statesmen responsible to law" is the necessary condition for a more democratic as well as for a more secure future.

WEB RESOURCES

AMERICAN CIVIL LIBERTIES UNION
http://www.aclu.org

AMNESTY INTERNATIONAL
http://www.ai.org

ANTIWAR.COM
http://www.antiwar.com

AVALON PROJECT AT YALE LAW
SCHOOL
http://www.yale.edu/lawweb/avalon/
avalon.htm

CENTER FOR CONSTITUTIONAL
RIGHTS
http://www-ccr-ny.org

CENTER FOR ECONOMIC AND
SOCIAL RIGHTS
http://www.cesr.org

CENTRAL COMMITTEE FOR
CONSCIENTIOUS OBJECTORS
http://www.objector.org/

CRIMES OF WAR PROJECT
http://www.crimesofwar.org

FELLOWSHIP OF RECONCILIATION
http://www.forusa.org

GUANTANAMO HUMAN RIGHTS
COMMISSION
http://www.guantanamohrc.org

HUMAN RIGHTS FIRST
http://www.humanrightsfirst.org

HUMAN RIGHTS WATCH
http://www.hrw.org

INSTITUTE FOR POLICY STUDIES
http://www.ips-dc.org

INTERNATIONAL COMMITTEE OF THE
RED CROSS
http://www.icrc.org

LAWYERS AGAINST THE WAR
http://www.lawyersagainstthewar.org

NATIONAL LAWYERS GUILD
http://www.nlg.org

NOT IN OUR NAME
http://www.notinourname.net

OCCUPATION WATCH
http://www.occupationwatch.org

PRO-SE INSTITUTE
http://www.internationallaw
.pro-se-institute.org/index.htm

UNITED FOR PEACE AND JUSTICE
http://www.unitedforpeace.org

UNITED NATIONS
http://www.un.org/law

WORLD TRIBUNAL ON IRAQ
http://www.worldtribunal.org

ACKNOWLEDGMENTS

The authors thank Steve Fraser, Tom Engelhardt, and Sara Bershtel for their belief in our project and Steve Fraser for his thoughtful editing. We thank Kate Levin, Rita Quintas, and Victoria Haire for their work in rushing a complicated manuscript through the production process.

We thank those who wrote contributions on a tight deadline especially for this book: Richard Falk, Michael Ferber, Elizabeth Holtzman, John Humphries, Bill Quigley, Bruce Shapiro, and Marela Zacarias. We thank those who revised previous work: John W. Dean, Lisa Hajjar, Nancy Lessin, and Mark LeVine. We thank those who gave us permission to use their previous writings, including Marjorie Cohn, Mark Danner, Oona Clare DeFlaun, Daniel Ellsberg, Ana Flores, Marie Grady, Jeremy Hinsman, Scott Horton, Sanford Levinson, Dr. Jim McDermott, Dr. Richard Rapport, and Anna Ritter.

We thank all those who provided us or helped us obtain permission to reprint materials. In particular we would like to thank Amnesty International, the Center for Constitutional Rights, the Center for Economic and Social Rights, Human Rights First, Human Rights Watch, and the American Civil Liberties Union, without whose work much of the information presented throughout this book would still be concealed from the public.

We thank the many people who helped us along the way. Chris Stone, Anne Mackinnon, Michael Ferber, and Susan Arnold helped us identify key themes. Emma Mackinnon asked penetrating questions that helped us clarify our goals at an early stage. Moira Cutler provided research assistance and identified many indispensable sources. Margaret Spillane and Bruce Shapiro pitched in above and beyond the call of duty. Herbert Bix gave generously of his time and energy. We thank Francis Boyle, Peter Canby, Tim Costello, John Gershman, Teresa Grady, John Humphries, Sylvia Madrigal, Roger Norman, Michael Pertschuk, Marcus Raskin, John Russell,

Christie Smith, Anna Sofaer, Katherine Stone, Aparna Sundaram, John Taylor, and Zeynep Toufe for a variety of special contributions.

Jeremy Brecher and Jill Cutler would like to provide special thanks to Fanya Cutler and Moira Cutler.

Brendan Smith would like to provide special thanks to Nicola for love and understanding, Gail Smith for editing and encouragement, and Wilfred and Sarah Armster for opening their home.

ABOUT THE EDITORS

The historian JEREMY BRECHER has written and edited more than a dozen books, including *Strike!* For his work in video documentaries, he earned five regional Emmy Awards and the Silver Gavel Award of the American Bar Association. His articles and opinion pieces have appeared in the *Chicago Tribune*, the *Nation*, and the *Los Angeles Times*.

JILL CUTLER is an assistant dean in Yale College and teaches nonfiction in the English Department. She has edited many books, including *Global Visions: Beyond the New World Order*.

BRENDAN SMITH (blsmith28@gmail.com) is a former senior congressional policy analyst specializing in human rights and international law. He is coauthor of *Globalization from Below*, coproducer of the documentary film *Global Village or Global Pillage?*, and has written for the *Los Angeles Times*, *The Nation*, and the *Baltimore Sun*. He received his law degree from Cornell University.

THE AMERICAN EMPIRE PROJECT

In an era of unprecedented military strength, leaders of the United States, the global hyperpower, have increasingly embraced imperial ambitions. How did this significant shift in purpose and policy come about? And what lies down the road?

The American Empire Project is a response to the changes that have occurred in America's strategic thinking as well as in its military and economic posture. Empire, long considered an offense against America's democratic heritage, now threatens to define the relationship between our country and the rest of the world. The American Empire Project publishes books that question this development, examine the origins of U.S. imperial aspirations, analyze their ramifications at home and abroad, and discuss alternatives to this dangerous trend.

The project was conceived by Tom Engelhardt and Steve Fraser, editors who are themselves historians and writers. Published by Metropolitan Books, an imprint of Henry Holt and Company, its titles include *Hegemony or Survival* by Noam Chomsky, *The Sorrows of Empire* by Chalmers Johnson, *Crusade* by James Carroll, *How to Succeed at Globalization* by El Fisgón, *Blood and Oil* by Michael Klare, and *Dilemmas of Domination* by Walden Bello.

For more information about the American Empire Project and for a list of forthcoming titles, please visit www.americanempireproject.com.